GRADE 8

McGraw Hill

Math

Third Edition

New York Chicago San Francisco Athens London Madrid
Mexico City Milan New Delhi Singapore Sydney Toronto

Copyright © 2022, 2018, 2011 by McGraw Hill. All rights reserved. Printed in the United States of America. Except as permitted under the United States Copyright Act of 1976, no part of this publication may be reproduced or distributed in any form or by any means, or stored in a database or retrieval system, without the prior written permission of the publisher.

1 2 3 4 5 6 7 8 9 LWI 27 26 25 24 22

ISBN 978-1-264-28571-6
MHID 1-264-28571-X

e-ISBN 978-1-264-28572-3
e-MHID 1-264-28572-8

McGraw Hill products are available at special quantity discounts for use as premiums and sales promotions, or for use in corporate training programs. To contact a representative please visit the Contact Us pages at www.mhprofessional.com.

McGraw Hill is committed to making our products accessible to all learners. To learn more about the available support and accommodations we offer, please contact us at accessibility@mheducation.com. We also participate in the Access Text Network (www.accesstext.org), and ATN members may submit requests through ATN.

McGraw Hill thanks Wendy Hanks for her invaluable contributions to this new edition.

Table of Contents

Table of Contents

Letter to Parents and Students

Welcome to McGraw Hill's Math!

Parents, this book will help your child succeed in eighth grade mathematics. It will give your eighth grader:

- **A head start** in the summer before eighth grade
- **Extra practice** during the school year
- **Helpful preparation** for standardized mathematics exams

The book is aligned to **National and State Standards**. A chart beginning on the next page summarizes those standards and shows how each state that does not follow the national standards differs from those standards. The chart also includes comparisons to Canadian standards.

If you live in a state that has adopted the national Common Core standards, you won't need the information in this table, although you may find its summary of Common Core standards helpful. Parents who live in Canada or states that have not adopted Common Core standards will find the table a useful tool and can be reassured that most of these regions have standards that are very similar to the national standards. This book contains ample instruction and practice for students in **any state** or in **Canada**.

Students, this book will help you do well in mathematics. Its lessons explain math concepts and provide lots of interesting practice activities.

Open your book and look at the **Table of Contents**. It tells what topics are covered in each lesson. Work through the book at your own pace.

Begin with the **Pretest**, which will help you discover the math skills you need to work on.

Each group of lessons ends with a **Unit Test**. The results will show you what skills you have learned and what skills you may need to practice more. A **Posttest** completes your work in this book and will show how you have done overall.

Take time to practice your math. Practicing will help you use and improve your math skills.

Good luck!

Eighth Grade National and State Math Standards

Eighth Grade U.S. Common Core Standards	Texas*	Virginia	Indiana	South Carolina
Know that there are numbers that are not rational, and approximate them by rational numbers.				
Expressions and Equations Work with radicals and integer exponents.	Omits estimation using scientific notation	Omits scientific notation	Omits estimation using scientific notation	
Understand the connections between proportional relationships, lines, and linear equations.				
Analyze and solve linear equations and pairs of simultaneous linear equations.		Omits 2-variable and simultaneous equations		
Define, evaluate, and compare functions.				
Use functions to model relationships between quantities.				
Understand congruence and similarity using physical models, transparencies, or geometry software.			Omits angles of triangles and parallel lines	
Understand and apply the Pythagorean Theorem.				
Solve real-world and mathematical problems involving volume of cylinders, cones, and spheres.		No cylinder or sphere. Includes volume and surface area of pyramid and prism		
Investigate patterns of association in bivariate data.	Omits two-way tables and using slope; includes standard deviation and rep. samples	Omits two-way tables and using slope; includes probability and boxplot	Omits two-way tables and using slope; includes probability	Also: use of matrices

*Texas also has a section on personal financial literacy.

**Also: parallel and perpendicular lines

Minnesota**	Oklahoma	Nebraska	Alaska	Canadian Provinces
		Omits estimation using scientific notation	Includes prime factorization	ON and WNCP omit scientific notation
		More work on solving equations		
	Omits 2-variable and simultaneous equations	Omits simultaneous equations		ON and WNCP omit equations with 0 or infinite solutions
		No related standards		
		No related standards		WNCP omits drawing function from verbal description
				WNCP adds tessellations
No related standards	No cone/sphere. Includes volume and surface area of rectangular prism			ON adds surface area of cylinder, circle construction, and Euler's theorem
Omits two-way tables and using slope	Omits two-way tables and using slope; includes probability	Omits two-way tables and using slope		ON adds probability, surveys, and graph choice

Pretest

Name ______________________________

Complete the following test items.

1. Kathy runs 16 miles a week. If she continues to run at this rate, how many miles will she run in a year?

2. The women's clothing department at Ms. Smith's store had a sale on jeans. There were 945 jeans in stock at the beginning of the sale and another 254 jeans were ordered. At the end of the sale the store still had 245 jeans in stock. How many jeans were sold during the sale?

3. Jack has 16 lengths of rope. Each is $6\frac{3}{4}$ meters long. How much rope does Jack have to divide among 20 people?

   How much rope will each person receive?

4. David has 176 ounces of hot sauce to divide among the 32 contestants in a chicken-wing eating contest. How many cups is that per contestant?

5. $4\frac{3}{10} + 3\frac{2}{5} + \frac{1}{3} + \frac{1}{2} =$

6. $-8 + 11 - (-9) + 4(-3) + \frac{12}{-4} =$

7. Solve for x: $x - 7 = 14$

8. Solve for x: $2x + 6 = 18$

9. Solve: $10 + (8 - 6)^2 - (12 \div 4) + 5(6 \times 2) + 3(7 - 4) =$ ______________

10. Restate in exponent form, then solve: $5 \times 5 + 2 \times 2 \times 2 + 3 \times 3 =$

11. 3.55 meters = ________ inches (Use 2.54 cm = 1 inch)

12. 10 yards = ________ centimeters

13. What is the area of the rectangle? ________

    What is the perimeter?

    12 cm

    8 cm

    What is the perimeter, in inches, using the conversion factor of 2.54 cm to the inch?

14. 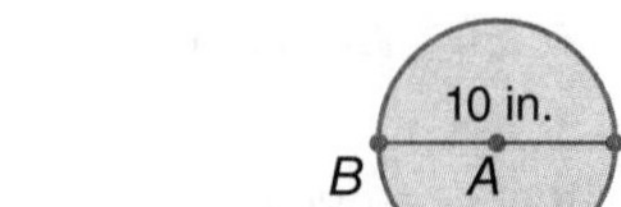

    What is the area of the circle? ________ (Use 3.14 for π.)

    What is the circumference of the circle?

15 Identify each angle as obtuse, acute, or right.

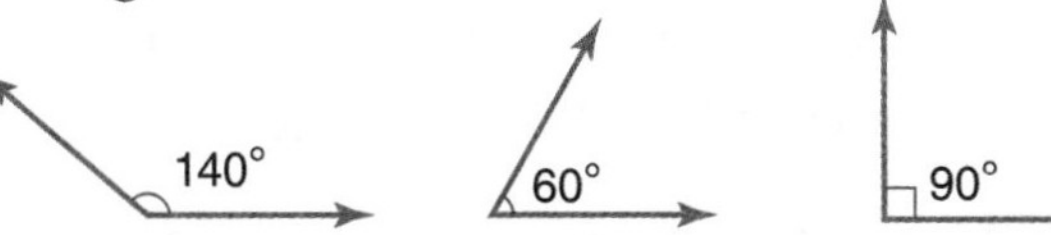

______ ______ ______

16 Identify each triangle as scalene, isosceles, or equilateral.

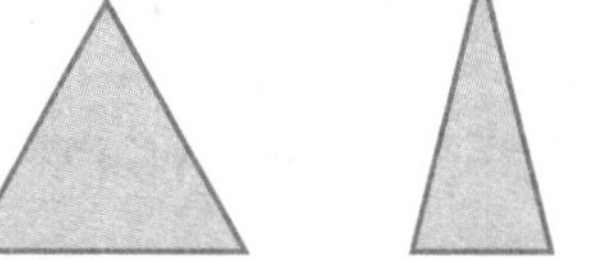

______ ______ ______

Calculate and reduce the fractions.

17 $4\frac{3}{5} \times 5\frac{1}{5} =$ ______

18 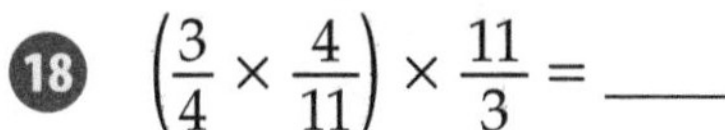 $\left(\frac{3}{4} \times \frac{4}{11}\right) \times \frac{11}{3} =$ ______

19 $\frac{12}{25} \div \frac{4}{5} =$ ______

20 Give the coordinates for points on the grid.

A ______ B ______

C ______ D ______

What is the slope of a line drawn between points A and B?

______

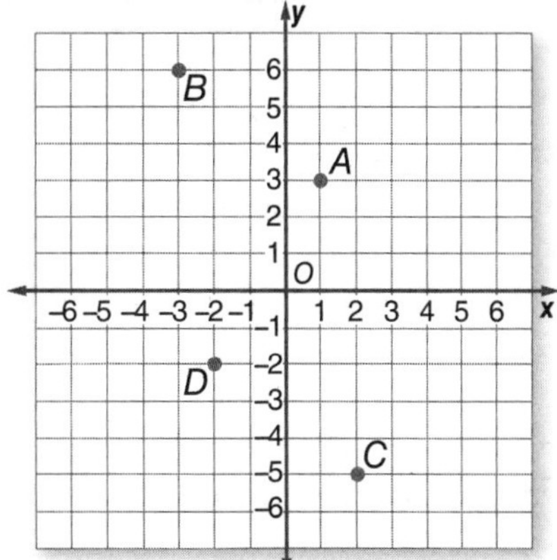

21 What is the measure of angle DBC?

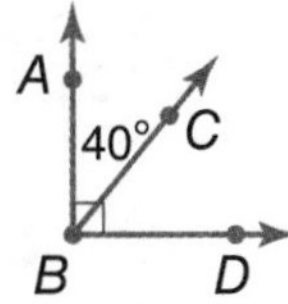

______

22 $0.15\overline{)0.235}$

23 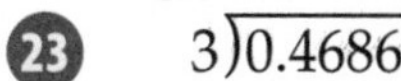 $3\overline{)0.4686}$

24 What is 40% of 0.775? ______

25 What is $\frac{5}{8}$ of 72%? ______

26 Restate 4.25 as an improper fraction and a mixed number.

Improper Fraction ______ Mixed Number ______

27 Put the following numbers in order from least to greatest.
1.162, 1.161, 2.16302, 2.163, 2.8022, 1.90688, 1.9122, 1.099

______

28 Solve for x. $\frac{15}{32} = \frac{x}{160}$ ______

29 Restate $2\frac{7}{16}$ as a decimal. ______

Pretest

Name ______________________

30 Sarah manufactured surfboards at a cost of $45.00 each. She wants to sell the surfboards at a 50% markup. What will be the selling price for each?

____

31 Dexter deposits $200 in a bank account that earns 3% simple interest. How much money will he have in the account after 1 year? __________

After 2 years? __________

32 Identify each quadrilateral.

    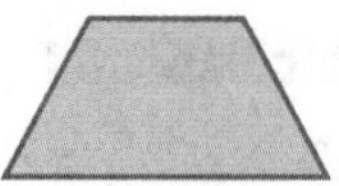

__________ __________ __________ __________ __________

33 The student council helped organize a jump rope competition for the school. During the competition, Team A jumped rope 1339 times in 20 minutes. Team B jumped rope 1448 times in 22 minutes, and Team C jumped rope 1552 times in 23 minutes. Which team had the fastest rate?

____

34 Larry spent Saturday afternoon reading a 600-page book. If he started the day on page 256, and stopped on page 539, what percent of the pages did he read on Saturday?

____

35 $\frac{4}{7} - \frac{5}{7} + \frac{3}{7} + \frac{4}{7} - \frac{3}{7} =$ __________

36 $\frac{5}{8} \times 3\frac{13}{25} =$ __________

37 $10^4 \times 10^5 =$ __________

38 $9^8 \div 9^4 =$ __________

39 What is 12^2? __________

40 What is the square root of 225? __________

41 What is the mode of the data distribution?

____

What is the median?

____

Stem	Leaf
2	2 3
3	1 6 8
4	2 7 7 7
5	3 4 4 6 6
6	1 4 4 5

Name ______________________________

Pretest

42 According to this graph, what frozen yogurt is the most preferred? ______________

The least preferred? ______________

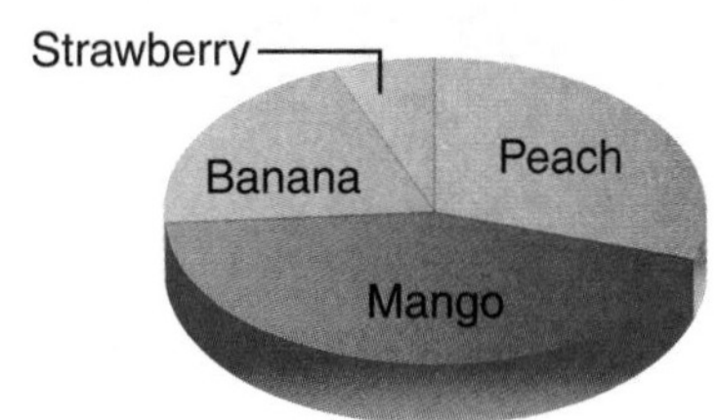

43 Brandon collected about 20 cans more than what person? ______________ Who collected the second fewest cans? ______________

44 How many possible combinations are there?

____

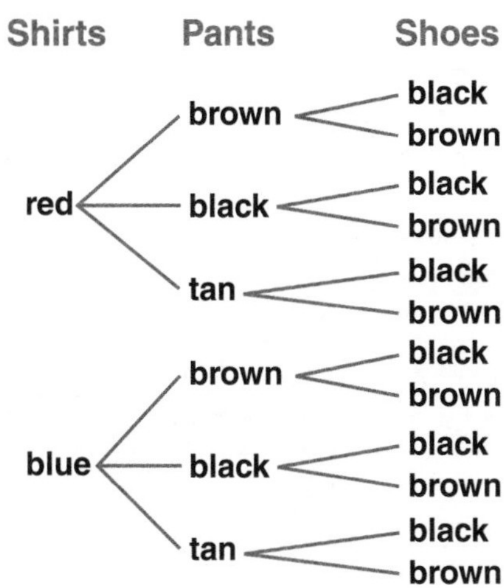

45 What is the range of the data in the box-and-whisker plot?

____

46 Use the Pythagorean Theorem to find the value of x.

____

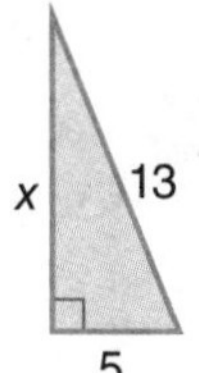

47 Name two pairs of alternate interior angles.

________ and ________ ________ and ________

Name two pairs of alternate exterior angles.

________ and ________ ________ and ________

Name a pair of vertical angles.

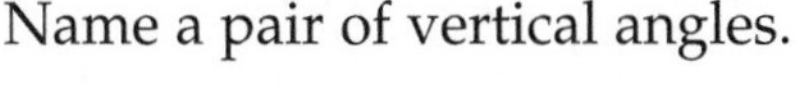

________ and ________

Name two pairs of supplementary angles.

________ and ________ ________ and ________

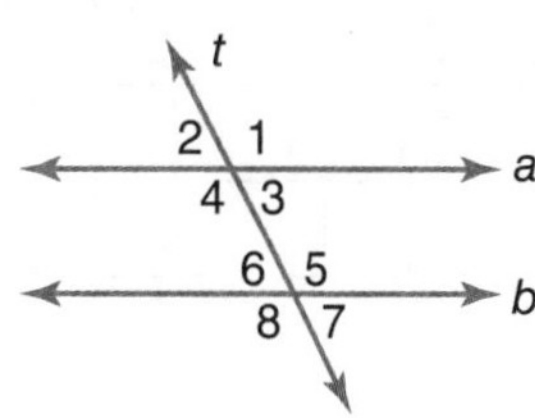

Pretest

Name ______________________

48 Name two line segments. ______________

Name four rays. ______________

Name a line. ______________

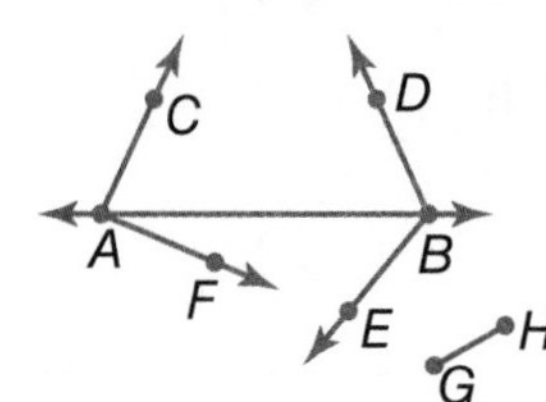

Calculate the volume and surface area of the figures shown.

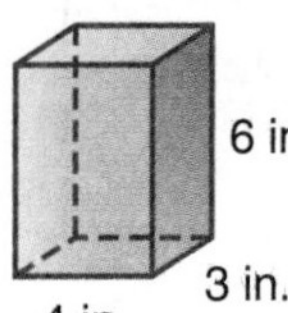

Volume ______________

Surface Area ______________

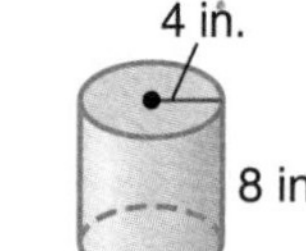

Volume ______________

Surface Area ______________

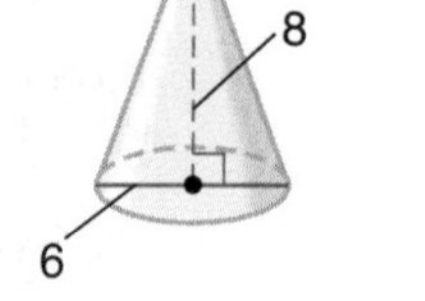

Volume ______________

52 Estimate the value of $\sqrt{30}$ ______________ Of $\sqrt{97}$. ______________

53 Convert 2.14 to an improper fraction. ______________

54 Solve $4x^2 + 14 - 4x^2 = 7$. ______________

55 Solve $4x^2 + 7 - 4x^2 = 7$. ______________

56 Complete and graph the function table for $y = 2x - 1$.

x	y
−2	
−1	
0	
1	
2	

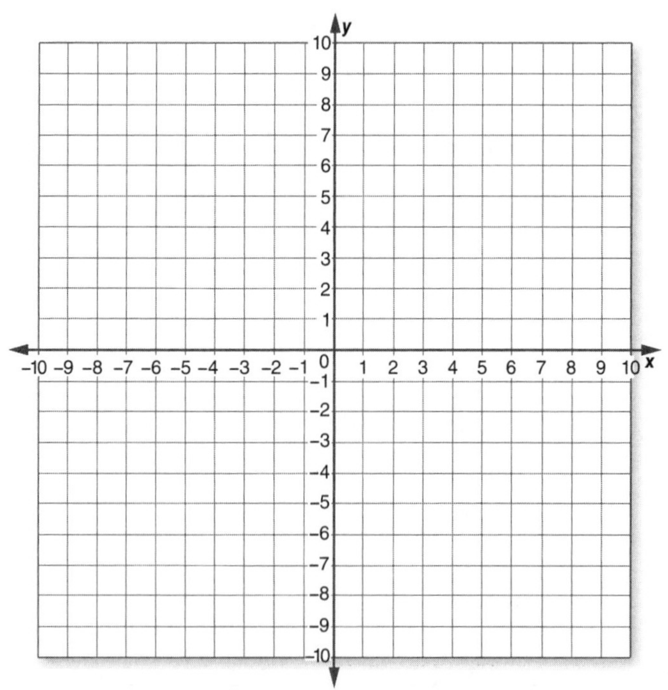

Name ____________________

Pretest

57 Look at the graph. Is this a linear or nonlinear function?

____

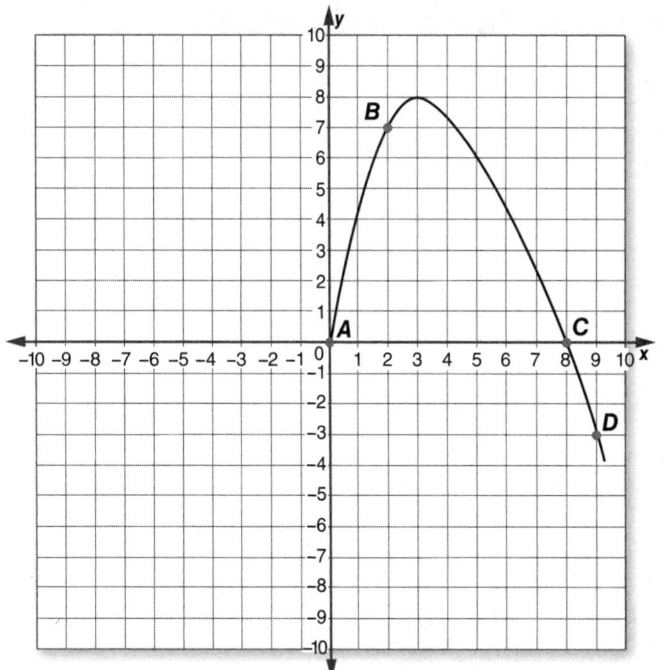

The function is increasing between points

____

The function is decreasing between points

____

The function is positive between points

____

The function is negative between points

____

58 How many times greater is 6×10^7 than 3×10^5?

59 In the graph below, is triangle ABC congruent to triangle ADC?

____

What type of transformation created triangle ADC?

____

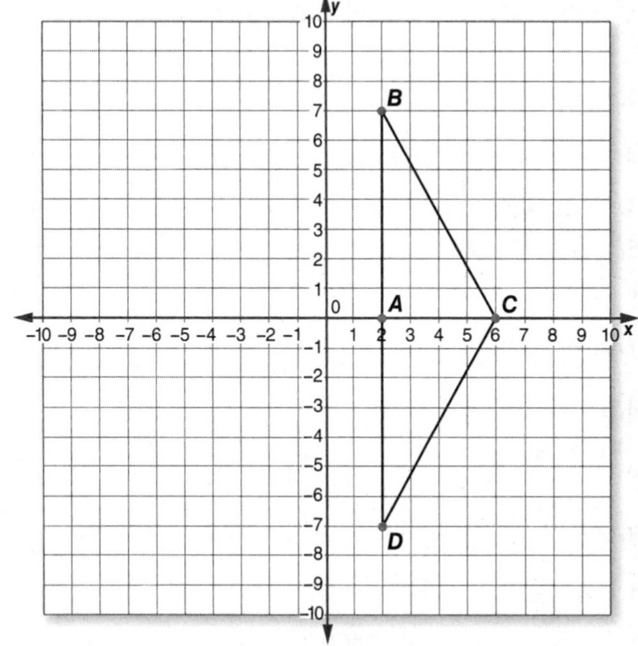

60 What type of transformation is shown below? ____________________

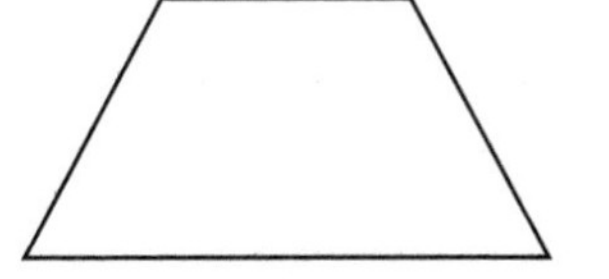

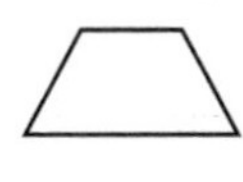

Pretest

Name ______________________________

Answers and Explanations for Pretest

1. 832 miles $\quad \dfrac{16 \text{ miles}}{1 \text{ week}} = \dfrac{x \text{ miles}}{52 \text{ weeks (1 year)}}; x = 16 \times 52 = 832$

2. 954 jeans $\quad 945 + 254 - 245 = 954$

3. 108 m; $5\frac{2}{5}$ m $\quad 6\frac{3}{4} \times 16 = \frac{27}{4} \times \frac{16}{1} = \frac{27}{1} \times \frac{4}{1} = 108; \frac{108}{20} = \frac{27}{5} = 5\frac{2}{5}$

4. $\frac{11}{16}$ c $\quad 176 \text{ oz} \div \frac{8 \text{ oz}}{1 \text{ cup}} = 22; \frac{22}{32} = \frac{11}{16}$

5. $8\frac{8}{15}$ $\quad 4 + 3 = 7; \frac{9}{30} + \frac{12}{30} + \frac{10}{30} + \frac{15}{30} = \frac{46}{30} = \frac{23}{15} = 1\frac{8}{15}; 7 + 1\frac{8}{15} = 8\frac{8}{15}$

6. -3 $\quad -8 + 11 - (-9) + 4(-3) + \frac{12}{-4} = -8 + 11 + 9 + 4(-3) + \frac{12}{-4} = -8 + 11 + 9 - 12 - 3 = -3$

7. $x = 21$

$$\begin{aligned} x - 7 &= 14 \\ +7 \quad & \ +7 \\ \hline x &= 21 \end{aligned}$$

8. $x = 6$

$$\begin{aligned} 2x + 6 &= 18 \\ -6 \quad & \ -6 \\ \hline \frac{2x}{2} &= \frac{12}{2} \\ x &= 6 \end{aligned}$$

9. 80 $\quad 10 + (8 - 6)^2 - (12 \div 4) + 5(6 \times 2) + 3(7 - 4) = 10 + 2^2 - 3 + 5(12) + 3(3)$
$= 10 + 4 - 3 + 5(12) + 3(3) = 10 + 4 - 3 + 60 + 9 = 80$

10. $5^2 + 2^3 + 3^2 = 25 + 8 + 9 = 42$

11. 139.76 inches $\quad 3.55 \text{ m} \times 100\frac{\text{cm}}{\text{m}} \div 2.54\frac{\text{cm}}{\text{in.}} = 139.76 \text{ in.}$

12. 914.4 cm $\quad 10 \text{ yd} \times 36\frac{\text{in.}}{\text{yd}} \times 2.54\frac{\text{cm}}{\text{in.}} = 914.4 \text{ cm}$

13. Area: 96 sq cm; Perimeter: 40 cm; 15.748 in. $\quad 8 \times 12 = 96; 8 + 8 + 12 + 12 = 40 \text{ cm}; 40 \text{ cm} \div 2.54\frac{\text{cm}}{\text{in.}} = 15.748 \text{ in.}$

14. Area: 78.5 sq in.; Circumference: 31.4 inches $\quad A = \pi r^2 = \pi \times (5^2) = 3.14 \times 25 = 78.5; C = \pi d = 3.14 \times 10 = 31.4$

15. Obtuse; Acute; Right

16. Scalene; Equilateral; Isosceles

17. $23\frac{23}{25}$ $\quad \frac{23}{5} \times \frac{26}{5} = \frac{598}{25} = 23\frac{23}{25}$

18. 1 $\quad \frac{3}{4} \times \frac{4}{11} = \frac{3}{1} \times \frac{1}{11} = \frac{3}{11}; \frac{3}{11} \times \frac{11}{3} = 1$

19. $\frac{3}{5}$ $\quad \frac{12}{25} \div \frac{4}{5} = \frac{12}{25} \times \frac{5}{4} = \frac{3}{5} \times \frac{1}{1} = \frac{3}{5}$

20. A (1, 3); B (−3, 6); C (2, −5), D (−2, −2); $\frac{-3}{4}$ $\quad s = \frac{y_2 - y_1}{x_2 - x_1} = \frac{6 - 3}{-3 - 1} = \frac{3}{-4}$

21. 50 degrees $\quad 90° - 40° = 50°$

22. 1.566667

```
          1.566...
0.15.)0.23.500
       15
        8 5
        7 5
        1 00
          90
         100
          90
          10...
```

23. 0.1562

$$\begin{array}{r} 0.1562 \\ 3\overline{)0.4686} \\ 3 \\ \hline 16 \\ 15 \\ \hline 18 \\ 18 \\ \hline 6 \\ 6 \\ \hline 0 \end{array}$$

24. 0.31 $0.4 \times 0.775 = 0.31$

25. 45% $\frac{5}{8} \times 72 = \frac{5}{1} \times 9 = 45$

26. $\frac{17}{4}$ or $4\frac{1}{4}$ $4.25 = \frac{425}{100} = \frac{17}{4} = 4\frac{1}{4}$

27. 1.099, 1.161, 1.162, 1.90688, 1.9122, 2.163, 2.16302, 2.8022

28. 75 $15 \times 160 = 32x; 2400 = 32x; x = 75$

29. 2.4375 2+

$$\begin{array}{r} 0.4375 \\ 16\overline{)7.0000} \\ 64 \\ \hline 60 \\ 48 \\ \hline 120 \\ 112 \\ \hline 80 \\ 80 \\ \hline 0 \end{array}$$

30. \$67.50 $45 \times 1.5 = \$67.50$

31. \$206.00; \$212.00 $\$200 \times 0.03 = \$6; \$200 + \$6 = \$206; \$6 \times 2 = \$12; \$200 + \$12 = \$212$

32. Square; rectangle; rhombus; kite; trapezoid

33. C $A: \frac{1339 \text{ jumps}}{20 \text{ min}} = \frac{66.95 \text{ jumps}}{1 \text{ min}}; B: \frac{1448 \text{ jumps}}{22 \text{ min}} = \frac{65.82 \text{ jumps}}{1 \text{ min}}; C: \frac{1552 \text{ jumps}}{23 \text{ min}} = \frac{67.48 \text{ jumps}}{1 \text{ min}}$

34. 41.17 $539 - 256 = 283; \frac{x}{100} \times 600 = 283; 6x = 283; x = 47.17$

35. $\frac{3}{7}$ $\frac{4-5+3+4-3}{7} = \frac{3}{7}$

36. $2\frac{1}{5}$ $\frac{5}{8} \times \frac{88}{25} = \frac{1}{1} \times \frac{11}{5} = \frac{11}{5} = 2\frac{1}{5}$

37. 10^9 $10^{4+5} = 10^9$

38. 9^4 or 6561 $9^{8-4} = 9^4$

39. 144 $12 \times 12 = 144$

40. 15 $15 \times 15 = 225$

41. 47; 50 The number 47 appears three times, more than any other number. There are 18 values, so the median is the average of #9 and #10: $\frac{47+53}{2} = \frac{100}{2} = 50$

42. Mango; strawberry

43. Molly; Megan

44. 12

 Name ______________________

45. 18 $22 - 4 = 18$

46. $x = 12$ $a^2 + b^2 = c^2;\ a^2 + 5^2 = 13^2;\ a^2 + 25 = 169;\ a^2 = 144;\ a = \sqrt{144} = 12$

47. Alternate interior angles: $\angle 4$ and $\angle 5$; $\angle 3$ and $\angle 6$;
Alternate exterior angles: $\angle 2$ and $\angle 7$; $\angle 1$ and $\angle 8$;
Vertical angles: $\angle 2$ and $\angle 3$: $\angle 1$ and $\angle 4$; $\angle 6$ and $\angle 7$; $\angle 5$ and $\angle 8$;
Supplementary angles: $\angle 1$ and $\angle 3$; $\angle 2$ and $\angle 4$; $\angle 5$ and $\angle 7$; $\angle 6$ and $\angle 8$

48. Line segment $\overline{AB}$, $\overline{AC}$, $\overline{AF}$, $\overline{DB}$, $\overline{BE}$, $\overline{HG}$; rays: $\overline{AC}$, $\overline{AF}$, $\overline{BE}$, $\overline{BD}$; Line $\overline{AB}$

49. Volume = 72 cu in.; SA = 108 sq in.
$V = lwh = 4 \times 3 \times 6 = 72;\ \text{SA} = 2(4 \times 3) + 2(4 \times 6) + 2(3 \times 6) = 2(12) + 2(24) + 2(18) = 24 + 48 + 36 = 108$

50. Volume = 128π cu in.; SA = 96π sq in.
$V = \pi r^2 h = \pi \times 4^2 \times 8 = \pi \times 16 \times 8 = 128\pi;\ \text{SA} = 2(\pi r^2) + (\pi dh) = 2(\pi 4^2) + \pi(8)(8) = 2(16\pi) + 64\pi = 32\pi + 64\pi = 96\pi$

51. Volume = 96π cu units $V = \frac{1}{3}Bh = \frac{1}{3}(\pi r^2)(h) = \frac{1}{3}(\pi 6^2)(8) = \frac{1}{3}(36\pi)(8) = 12\pi(8) = 96\pi$

52. 5.5; 9.8 $\sqrt{36} = 6$ and $\sqrt{25} = 5$, so $\sqrt{30} \approx 5.5$; $\sqrt{100} = 10$ and $\sqrt{81} = 9$, so $\sqrt{97} \approx 9.8$

53. $\frac{107}{50}$ $\frac{214}{100} = \frac{107}{50}$

54. No solution $4x^2 - 4x^2 = 0$, so we are left with $14 = 7$ which is not true.

55. Infinite solutions $4x^2 - 4x^2 = 0$, so we are left with $7 = 7$ which is true no matter what x is.

56.

x	y
–2	–5
–1	–3
0	–1
1	1
2	3

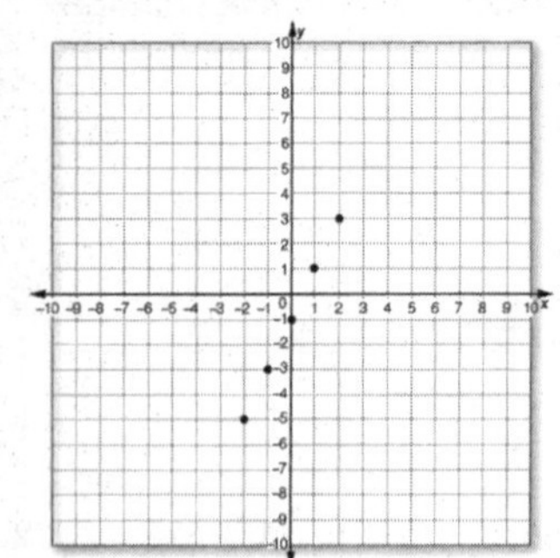

57. Nonlinear; A and B; C and D; A and B or B and C; C and D

58. 200 $\frac{6 \times 10^7}{3 \times 10^5} = 2 \times 10^2 = 2 \times 100 = 200$

59. Yes; reflection

60. dilation

Name ____________________

Order of Operations

What happens if you see a long string of mathematical calculations to perform? Is there some way to know where to begin? Yes, you can use a rule called the **order of operations**. It tells you in what order you should do calculations for equations in a long string.

There is even a simple word that can help you remember the order of operations: **PEMDAS**. This stands for **P**arentheses, **E**xponents, **M**ultiplication, **D**ivision, **A**ddition, and **S**ubtraction.

Example:

Solve: $20 - 5 \times 2 + 36 \div 3^2 - (9 - 2) = ?$

We can solve this problem using the order of operations. Remember PEMDAS.

1. Parentheses $(9 - 2) = 7$

   $20 - 5 \times 2 + 36 \div 3^2 - 7 = ?$

2. Exponents $3^2 = 9$

   $20 - 5 \times 2 + 36 \div 9 - 7 = ?$

3. Multiplication and Division $5 \times 2 = 10$

   $36 \div 9 = 4$

   $20 - 10 + 4 - 7 = ?$

4. Addition and Subtraction $20 - 10 = 10$

   $10 + 4 = 14$

   $14 - 7 = 7$

Exercises CALCULATE

1. $(5 + 2) \times (5 - 3) - (3 \times 3) + 2^{(5 - 2)}$

2. $(6 - 5) \times (6 - 4) - 2^3 + 6$

3. $(7 - 4)^3 + (7 - 2)^2 + 5 - 2 + 3^{(5 - 3)}$

4. $(8 + 2) \times (8 - 5) + 42 - (7 - 4)^3$

5. $(8 - 6)^3 - (7 - 5)^3 + 9 - (5 - 2)$

6. $(4)^2 - (2^3 - 5) + (2^2 + 2) - 2^3$

7. $(7 - 2) + (8 - 5) - (4 - 1) - 2$

8. $(4 + 3) \times (5 - 2) \times (2 - 1)^2$

Name ______________________

Properties

Commutative and Associative Properties

Numbers behave in specific ways. Each kind of number behavior is called a property.

Commutative Property of Addition: You can add addends *in any order* without changing the sum. $7 + 3 + 6 = 6 + 3 + 7$

Commutative Property of Multiplication: You can multiply factors *in any order* without changing the product. $5 \times 2 \times 9 = 9 \times 5 \times 2$

Associative Property of Addition: You can group addends any way you like without changing the sum. $(7 + 8) + 3 = 7 + (8 + 3)$

Associative Property of Multiplication: You can group factors any way you like without changing the product. $(3 \times 12) \times 4 = 3 \times (12 \times 4)$

Distributive and Identity Properties

Distributive Property of Multiplication: To multiply a sum of two or more numbers, you can multiply by each number separately, and then *add* the products. To multiply the difference of two numbers, multiply separately and *subtract* the products.

Some numbers in a problem do not affect the answer. These numbers are called **Identity Elements**.

With adding, the identity element is 0, because any addend or addends + 0 will not change the total. In multiplication, the identity element is 1, because any factor or factors × 1 will not change the product. However, subtraction and division do not have identity elements.

Examples:

$9 \times (2 + 5) = (9 \times 2) + (9 \times 5)$
$5 \times (12 - 10) = (5 \times 12) - (5 \times 10)$

You can also use the Distributive Property for dividing, but *only* if the numbers you are adding or subtracting are in the dividend.
$(28 + 8) \div 4 = (28 \div 4) + (8 \div 4)$

However, you *cannot* use the Distributive Property when the numbers you are adding or subtracting are in the divisor.
$28 \div (4 + 2)$ *does not* $= (28 \div 4) + (28 \div 2)$

Properties of Equality and Zero

Zero Property of Multiplication: Any number multiplied by zero will be zero. $16 \times \mathbf{0} = \mathbf{0}$

Equality Property of Addition: You can keep an equation equal if you add *the same number* to both sides. $(6 + 4) \mathbf{+ 3} = (9 + 1) \mathbf{+ 3}$

Equality Property of Subtraction: You can keep an equation equal if you subtract *the same number* from both sides.
$(6 + 4) \mathbf{- 5} = (9 + 1) \mathbf{- 5}$

Equality Property of Multiplication: You can keep an equation equal if you multiply both sides by *the same number*. $(6 + 4) \mathbf{\times 10} = (9 + 1) \mathbf{\times 10}$

Equality Property of Division: You can keep an equation equal if you divide both sides by *the same number*. $(6 + 4) \mathbf{\div 2} = (9 + 1) \mathbf{\div 2}$

Remember...

You may **never** divide a number by zero.

Name ______________________________

Negative Numbers

Negative numbers are numbers that are less than zero. You identify them by adding a minus sign to the front of a number. So −1 is 1 less than 0. −53.5 is 53.5 less than 0. There are special symbols used in comparing the number value parts.

< means "less than"
> means "greater than"
≤ means "less than or equal to"
≥ means "greater than or equal to"
= means "equal to"

Remember...

Zero (0) is neither positive nor negative.

Examples:

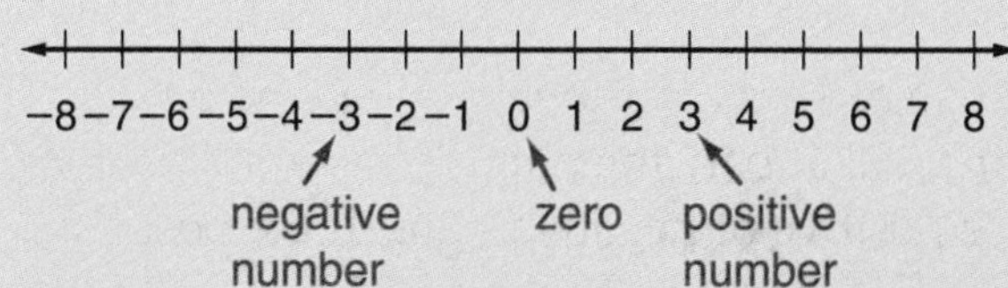

Look at the number line. Notice that −3 is three spaces to the left of 0 on the negative side. Also note that 3 is three spaces to the right of 0, on the positive side.

The Property of Additive Inverse: When you add a negative number to its inverse (its exact opposite on the other side of the number line), the total is 0.

For example, $-7 + 7 = 0$.

Exercises CALCULATE

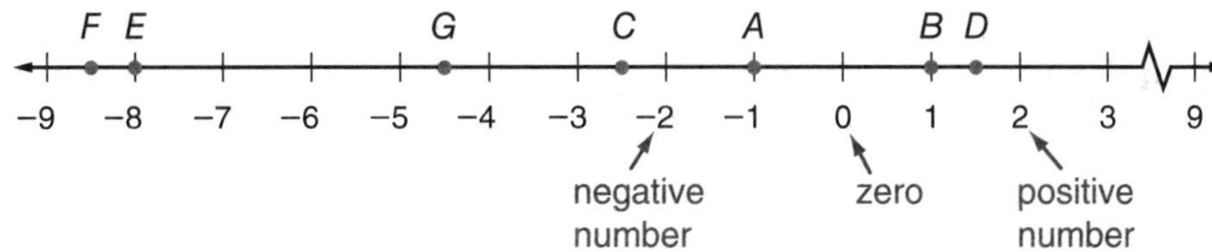

1. On the number line, place and label the number values as points on the number line.
A (−1), B (1), C (−2.5), D (1.5), E (−8), F (−8.5), G (−4.5)
Then order values from least to greatest.

____

2. Order the number values from greatest to least.
4.6, −6.6, −6, −6.7, −4.3, 3, 3.3, −3.3, 8, −8.1

____

Use > (is greater than), < (is less than), or = (is equal to) in comparing the number value pairs.

3. −4.5 ________ 4.5

4. −3.3 ________ −3.0

5. 7.5 ________ −7.5

6. −7.5 ________ 1.5

7. −6.1 ________ −6.25

8. −5 ________ −4.95

9. 13.9 ________ 13.9

10. −9 ________ 9

11. −8 ________ −0.888

Name ______________________

Adding and Subtracting Negative Numbers

When you add a positive number and a negative number, compare the numbers as if they do not have positive or negative signs. If the positive number is larger, just subtract.

Example: $6 + (-4) = ?$

Step 1: Remove the + sign and the parentheses.

Step 2: Subtract: $6 - 4 = 2$

If the negative number is larger, subtract the smaller number from the larger one. Then put a minus sign in front of the difference.

Example: $1 + (-3) = ?$

Step 1: Subtract the smaller from the greater number: $3 - 1 = 2$

Step 2: Write a minus sign in front of the difference: $1 + (-3) = -2$

When adding two negative numbers, ignore the minus sign and add. Then write a minus sign in front of the total.

Example: $(-1) + (-6) = ?$

Step 1: Ignore the minus signs and add: $1 + 6 = 7$

Step 2: Write a minus sign in front of the total: $(-1) + (-6) = -7$

Exercises ADD OR SUBTRACT

1. $171 + (-32) =$ ______
2. $(-145) + 61 =$ ______
3. $111 + (-112) =$ ______
4. $715 + (-316) =$ ______
5. $1101 + (-561) - 114 =$ ______
6. $295 + (-365) + (-111) =$ ______
7. $(-210) + (-210) - 427 =$ ______
8. $71 + (-53) + 10 =$ ______
9. $301 + (-222) =$ ______
10. $118 - 181 - (-128) =$ ______
11. $(-125) + 214 =$ ______
12. $85 - 19 + 24 + (-110) =$ ______
13. $27 + (-79) - 30 =$ ______
14. $(-213) + 163 + (-119) =$ ______
15. $42 + 22 + (-67) - (-31) =$ ______
16. $12 - (-29) - 29 =$ ______

Name ________________________________

Multiplying and Dividing Negative Numbers

Negative numbers can also be multiplied and divided. You just need to remember these two rules:

When two numbers have the same sign, either negative or positive, their product, or quotient, is *positive*.

When two numbers have different signs, one negative and one positive, their product, or quotient, is *negative*.

Examples:

$5 \times 4 = 20$	$(-5) \times (-4) = 20$
$(-5) \times 4 = -20$	$5 \times (-4) = -20$
$6 \div 2 = 3$	$(-6) \div (-2) = 3$
$(-6) \div 2 = -3$	$6 \div (-2) = -3$

Exercises MULTIPLY OR DIVIDE

1. $-5 \times (-3) =$ ____________
2. $15 \times (-10) =$ ____________
3. $-100 \div 10 =$ ____________
4. $-25 \times -3 =$ ____________
5. $-15 \times 15 =$ ____________
6. $-12 \times -5 \times -5 =$ ____________
7. $-2 \times 14 =$ ____________
8. $-11 \times 21 =$ ____________
9. $-15 \times -5 \times 3 =$ ____________
10. $-3 \times -103 \times -2 =$ ____________
11. $-20 \div -20 \times 14 =$ ____________
12. $-22 \times 11 \times -10 =$ ____________
13. $-8 \times -14 =$ ____________
14. $-132 \div 44 =$ ____________
15. $(150 \div -30) \times -3 =$ ____________
16. $55 \div -55 \times -12 =$ ____________
17. $(-90 \div -3) \div -15 =$ ____________
18. $52 \times -13 \div -4 =$ ____________

Name ______________________________

Changing Improper Fractions to Mixed Numbers

To understand fractions, there are some terms you need to know. For instance, the number on the bottom is the **denominator**. The denominator tells you what kind of units the whole is divided into: fifths, halves, quarters, and so on. The number on the top is the **numerator**, which tells how many of those units there are.

A fraction is less than 1 when the numerator is less than the denominator. Any fraction greater than 1 is an **improper fraction**. An improper fraction can be changed into a **mixed number**, which is part whole number and part fraction.

Example: Change $\frac{13}{4}$ to a mixed number.

To change an improper fraction into a mixed number, divide the numerator by the denominator. The whole number part is the quotient. The remainder becomes the numerator of the fraction. The denominator remains the same.

Step 1: $13 \div 4 = 3$ with a remainder of 1

Step 2: Write the 3 as your quotient, the 1 as your numerator, and keep the denominator as 4.

$$\frac{13}{4} = 3\frac{1}{4}$$

Exercises CONVERT TO A MIXED NUMBER

1. $\frac{64}{3}$
2. $\frac{101}{4}$
3. $\frac{15}{2}$
4. $\frac{52}{3}$
5. $\frac{66}{12}$
6. $\frac{137}{11}$
7. $\frac{176}{16}$
8. $\frac{61}{8}$
9. Gerrie collects honey from a few beehives. She scoops out the honey with a small jar that holds $\frac{1}{3}$ of a cup. Over the last two weeks Gerrie has filled this jar 158 times. How many cups of honey has she collected?

   ____

10. To finish sewing her tapestry, Petra needs 142 strips of cloth that are each one quarter of a yard. How many yards of cloth is that?

    ____

Name ______________________________

Changing Mixed Numbers to Improper Fractions

Now you know how to change an improper fraction to a mixed number. But can you also change a mixed number into an improper fraction? Yes, and it is simple. First, multiply the whole number by the denominator of the fraction. Then, add the numerator to that product. Finally, place the total over the denominator.

Example: Change $8\frac{3}{5}$ into an improper fraction.

Step 1: $5 \times 8 = 40$

Step 2: $40 + 3 = 43$

$8\frac{3}{5} = \frac{43}{5}$

Exercises CONVERT TO AN IMPROPER FRACTION

1. $5\frac{3}{4}$
2. $7\frac{5}{7}$
3. $25\frac{7}{11}$
4. $24\frac{4}{5}$
5. $16\frac{5}{13}$
6. $14\frac{9}{14}$
7. $53\frac{4}{9}$
8. $17\frac{3}{4}$

9. Gene's bucket holds $\frac{1}{3}$ of a pound of soil. Gene needs to move $10\frac{2}{3}$ pounds of topsoil to his grandmother's garden. How many times will he need to fill his bucket if he wants to move the entire pile of topsoil to the garden?

____

10. Kayla wants to give a third of a pie to each of her 25 relatives. She has already baked 6 pies. How many more pies will she need to bake so that each relative can have a third?

____

Name ______________________________

Adding and Subtracting Fractions with Like Denominators

ADDITION Two denominators that are exactly the same are called **like denominators**. They are easy to add, because you ignore the denominators when you add them.

Example: $\frac{5}{9} + \frac{2}{9} = ?$

In this example, all you do is add the numerators. Then place the total over the denominator in both fractions.

Step 1: $5 + 2 = 7$

$$\frac{5}{9} + \frac{2}{9} = \frac{7}{9}$$

Exercises ADD

1. $\frac{3}{4} + \frac{3}{4}$

2. $\frac{1}{5} + \frac{4}{5}$

3. $\frac{5}{8} + \frac{5}{8}$

4. $\frac{7}{9} + \frac{4}{9}$

5. $\frac{4}{11} + \frac{3}{11}$

6. $\frac{15}{17} + \frac{5}{17}$

7. $\frac{7}{9} + \frac{14}{9}$

8. $\frac{2}{3} + \frac{5}{3}$

9. Manny combined $\frac{1}{7}$ quarts of orange juice, $\frac{2}{7}$ quarts of lemonade, and $\frac{5}{7}$ quarts of raspberry tea into one container. How much liquid is now in the container? Express your answer as a mixed number.

____

10. James, Riley, and Nancy surveyed their class about the cafeteria food. James surveyed $\frac{2}{9}$ of the class, Riley surveyed another $\frac{5}{9}$ of the class, and Nancy surveyed another $\frac{1}{9}$ of the class. Were the three of them able to poll the entire class?

____

Name ______________________________

Adding and Subtracting Fractions with Like Denominators (cont.)

SUBTRACTION Do you use the same process when you subtract fractions with like denominators? Yes, the process is exactly the same! Ignore the denominator when doing your work.

Example: $\frac{14}{17} - \frac{9}{17} = ?$

Step 1: $14 - 9 = 5$

$\frac{14}{17} - \frac{9}{17} = \frac{5}{17}$

Remember...

To add or subtract fractions with like denominators, you only need to work with the numerators. Then put your total, or difference, over the like denominator.

Exercises **SUBTRACT**

11. $\frac{3}{4} - \frac{1}{4}$
12. $\frac{3}{3} - \frac{2}{3}$
13. $\frac{8}{9} - \frac{5}{9}$
14. $\frac{7}{8} - \frac{1}{8}$
15. $\frac{5}{7} - \frac{3}{7}$
16. $\frac{1}{2} - \frac{1}{2}$
17. $\frac{2}{3} - \frac{1}{3}$
18. $\frac{5}{3} - \frac{2}{3}$
19. Kira made $\frac{7}{8}$ quarts of grape juice and served $\frac{3}{8}$ quarts for dinner. How much juice does she have left?

    ____

20. Ellen bought $\frac{19}{16}$ pounds of flour from the store. On her way home, she spilled $\frac{11}{16}$ pounds of flour. If she needs $\frac{7}{16}$ pounds of flour to make bread, will she have enough flour?

    ____

Name ______________________________

Adding or Subtracting Fractions with Unlike Denominators

How do you add or subtract fractions if the denominators are different?

First you have to change the fractions so that they have like denominators. You must find the **common denominator**, another term for like denominator.

Remember...

When you multiply the numerator and the denominator by the same number, the value of the fraction does not change.

Example: $\frac{5}{8} + \frac{1}{6} = ?$

Look at the denominators, 8 and 6. The first thing you have to do is find a number that is a **common multiple** of both numbers. The simplest way to do that is to multiply the two numbers. $8 \times 6 = 48$. There might be a smaller common multiple that is easier to work with. Make a chart of multiples.

	2	3	4
8	16	(24)	32
6	12	18	(24)

When you find the lowest common multiple, take each fraction one at a time. Multiply the original denominator to make it become the common denominator, and multiply the numerator by the same number.

Step 1: Find a common multiple.

Step 2: $\frac{5}{8} = \frac{5 \times 3}{8 \times 3}$

Step 3: $\frac{1}{6} = \frac{4 \times 1}{4 \times 6}$

$\frac{15}{24} + \frac{4}{24} = \frac{19}{24}$

Exercises ADD OR SUBTRACT

1. $\frac{3}{4} + \frac{2}{5}$
2. $\frac{5}{7} + \frac{1}{3}$
3. $\frac{11}{20} + \frac{2}{3}$
4. $\frac{1}{4} - \frac{1}{13}$
5. $\frac{1}{4} - \frac{1}{9}$
6. $\frac{2}{21} + \frac{1}{3}$
7. $\frac{34}{11} - \frac{1}{3}$
8. $\frac{11}{7} + \frac{1}{6}$
9. $\frac{11}{15} - \frac{2}{3}$
10. $\frac{5}{8} - \frac{2}{7}$
11. $\frac{14}{11} + \frac{3}{7}$
12. $\frac{11}{12} - \frac{3}{5}$

Name ____

Adding or Subtracting Mixed Numbers with Unlike Denominators

ADDITION How do you add mixed numbers with unlike denominators?

There are *two* ways to do this. However, in both ways you will first have to find a common denominator for the fractions. One way is to change each mixed number to an improper fraction, then find the common denominator and add the fractions. The other way is even easier. Just add the whole number parts first. Find the common denominator for the fractions and add the fractions. Then add the total fraction to the total of the whole numbers.

Example: $3\frac{2}{3} + 6\frac{1}{2} = ?$

Step 1: Add the whole numbers.

$3 + 6 = 9$

Step 2: Find the common denominator.

$\frac{2}{3} = \frac{4}{6}$ and $\frac{1}{2} = \frac{3}{6}$

Step 3: Add the fractions.

$\frac{4}{6} + \frac{3}{6} = \frac{7}{6} = 1\frac{1}{6}$

$3\frac{2}{3} + 6\frac{1}{2} = 9 + 1\frac{1}{6} = 10\frac{1}{6}$

Remember...

Sometimes, when you add fractions, their total will be an improper fraction. You need to change it to a mixed number before adding it to the total of the whole numbers.

Exercises **ADD**

1. $12\frac{1}{2} + 3\frac{3}{4}$
2. $13\frac{3}{7} + 4\frac{3}{11}$
3. $5\frac{2}{7} + 3\frac{3}{8}$
4. $3\frac{1}{6} + 7\frac{1}{4}$
5. $4\frac{3}{11} + 3\frac{1}{3}$
6. $11\frac{1}{2} + 5\frac{2}{5}$
7. $4\frac{7}{9} + 5\frac{2}{7}$
8. $13\frac{3}{5} + 15\frac{7}{11}$
9. $22\frac{5}{6} + 27\frac{5}{13}$
10. $1\frac{1}{11} + 7\frac{2}{5}$
11. $44\frac{1}{2} + 14\frac{2}{9}$
12. $9\frac{5}{7} + 10\frac{1}{3}$

Name ______________________________

Adding or Subtracting Mixed Numbers with Unlike Denominators (cont.)

SUBTRACTION How do you subtract mixed numbers with unlike denominators? First, you need to find a common denominator for the fractions.

Example: $12\frac{5}{7} - 9\frac{2}{5} = ?$

Step 1: $12 - 9 = 3$

Step 2: Find a common multiple for the fraction.

$\frac{5}{7} = \frac{25}{35}$ and $\frac{2}{5} = \frac{14}{35}$

Step 3: Subtract the fraction.

$\frac{25}{35} - \frac{14}{35} = \frac{11}{35}$

Step 4: Add the difference of the whole numbers to the difference of the fractions.

$3 + \frac{11}{35} = 3\frac{11}{35}$

What do you do if the second fraction—the one you are supposed to subtract—is *larger* than the first fraction? In this case, subtract the *smaller* fraction from the *larger* fraction. Then, *subtract* the remainder of the fractions from the difference of the whole numbers. The following example will show you how to do this.

Example: $12\frac{5}{7} - 9\frac{4}{5} = ?$

Step 1: $12 - 9 = 3$

Step 2: Find a common multiple for the fraction.

$\frac{5}{7} = \frac{25}{35}$ and $\frac{4}{5} = \frac{28}{35}$

Step 3: Subtract the smaller fraction from the larger one.

$\frac{28}{35} - \frac{25}{35} = \frac{3}{35}$

Step 4: Subtract the fraction from the whole number.

$3 - \frac{3}{35} = 2\frac{32}{35}$

$12\frac{5}{7} - 9\frac{4}{5} = 2\frac{32}{35}$

Exercises SUBTRACT

13. $11\frac{5}{9} - 4\frac{9}{13}$
14. $13\frac{1}{6} - 10\frac{2}{15}$
15. $15\frac{2}{3} - 14\frac{1}{6}$
16. $20\frac{3}{4} - 11\frac{4}{9}$
17. $13\frac{5}{6} - 3\frac{5}{7}$
18. $23\frac{4}{5} - 19\frac{5}{11}$
19. $13\frac{4}{11} - 3\frac{1}{2}$
20. $11\frac{2}{3} - 10\frac{7}{9}$
21. $77\frac{1}{3} - 41\frac{5}{17}$
22. $9\frac{5}{7} - 3\frac{3}{14}$
23. $31\frac{7}{8} - 12\frac{2}{5}$
24. $45\frac{1}{3} - 32\frac{3}{7}$

Name ______________________________

Reducing Fractions

Reducing fractions to their lowest form requires you to divide the numerator and the denominator by a number that divides evenly into both numbers. The way to be certain that you have reduced a fraction correctly is to make sure that there is no number that will divide evenly into both the numerator and denominator. Remember that you will not change the value of a fraction if you multiply or divide its numerator and its denominator by the same number.

Example: Reduce $\frac{48}{120}$ to its lowest form.

Step 1: Find a common factor for both the numerator and the denominator: 12

Step 2: Divide both the numerator and the denominator by that factor:
$48 \div 12 = 4, 120 \div 12 = 10$

Step 3: Can the numerator and denominator be reduced further? Yes

Step 4: Find another common factor and divide both numbers by that factor:
$4 \div 2 = 2, 10 \div 2 = 5$

$\frac{2}{5}$ is the lowest you can reduce $\frac{48}{120}$

Exercises REDUCE

1. $\frac{8}{20}$
2. $\frac{49}{588}$
3. $\frac{525}{1890}$
4. $\frac{168}{3080}$
5. $\frac{24}{150}$
6. $\frac{18}{546}$
7. $\frac{120}{336}$
8. $\frac{220}{650}$
9. $\frac{3}{18}$
10. $\frac{42}{110}$
11. $\frac{3276}{5712}$
12. $\frac{686}{2000}$
13. $\frac{210}{315}$
14. $\frac{66}{528}$
15. $\frac{360}{1650}$
16. $\frac{182}{512}$

Name ___________________________

Multiplying Fractions and Whole Numbers

Is there a simple way to multiply a fraction by a whole number? Yes, you multiply the fraction's numerator by the whole number. Then write that product over the fraction's denominator.

Example: $17 \times \frac{2}{3} = ?$

Step 1: Multiply the whole number by the numerator. $17 \times 2 = 34$

Step 2: Place the number in the denominator.
$17 \times \frac{2}{3} = \frac{34}{3}$
If the final fraction is an improper fraction, you need to change it to a mixed number.

Step 3: Convert to a mixed number: $\frac{34}{3} = 11\frac{1}{3}$
$17 \times \frac{2}{3} = 11\frac{1}{3}$

Exercises **MULTIPLY**

1. $13 \times \frac{1}{4}$
2. $15 \times \frac{2}{7}$
3. $22 \times \frac{3}{8}$
4. $24 \times \frac{3}{4}$
5. $18 \times \frac{7}{20}$
6. $31 \times \frac{2}{17}$
7. $6 \times \frac{7}{24}$
8. $14 \times \frac{10}{11}$
9. $16 \times \frac{5}{36}$
10. $7 \times \frac{2}{3}$
11. $16 \times \frac{3}{5}$
12. $14 \times \frac{11}{28}$
13. $44 \times \frac{6}{7}$
14. $20 \times \frac{23}{40}$
15. $33 \times \frac{6}{11}$
16. $25 \times \frac{16}{45}$
17. Before setting out on a bike ride, each rider was given $\frac{5}{8}$ gallons of water to carry with them on the trip. If there are 28 people on the bike ride, how much water was dispensed?

    ____

18. Norbert estimates that it takes $1\frac{2}{7}$ hours to complete one load of laundry. If Norbert's dad has 8 loads of laundry to do, how long will it take him to finish?

    ____

Name ______________________________

Multiplying Two Fractions; Reciprocals

Is it difficult to multiply two fractions? No, it is simple. Multiply the numerators to get the numerator of the product. Then multiply the denominators to get the denominator of the product.

Example: $\frac{3}{5} \times \frac{8}{9} = ?$

Step 1: Multiply the numerators. $3 \times 8 = 24$

Step 2: Multiply the denominators. $5 \times 9 = 45$

$\frac{3}{5} \times \frac{8}{9} = \frac{24}{45}$

Step 3: Reduce to lowest form. $\frac{24}{45} = \frac{8}{15}$

$\frac{3}{5} \times \frac{8}{9} = \frac{8}{15}$

If the fractions are **reciprocals**, you do not have to multiply at all. Reciprocals are two fractions that look like each other upside-down. The numerator of the first is the denominator of the second, and the numerator of the second is the denominator of the first. The product of reciprocals is *always* 1.

Example: $\frac{2}{3} \times \frac{3}{2} = ?$

Step 1: Multiply the numerators. $2 \times 3 = 6$

Step 2: Multiply the denominators. $3 \times 2 = 6$

$\frac{2}{3} \times \frac{3}{2} = \frac{6}{6} = 1$

Exercises MULTIPLY

1. $\frac{3}{2} \times \frac{4}{9}$
2. $\frac{5}{9} \times \frac{12}{30}$
3. $\frac{15}{21} \times \frac{6}{25}$
4. $\frac{1}{2} \times \frac{1}{2}$
5. $\frac{2}{3} \times \frac{3}{4}$
6. $\frac{5}{4} \times \frac{16}{35}$
7. $\frac{5}{18} \times \frac{9}{25}$
8. $\frac{4}{14} \times \frac{28}{64}$
9. $\frac{13}{22} \times \frac{11}{13}$
10. $\frac{12}{13} \times \frac{52}{72}$
11. $\frac{2}{15} \times \frac{2}{15}$
12. $\frac{21}{24} \times \frac{8}{35}$
13. $\frac{48}{21} \times \frac{42}{64}$
14. $\frac{7}{9} \times \frac{9}{14}$
15. $\frac{15}{18} \times \frac{9}{25}$
16. $\frac{10}{13} \times \frac{26}{45}$
17. Daisy runs on an oval track that is $\frac{1}{4}$ of a mile long. If she runs $\frac{5}{16}$ of the way around the track, how far did she run?

    ____

18. Bart's family's motorboat uses $\frac{22}{6}$ gallons of gas every hour. If they run the boat for $\frac{1}{3}$ of an hour, how much gas will they be using?

    ____

Name ______________________

Multiplying Fractions and Mixed Numbers

How do you multiply a fraction and a mixed number? The easiest way is to change the mixed number into an improper fraction. Then multiply the fractions as you would normally.

Example: $4\frac{1}{8} \times \frac{1}{3} = ?$

Step 1: Change the mixed number into an improper fraction. $4\frac{1}{8} = \frac{33}{8}$

Step 2: Multiply the fractions. $\frac{33}{8} \times \frac{1}{3} = \frac{33}{24}$

Step 3: Convert the improper fraction to a mixed number and reduce. $\frac{33}{24} = 1\frac{3}{8}$

$4\frac{1}{8} \times \frac{1}{3} = 1\frac{3}{8}$

Remember...

You do not always have to wait until you finish multiplying to reduce. Sometimes you can reduce *before* you multiply. If you are multiplying two fractions, look at both numerators and then at both denominators. If you can divide *either* numerator by the same number as *either* denominator, you can reduce! For example: The denominator 10 and the numerator 15 can both be divided evenly by 5.

$\frac{17}{10} \times \frac{15}{4} = \frac{17}{(10 \div 5)} \times \frac{(15 \div 5)}{4} = \frac{17}{2} \times \frac{3}{4} = \frac{51}{8}$

Exercises MULTIPLY

1. $6\frac{3}{4} \times \frac{1}{9}$
2. $\frac{1}{10} \times 4\frac{1}{6}$
3. $12\frac{1}{4} \times \frac{2}{7}$
4. $3\frac{1}{7} \times \frac{14}{11}$
5. $\frac{2}{5} \times 3\frac{3}{4}$
6. $4\frac{5}{7} \times \frac{7}{11}$
7. $4\frac{2}{5} \times \frac{3}{11}$
8. $3\frac{1}{4} \times \frac{4}{13}$
9. $3\frac{3}{5} \times \frac{10}{9}$
10. $\frac{3}{13} \times 4\frac{1}{3}$
11. $3\frac{2}{3} \times \frac{2}{11}$
12. $5\frac{1}{5} \times \frac{3}{13}$
13. $5\frac{1}{4} \times \frac{1}{3}$
14. $2\frac{4}{5} \times \frac{2}{7}$
15. $2\frac{1}{4} \times \frac{3}{10}$
16. $3\frac{1}{3} \times \frac{3}{5}$
17. Thomas can walk on his hands $20\frac{2}{5}$ yards in a minute. How far can he go in $\frac{3}{4}$ minutes?

    ____

18. Peyton plays a round of golf in $3\frac{3}{8}$ hours. How long would it take him to play $\frac{2}{3}$ rounds of golf?

    ____

Name ____

Multiplying Mixed Numbers

You know that mixed numbers can be changed into improper fractions. You also know how to multiply fractions. Can you figure out how to multiply mixed numbers? First you need to change the mixed numbers into improper fractions!

Example: $1\frac{7}{10} \times 3\frac{3}{4} = ?$

Step 1: Convert both mixed numbers into improper fractions. $1\frac{7}{10} = \frac{17}{10}$ and $3\frac{3}{4} = \frac{15}{4}$

Step 2: Multiply the improper fractions and reduce. $\frac{17}{10} \times \frac{15}{4} = \frac{255}{40} = \frac{51}{8}$

Step 3: Convert your fraction to a mixed number. $\frac{51}{8} = 6\frac{3}{8}$

$1\frac{7}{10} \times 3\frac{3}{4} = 6\frac{3}{8}$

Exercises MULTIPLY

1. $5\frac{1}{2} \times 3\frac{3}{4}$
2. $2\frac{1}{3} \times 2\frac{4}{5}$
3. $8\frac{1}{5} \times 3\frac{1}{7}$
4. $1\frac{3}{4} \times 12\frac{1}{3}$
5. $2\frac{1}{2} \times 4\frac{2}{3}$
6. $3\frac{1}{8} \times 3\frac{1}{7}$
7. $11\frac{1}{5} \times 6\frac{2}{3}$
8. $9\frac{1}{2} \times 5\frac{1}{5}$
9. $1\frac{2}{3} \times 7\frac{1}{5}$
10. $8\frac{3}{4} \times 3\frac{1}{2}$
11. $3\frac{5}{8} \times 5\frac{1}{4}$
12. $4\frac{2}{3} \times 4\frac{1}{2}$
13. $3\frac{1}{5} \times 2\frac{1}{10}$
14. $10\frac{4}{5} \times 2\frac{1}{11}$
15. $22\frac{5}{9} \times 1\frac{3}{5}$
16. $14\frac{3}{4} \times 2\frac{5}{7}$

Name ______________________________

Dividing Fractions by Whole Numbers

Dividing fractions differs from the method you used to divide whole numbers. You actually divide fractions by *multiplying*! To divide a fraction by a whole number, multiply the denominator by the whole number.

Example: $\frac{7}{9} \div 3 = ?$

Step 1: Multiply the denominator by the whole number. $9 \times 3 = 27$

Step 2: Reduce, if necessary.

$\frac{7}{9} \div 3 = \frac{7}{27}$

Exercises DIVIDE

1. $\frac{3}{2} \div 4$
2. $\frac{6}{16} \div 4$
3. $\frac{6}{27} \div 3$
4. $\frac{1}{12} \div 4$
5. $\frac{18}{57} \div 2$
6. $\frac{14}{15} \div 7$
7. $\frac{4}{9} \div 9$
8. $\frac{12}{18} \div 12$
9. $\frac{16}{22} \div 4$
10. $\frac{15}{19} \div 3$
11. $\frac{12}{31} \div 6$
12. $\frac{55}{63} \div 20$
13. $\frac{33}{477} \div 11$
14. $\frac{3}{14} \div 9$
15. $\frac{15}{31} \div 5$
16. $\frac{16}{63} \div 4$
17. Julius receives $\frac{3}{4}$ pounds of Swiss chocolate from his grandmother and wants to divide the chocolate evenly among his 8 friends. How much chocolate will each friend receive?

    ____

18. Paola has $\frac{18}{25}$ yard of yarn. She wants to cut the yarn into 3 equal pieces to make button loops. How long should she cut each piece?

    ____

Name ________________________________

Dividing Whole Numbers by Fractions

Dividing a whole number by a fraction also involves multiplication. To divide a whole number by a fraction, you multiply the whole number by the reciprocal of the fraction.

Example: $5 \div \frac{2}{3} = ?$

Step 1: Multiply the whole number by the reciprocal of the fraction. $5 \times \frac{3}{2} = \frac{15}{2}$

Step 2: Reduce, if necessary, and convert to a mixed number. $\frac{15}{2} = 7\frac{1}{2}$

$5 \div \frac{2}{3} = 7\frac{1}{2}$

Exercises DIVIDE

1. $5 \div \frac{1}{10}$
2. $9 \div \frac{3}{5}$
3. $14 \div \frac{7}{8}$
4. $12 \div \frac{4}{9}$
5. $12 \div \frac{3}{4}$
6. $42 \div \frac{7}{9}$
7. $45 \div \frac{5}{8}$
8. $24 \div \frac{2}{7}$
9. $16 \div \frac{2}{5}$
10. $5 \div \frac{3}{8}$
11. $16 \div \frac{4}{7}$
12. $39 \div \frac{3}{11}$
13. $15 \div \frac{3}{11}$
14. $14 \div \frac{7}{4}$
15. $27 \div \frac{3}{11}$
16. $33 \div \frac{3}{8}$
17. Brandon worked with his community to provide aid packages for recent hurricane victims. Each package was to contain $\frac{4}{15}$ pounds of sugar. How many packages could Brandon fill if he had 60 pounds of sugar to distribute?

    ____

18. Dahlia is planning a bike trip with her friends. Her plan is to ride for $\frac{3}{5}$ hour and then rest for $\frac{1}{5}$ hour. If the entire trip will take 20 hours to complete, how many rest stops will the team make during the ride?

    ____

Name ______________________________

Dividing Fractions by Fractions

How do you divide a fraction by another fraction? You multiply the first fraction by the reciprocal of the second.

Example: $\frac{3}{10} \div \frac{2}{3} = ?$

Step 1: Multiple the first fraction by the reciprocal of the second. $\frac{3}{10} \times \frac{3}{2} = \frac{9}{20}$

Step 2: Reduce, if necessary.

$\frac{3}{10} \div \frac{2}{3} = \frac{9}{20}$

Exercises DIVIDE

1. $\frac{6}{7} \div \frac{3}{8}$
2. $\frac{4}{14} \div \frac{2}{16}$
3. $\frac{2}{9} \div \frac{3}{7}$
4. $\frac{1}{4} \div \frac{1}{8}$
5. $\frac{5}{13} \div \frac{5}{9}$
6. $\frac{7}{9} \div \frac{1}{7}$
7. $\frac{1}{13} \div \frac{1}{3}$
8. $\frac{5}{17} \div \frac{2}{17}$
9. $\frac{4}{5} \div \frac{1}{4}$
10. $\frac{15}{24} \div \frac{5}{3}$
11. $\frac{6}{11} \div \frac{11}{7}$
12. $\frac{13}{17} \div \frac{26}{17}$
13. $\frac{3}{11} \div \frac{22}{33}$
14. $\frac{4}{7} \div \frac{4}{21}$
15. $\frac{9}{14} \div \frac{3}{7}$
16. $\frac{3}{5} \div \frac{5}{3}$

17. A recipe calls for the use of $\frac{1}{16}$ ounce of batter for each muffin. How many muffins can be made from $\frac{7}{8}$ ounces of batter?

____

18. How many miles can a go-cart travel on a full tank of gas if the gas tank holds $\frac{15}{16}$ gallons and burns $\frac{1}{8}$ gallons for each mile traveled?

____

Name ______________________________

Dividing Mixed Numbers

How can you use a reciprocal to divide one mixed number by another mixed number? First, change both mixed numbers into improper fractions. Then multiply the first fraction by the reciprocal of the second.

Example: $3\frac{3}{5} \div 2\frac{3}{6} = ?$

Step 1: Convert both mixed numbers to improper fractions. $3\frac{3}{5} = \frac{18}{5}$ and $2\frac{3}{6} = \frac{15}{6}$

Step 2: Multiply the first fraction by the reciprocal of the second. $\frac{18}{5} \times \frac{6}{15} = \frac{108}{75}$

Step 3: Reduce, if necessary, and convert to a mixed number. $\frac{108}{75} = \frac{36}{25} = 1\frac{11}{25}$

$3\frac{3}{5} \div 2\frac{3}{6} = 1\frac{11}{25}$

Exercises **DIVIDE**

1. $3\frac{1}{6} \div 2\frac{1}{3}$
2. $4\frac{3}{7} \div 3\frac{3}{8}$
3. $5\frac{3}{7} \div 2\frac{2}{3}$
4. $5\frac{2}{9} \div 3\frac{2}{7}$
5. $7\frac{2}{5} \div 3\frac{3}{5}$
6. $4\frac{1}{4} \div 2\frac{3}{7}$
7. $3\frac{4}{9} \div 3\frac{2}{9}$
8. $3\frac{4}{11} \div 5\frac{1}{2}$
9. $4\frac{7}{13} \div 2\frac{2}{3}$
10. $3\frac{7}{13} \div 1\frac{5}{8}$
11. $1\frac{6}{7} \div 2\frac{2}{9}$
12. $3\frac{5}{8} \div 1\frac{7}{8}$
13. $2\frac{4}{7} \div 4\frac{1}{3}$
14. $6\frac{1}{2} \div 2\frac{1}{2}$
15. $7\frac{3}{5} \div 1\frac{4}{5}$
16. $1\frac{2}{9} \div 3\frac{1}{7}$
17. Ursula ran for $1\frac{3}{4}$ hours. If she ran $3\frac{3}{4}$ miles in total, how fast did she run in miles per hour?

    ____

18. Mason sorted $14\frac{5}{8}$ pounds of laundry into $2\frac{1}{2}$ loads. How many pounds were in each load?

    ____

Name ______________________________

Place Value and Rounding

Understanding place value can help you work with decimals.

Tens	Ones		Tenths	Hundredths	Thousandths
1	5	.	4	0	7

Look at the chart. Suppose you are asked to round a decimal to its highest whole number. You can do that by looking at the digit in the tenths place. If that digit is less than 5, round down and keep the whole number that is already there. If the digit in the tenths place is 5 or greater, add 1 to the whole number.

You can also round a decimal to its nearest tenth, its nearest hundredth, its nearest thousandth, and so on. Just look at the digit to the *right* of the rounding place. If that digit is less than 5, keep the digit you see in the rounding place. If that digit is 5 or greater, add 1 to the digit in the rounding place.

Exercises ROUND

Round to the nearest whole number.

1. 48.6
2. 98.3
3. 156.67
4. 3026.92
5. 189.41233
6. 2244.66795
7. 279.99556
8. 428.5

Round to the nearest tenth.

9. 124.5755
10. 175.5133
11. 349.49888
12. 313.35664
13. 375.77454
14. 44.00913
15. 566.9943
16. 61.15

Round to the nearest hundredth.

17. 1536.3357
18. 32.4589
19. 118.9977
20. 523.75776
21. 1099.989877
22. 1.11881
23. 33.43718
24. 555.555

Round to the nearest thousandth.

25. 729.239788
26. 409.13391
27. 8056.708035
28. 549.594959
29. 99.80007
30. 177.555901
31. 2012.20507
32. 901.901445

Name ______________________________

Changing Fractions to Decimals

What is the difference between a decimal and a fraction?

Actually, a decimal *is* a fraction expressed in a different way.

So $0.7 = \frac{7}{10}$ and $5.023 = 5\frac{23}{1000}$

However, decimals are expressed only in tenths, hundredths, thousandths, and so on. So some fractions cannot be converted to simple decimals.

Example: $\frac{5}{8} = ?$

Every fraction represents its numerator divided by its denominator. So $\frac{5}{8} = 5 \div 8$. Set up a simple division problem. Add a decimal point and as many placeholder zeros as you need in your dividend.

$$\begin{array}{r} 0.625 \\ 8\overline{)5.000} \\ \underline{4.8} \\ 20 \\ \underline{16} \\ 40 \\ \underline{40} \\ 0 \end{array}$$

As you can see,

$\frac{5}{8} = 0.625$, or six hundred twenty-five thousandths

Exercises CONVERT TO DECIMAL

Round to the nearest thousandth.

1. $1\frac{5}{16}$
2. $2\frac{4}{7}$
3. $\frac{48}{200}$
4. $3\frac{375}{500}$
5. $\frac{6}{200}$
6. $7\frac{13}{33}$
7. $\frac{52}{156}$
8. $4\frac{11}{15}$
9. $1\frac{1}{2000}$
10. $2\frac{33}{75}$

Name ______________________________

Changing Decimals to Fractions

Can you also change decimals to fractions? Yes, and it is much easier to do than changing fractions into decimals. Begin by looking at the *place value* farthest to the right. Use that as your denominator. The decimal number becomes the numerator. After you have changed the decimal into a fraction, you might even be able to reduce it.

Example: $0.72 = \frac{72}{100} = \frac{18}{25}$

Exercises **CONVERT TO FRACTION**

1. 1.3 ______________________________

2. 0.60 ______________________________

3. 0.588 ______________________________

4. 3.875 ______________________________

5. 6.75 ______________________________

6. 1.125 ______________________________

7. 3.26 ______________________________

8. 0.325 ______________________________

9. Chad had 0.625 gallons of gas left in his lawnmower at the end of summer. Restate the amount as a fraction.

____

10. Wanda toured the milk processing plant with her class. The guide said there were over 0.75 miles of conveyor belts in the plant. Restate that number as a fraction.

____

Name ____________________

Comparing and Ordering Decimals

If you look at place values, you can compare and order decimals just as you can compare and order whole numbers. Remember to line up your decimals so that the decimal points are all in the same column. As with whole numbers, each digit is one place value *higher* than the digit to its immediate right.

When comparing whole numbers with decimals, always look at the whole numbers first. If two whole numbers are the same, *then* compare by moving right from the decimal point. To compare decimals like 0.07 and 0.072, you can imagine a placeholder zero to make them both fill the same number of places. So 0.07 = 0.070. That is less than 0.072!

Example:

Order these decimals:
5.62 6.186 0.2 0.07 5.65 0.071 0.009

Decimals: 5.62
6.186
0.2
0.07
5.65
0.071
0.009

The order, reading from greatest to least is:
6.186, 5.65, 5.62, 0.2, 0.071, 0.07, 0.009

Remember...

When comparing numbers with decimals, always look at the whole numbers first. If two whole numbers are the same, then compare the numbers *to the right* of the decimal point.

Exercises COMPARE

Order from least to greatest.

1. 1.3, 1.031, 1.322, 13.1, 0.1332, 1.5, 1.55, 1.505

____

2. 0.751, 0.75, 7.51, 0.705, 0.075, 0.34, 1.675, 1.68

____

3. 0.17, 1.7, 0.017, 0.00175, 0.01695, 0.107, 1.07

____

4. 0.45, 0.625, 0.405, 0.420, 0.415, 0.451, 1.4

____

Order from greatest to least.

5. 0.25, 0.333, 0.15, 0.155, 0.125, 0.33

____

6. 0.332, 0.3334, 0.334, 0.3, 0.3033, 0.0335, 1.0001

____

7. 0.6667, 0.7501, 0.6, 0.75, 0.751, 0.707, 0.667

____

8. 0.68, 0.55, 0.6, 0.63, 0.6665, 0.06665, 0.59996

____

Name ______________________________

Adding Decimals

Is there anything special you need to know in order to add decimals? Yes, you need to make sure to line up your addends by place value. Once you do that, adding decimals is *exactly* the same as adding whole numbers.

Example: 79.46 + 8.65

```
  79.46
+ 08.65
  88.11
```

Remember...

You also need to put a decimal point in its proper column in the total!

Exercises ADD

1.
```
  145.415
   22.1
+  0.4667
```

2.
```
  436.911
+ 401.22
```

3.
```
  57.477
  81.534
+ 0.000543
```

4.
```
  12.232
   3.001
+  5.0019
```

5.
```
  73.045
   0.011
+  3.1
```

6.
```
  11.0809
+ 13.2291
```

7.
```
   0.882
  15.6
+  0.466
```

8.
```
  44.32
+  2.1109
```

9. Troy plays for the football team as a punter. Last week Troy made three punts of 11.324 meters, 12.6742 meters, and 10.227 meters. What was the total length of these three punts?

____

10. Kate measured the amount of rain that fell during the last three rainstorms. She measured 0.903 inches of rainfall for the first storm, 1.6778 inches for the second storm, and 1.2655 inches for the third storm. What was the total rainfall for the three storms?

____

Name ______________________________

Subtracting Decimals

Is subtracting decimals similar to subtracting whole numbers? Yes, but you have to remember to line up the decimals. Insert placeholder zeros if necessary.

Example: 243 − 178.861

$$\begin{array}{r} 243.\mathbf{000} \\ -\ 178.861 \\ \hline 64.139 \end{array}$$

Remember...

The value of a number does *not* change if you add a decimal point at the end and insert placeholder zeros. You can use as many placeholder zeros as you need to complete your calculations.

Exercises SUBTRACT

1. $\begin{array}{r} 17.382 \\ -\ 5.4445 \\ \hline \end{array}$

2. $\begin{array}{r} 28.001 \\ -\ 15.5628 \\ \hline \end{array}$

3. $\begin{array}{r} 102.87 \\ -\ 2.4801 \\ \hline \end{array}$

4. $\begin{array}{r} 38.3102 \\ -\ 33.5305 \\ \hline \end{array}$

5. $\begin{array}{r} 13.3333 \\ -\ 7.777 \\ \hline \end{array}$

6. $\begin{array}{r} 19.1113 \\ -\ 5.3741 \\ \hline \end{array}$

7. $\begin{array}{r} 575.002 \\ -\ 112.3145 \\ \hline \end{array}$

8. $\begin{array}{r} 9.0701 \\ -\ 6.90941 \\ \hline \end{array}$

9. The winner of the pole vault recorded a best vault of 5.8833 meters. The second place winner recorded a best vault of 5.4993 meters. What was the difference between the winning vault and the second-place vault?

____

10. Annie measured the depth of the water in the school's fountain and found there were 9.774 inches of water. Annie measured the depth of the water again the next day and noted that the water level was 1.7456 inches lower. What was the new depth of the water?

____

Name ______________________________

Multiplying with Decimals

When multiplying decimals, you do *not* line up the decimal points. You just multiply as if there were no decimal points at all. When you are finished multiplying, count the total number of decimal places in the **factors**, the numbers you have multiplied. Then, starting from the right of your product, count that number of places, and put your decimal point to the *left* of the last place you counted.

Example: 33.2 × 0.46

$$\begin{array}{r} 332 \\ \times \quad 46 \\ \hline 1992 \\ 13280 \\ \hline 15.272 \end{array}$$

Exercises MULTIPLY

1. $\begin{array}{r} 189 \\ \times\ 2.53 \\ \hline \end{array}$

2. $\begin{array}{r} 7.18 \\ \times\ 2.431 \\ \hline \end{array}$

3. $\begin{array}{r} 15 \\ \times\ 4.175 \\ \hline \end{array}$

4. $\begin{array}{r} 1.7 \\ \times\ 7.023 \\ \hline \end{array}$

5. $\begin{array}{r} 77 \\ \times\ 7.770 \\ \hline \end{array}$

6. $\begin{array}{r} 15 \\ \times\ 2.42 \\ \hline \end{array}$

7. $\begin{array}{r} 16 \\ \times\ 9.1 \\ \hline \end{array}$

8. $\begin{array}{r} 55 \\ \times\ 6.333 \\ \hline \end{array}$

9. Pauline's mom drives the soccer team to and from each of their away games. If the team has 12 away games, and on average Pauline's mom uses 2.775 gallons of gas to make the round trip, how much gas will she use for the whole season?

   ____

10. The delivery truck driver has 64 packages to deliver to the school. The average weight of a package is 13.7552 pounds. If the delivery truck has a load capacity of 900 pounds, can the delivery driver deliver all 64 packages in one load?

   ____

Name ______________________________

Dividing with Decimals

When dividing a decimal by a whole number, *only* the dividend has a decimal point. To calculate correctly, you must line up a decimal point in the quotient with the decimal point in the dividend.

When dividing either a decimal or a whole number by a decimal, you must move the decimal point of the divisor all the way to the right. So you must multiply the divisor by whatever power of 10 will do that. Then, you have to also multiply the dividend by that same power of 10.

Examples:

$92.4 \div 7$

Step 1: Complete the division problem, and make sure the decimal in the quotient aligns with the decimal in the dividend:

```
   13.2
7)92.4
  7
  22
  21
   14
   14
    0
```

$27 \div 0.08$

Step 1: Multiply both numbers by 100:
$0.08 \times 100 = 8$ $27 \times 100 = 2700$

Step 2: Complete the division problem:

```
   337.5
8)2700.0
  24
   30
   24
    60
    56
     40
     40
      0
```

Exercises DIVIDE. ROUND TO THE NEAREST HUNDREDTH.

1. 4.51)335
2. 7.1)416
3. 7.71)214
4. 88)145.2
5. 37)24.05
6. 2.24)44.8
7. 25)55.5
8. 7.8)273

Name ______________________________

Rational Numbers

A **rational number** is any real number that can be made by dividing two integers. In other words, any number that can be expressed as a fraction. Rational numbers include the set of whole numbers, the set of integers, plus fractions.

Examples:

The whole number 1 is rational because you can write it as $\frac{1}{1}$.

The negative integer −6 is rational because you can write it as $\frac{-6}{1}$.

The mixed number $3\frac{1}{3}$ is rational because you can write it as $\frac{10}{3}$.

The decimal 0.8 is rational because you can write it as $\frac{8}{10}$.

The repeating decimal $0.33\overline{3}$ is rational because you can write it as $\frac{1}{3}$.

Any rational number can be written as a decimal that is finite (ends) or eventually repeats.

To convert a repeating decimal to a fraction, set the repeating decimal equal to x. Find a power of 10 that you can multiply the number by to capture the repeating section, then subtract the original number and solve for x.

Example:

Convert 3.151515... to a fraction.

First, set the whole number 3 aside to isolate the repeating decimal: 0.151515...

Let $x = 0.151515...$

The repeating part is 15. You will need to go out 2 decimal places to capture the repeating part, so multiply by 10^2 to capture the repeating section.

$$100x = 15.1515...$$

Subtract x and the repeating decimal disappears.

$$\begin{aligned} 100x &= 15.1515... \\ -x &= \ \ 0.1515... \\ \hline 99x &= 15 \\ x &= \frac{15}{99} = \frac{5}{33} \end{aligned}$$

Now add back the whole integer 3 that we set aside in the beginning: $x = 3\frac{5}{33}$ or $\frac{104}{33}$.

Exercises CALCULATE

Circle each group the number belongs to (there can be more than one).

1. −16 whole integer rational
2. 0.006 whole integer rational
3. 7 whole integer rational

Name ____

Rational Numbers (cont.)

4. -1.953 whole integer rational

5. $-\frac{8}{17}$ whole integer rational

6. $3\frac{4}{5}$ whole integer rational

7. $-1\frac{3}{4}$ whole integer rational

8. $\frac{78}{79}$ whole integer rational

Change each number to a fraction.

9. -23 ________________

10. 0.156 ________________

11. 19.36 ________________

12. $8\frac{2}{3}$ ________________

13. -8 ________________

14. $2\frac{7}{9}$ ________________

15. 1.945 ________________

16. 7.8 ________________

17. $13\frac{1}{2}$ ________________

18. 76.38 ________________

19. -302 ________________

20. $9.\overline{3}$ ________________

Name ______________________________

Round to the nearest tenth.

1. 3406.997 ____________
2. 2,467,891.3554 ____________
3. 17.99986 ____________

Convert the decimal to a fraction.

4. 0.8 = ____________
5. 0.875 = ____________
6. 0.08 = ____________

Convert the fraction to a decimal.

7. $\frac{3}{5} =$ ____________
8. $\frac{8}{15} =$ ____________
9. $\frac{3}{16} =$ ____________

Put the decimals in order from least to greatest.

10. 0.122, 0.1145, 0.616, 0.6165, 0.513, 0.3132, 0.2126, 0.819

____

Add or Subtract.

11. $\begin{array}{r} 1.1564 \\ 2.1667 \\ +\ 3.337833 \\ \hline \end{array}$

12. $\begin{array}{r} 4.15466 \\ -\ 2.2355 \\ \hline \end{array}$

Multiply or Divide.

13. $\begin{array}{r} 0.4033 \\ \times\ \ 90 \\ \hline \end{array}$

14. $25\overline{)\$2.67}$

15. $0.025\overline{)0.5805}$

16. $\begin{array}{r} \$1.58 \\ \times\ 0.65 \\ \hline \end{array}$

Name ______________________________

17 Chad and his service club collected a total of 954.75 pounds of canned food for the local animal shelter. There are 15 people in the club. If each member collected the same amount of canned food, how many pounds did each member collect?

______________________________ pounds

18 Jane went to the store to buy food for a party of 6 neighbors. For each guest, she spent $2.55 for salad, $1.75 for a cold beverage, and $1.25 for a fruit cup. How much did she spend in total to buy the food?

____

Jane has $35. Does she have enough money to buy everything she needs?

____

If so, then how much change will Jane get back?

____

19 Rodney runs on a cross-country course that is 2.35 miles in length. During the week he ran the course $5\frac{1}{2}$ times. How far did he run that week?

____

20 Stan is preparing pots for planting flowers. He has 23.5 pounds of potting soil. If Stan fills each pot with 1.35 pounds of potting soil, how many pots can he fill?

____

21 Billy charges 45¢ per square foot to varnish patio decks. If the patio deck he is varnishing is 220.25 square feet in area, how much should Billy charge for the job?

____

22 Tracy mixed cold beverages for all of the teams participating in a local baseball tournament. For each batch, she mixed 3.25 gallons of lemonade with 1.3 gallons of iced tea. If Tracy made $8\frac{3}{4}$ batches, how many gallons of cold beverage did she make?

______________________________ gallons

Name ____________________

Solve.

23. Edie's local newspaper has 4476 pages of advertising each year. If the magazine is published once a week, about how many pages of advertising are in each issue? (Calculate using 52 weeks in a year.)

____

How many pages exactly?

____

Change each to a mixed number.

24. $\frac{45}{7}$

25. $\frac{66}{8}$

26. $\frac{1}{2} \times 44$

27. $\frac{1}{4} \times 22$

28. $\frac{11}{18} \times \frac{11}{22}$

29. $\frac{2}{3} \times 4\frac{3}{5}$

30. $18 \times \frac{7}{9}$

31. $\frac{15}{29} \div 45$

Calculate using Order of Operations (PEMDAS).

32. $4 \times 2(8 - 4) + (12 - 6) \times 2 + (6 - 4) \times 3 + 22$

____

33. $12 + 2(7 - 5) + (5 - 2) \times 2 + 2(6 - 2)$

____

34. $22 + (2 \times 5) \times 2 + 2(7 - 3)$

____

35. $36 - 3(6 - 2) + 7 \times 3 + 2(5) - 4$

____

Name ______________________________

Solve the equation and indicate the point on the number line that corresponds with the answer.

36 $-5 + 5 - 5$ ______

37 $-10 + 4 - 1$ ______

38 $-7 + (-4) + 3$ ______

39 $9 - 5 + (-7)$ ______

Calculate.

40 -60×25 ______

41 $-135 \div 15$ ______

42 $12 \times (-5 - 7) \div (8 - 16)$ ______

43 $630 \div -70$ ______

44 $14(-6) \div -7$ ______

45 $-5 \times (-3) \times (14 - 18)$ ______

46 $-24 \times -3 \div -2$ ______

47 $15 \times -3 \div 9$ ______

48 $(19 - 23) \times (5 - 4) \times (17 - 15)$ ______

Name ______________________

Answers and Explanations

1. 3407.0
2. 2,467,891.4
3. 18.0
4. $\frac{4}{5}$ $\frac{8}{10}=\frac{4}{5}$
5. $\frac{7}{8}$ $\frac{875}{1000}=\frac{35}{40}=\frac{7}{8}$
6. $\frac{2}{25}$ $\frac{8}{100}=\frac{2}{25}$
7. 0.6 $5\overline{)3.0}$ = 0.6; 30; 0
8. 0.5333 $15\overline{)8.000}$ = 0.533…; 75; 50; 45; 50; 45; 5…
9. 0.1875 $16\overline{)3.0000}$ = 0.1875; 16; 140; 128; 120; 112; 80; 80; 0
10. 0.1145, 0.122, 0.2126, 0.3132, 0.513, 0.616, 0.6165, 0.819
11. 6.660933

$$\begin{array}{r} \scriptsize{121} \\ 1.1564 \\ 2.1667 \\ +3.337833 \\ \hline 6.660933 \end{array}$$

12. 1.91916

$$\begin{array}{r} \scriptsize{3\ 1\ 4\ 1} \\ \not{4}.1\not{5}466 \\ -\ 2.23550 \\ \hline 1.91916 \end{array}$$

13. 36.2970

$$\begin{array}{r} \scriptsize{2\ 2} \\ 0.4033 \\ \times\ \ 90 \\ \hline 36.2970 \end{array}$$

14. $0.11

$25\overline{)2.6700}$ = 0.1068; 25; 170; 150; 200; 200; 0

15. 23.22

$0.025.\overline{)0.580.50}$ = 23.22; 50; 80; 75; 55; 50; 50; 50; 0

16. $1.03

$$\begin{array}{r} \scriptsize{3\ 4} \\ \scriptsize{2\ 4} \\ 1.58 \\ \times\ 0.65 \\ \hline 7^{1}90 \\ 9^{1}480 \\ \hline 1.0270 \end{array}$$

17. 63.65

$15\overline{)954.75}$ = 63.65; 90; 54; 45; 97; 90; 75; 75; 0

18. $33.30, yes, $1.70

$2.55 + $1.75 + $1.25 = $5.55;
6 × $5.55 = $33.30;
$35.00 − $33.30 = $1.70

19. 12.925 miles

$2.35 \times 5.5 = 12.925$

20. 17 pots $23.5 \div 1.35 = 17.41$
21. $99.11

220.25 × $.45 = $99.11

22. 39.8 gallons

$3.25 + 1.3 = 4.55;$
$8.75 \times 4.55 = 39.8125$

23. 90; 86 $4500 \div 50 = 90;$
$4{,}476 \div 52 = 86.08$
24. $6\frac{3}{7}$ $45 \div 7 = 6$ R3, so $6\frac{3}{7}$
25. $8\frac{1}{4}$ $66 \div 8 = 8$ R2, so $8\frac{2}{8} = 8\frac{1}{4}$
26. 22

$$\frac{1}{\not{2}_{1}} \times \frac{\not{44}^{22}}{1} = \frac{22}{1} = 22$$

27. $5\frac{1}{2}$

$$\frac{1}{\not{4}_{2}} \times \frac{\not{22}^{11}}{1} = \frac{11}{2} = 5\frac{1}{2}$$

28. $\frac{11}{36}$

$$\frac{11}{18} \times \frac{\not{11}^{1}}{\not{22}_{2}} = \frac{11}{18} \times \frac{1}{2} = \frac{11}{36}$$

29. $3\frac{1}{15}$

$$\frac{2}{3} \times \frac{23}{5} = \frac{46}{15} = 3\frac{1}{15}$$

30. 14

$$\frac{\not{18}^{2}}{1} \times \frac{7}{\not{9}_{1}} = \frac{14}{1} = 14$$

31. $\frac{1}{87}$

$$\frac{\not{15}^{1}}{29} \times \frac{1}{\not{45}_{3}} = \frac{1}{87}$$

Name ______________________________

32. 72

$4 \times 2(4) + (6) \times 2 + (2) \times 3 + 22$
$= 4 \times 8 + 12 + 6 + 22$
$= 32 + 12 + 6 + 22$
$= 72$

33. 30

$12 + 2(2) + (3) \times 2 + 2(4) = 12 + 4 + 6 + 8 = 30$

34. 50

$22 + (10) \times 2 + 2(4) = 22 + 20 + 8 = 50$

35. 51

$36 - 3(4) + 7 \times 3 + 2(5) - 4 = 36 - 12 + 21 + 10 - 4 = 51$

36. –5; Point A $-5 + 5 - 5 = 0 - 5 = -5$

37. –7; Point B $-10 + 4 - 1 = -6 - 1 = -7$

38. –8; Point D $-7 + (-4) + 3 = -7 - 4 + 3 = -11 + 3 = -8$

39. –3; Point C $9 - 5 + (-7) = 9 - 5 - 7 = 4 - 7 = -3$

40. –1500 $-60 \times 25 = -1500$

41. –9 $\frac{-135}{15} = -\frac{135}{15} = -9$

42. 18 $12 \times -12 \div -8 = -144 \div -8 = 18$

43. –9 $\frac{630}{-70} = -\frac{630}{70} = -\frac{63}{7} = -9$

44. 12 $\frac{14(-6)}{-7} = \frac{-84}{-7} = 12$

45. –60 $-5 \times (-3) \times (-4) = 15 \times (-4) = -60$

46. –36 $\frac{-24 \times -3}{-2} = \frac{72}{-2} = -36$

47. –5 $\frac{15 \times -3}{9} = \frac{-45}{9} = -5$

48. –8 $(-4) \times 1 \times 2 = -4 \times 2 = -8$

Name ______________________________

Ratios

What is a ratio? A **ratio**, often expressed as a fraction, compares two numbers.

Examples:

Eight people want equal shares of one pie. You could set up a ratio.

$$\frac{\text{1 pie}}{\text{8 people}}$$

When you remove the words, you can see that each person should get $\frac{1}{8}$ of the pie.

You can compare *any* two numbers with a ratio. For example: Shaundra read 5 books last month, and Carmen read 4.

$$\frac{\text{5 Shaundra books}}{\text{4 Carmen books}}$$

So the ratio of Shaundra's reading to Carmen's reading was 5:4 (say "five to four"). You can also express this as a mixed number. Shaundra read $1\frac{1}{4}$ times as many books as Carmen.

Exercises SOLVE

State the ratio as a fraction.

1. Paul is making a plaster mixture for his sculpture class. If he mixes 5 ounces of plaster with 4 ounces of water, what is the ratio of plaster to water?

   ____

2. Erika's mom separates the laundry into sets. If she puts two sheets and three pillow cases into each set, what is the ratio of pillowcases to sheets?

   ____

3. Floyd is setting tables for a sports banquet. For each place setting, he puts two forks to the left of the plate and a knife and a spoon to the right of the plate. What is the ratio of forks to knives?

   ____

4. Jean is making pizza. She adds 4 slices of pepperoni and 3 olives to each slice of pizza. What is the ratio of pepperoni to olives?

   ____

   What is the ratio of olives to pepperoni?

   ____

5. If the junior high has a ratio of 6 eighth graders for every 8 seventh graders, what is the ratio of seventh graders to eighth graders?

   ____

6. A peanut butter cookie recipe calls for 1 egg, 1 cup of peanut butter, and 1 cup of sugar. What is the ratio of sugar to peanut butter?

   ____

7. There are 15 boys in a class that has a ratio of 5:6 boys to girls. How many girls are in the class?

   ____

8. There are 12 boys in a class that has a ratio of 4:3 boys to girls. How many students are in the class?

   ____

Name ______________________________

Proportions and Cross-Multiplying

Do you ever have to use more than one ratio to solve a problem? Yes, a **proportion** is a problem that contains two ratios that are equal.

Example:

Suppose you want to give a party for 20 people. You know that two quarts of potato salad will feed 10 people, but how much potato salad will you need if you are feeding 20 people? When you have two ratios, but don't know the value of one of the numerators or one of the denominators, set up a proportion problem. This kind of problem is called an **equation**, a mathematical statement that two things are equal. You can use *q* to stand for the unknown number of *quarts.*

$$\frac{2 \text{ quarts}}{10 \text{ people}} = \frac{q}{20 \text{ people}}$$

Cross-multiplying is the way to find the missing number. Multiply the numerator of the first fraction by the denominator of the second fraction and write that on one side of the equation. Then multiply the denominator of the first fraction by the numerator of the second fraction and write that on the other side of the equation. To get the answer, look at the side of the equation that has both a known number and the unknown number. Divide *both* sides of the equation by that known number.

Step 1: Set up your equation. $\frac{2}{10} = \frac{q}{20}$

Step 2: Cross-multiply. $2 \times 20 = 10 \times q$

Step 3: Find the side of the equation with the unknown number. Then look at the known number on that side. (In this equation, it's 10.) Divide *both* sides of the equation by that known number. $40 \div 10 = 4$

$q = 4$

You will need four quarts of potato salad for 20 people!

Exercises SOLVE

Indicate (True or False) whether the ratios are equal.

1. $\frac{4}{9} = \frac{36}{81}$ ______
2. $\frac{5}{7} = \frac{35}{42}$ ______
3. $\frac{4}{3} = \frac{12}{9}$ ______
4. $\frac{9}{8} = \frac{16}{18}$ ______
5. $\frac{5}{12} = \frac{125}{300}$ ______
6. $\frac{6}{5} = \frac{36}{32}$ ______
7. $\frac{7}{11} = \frac{84}{132}$ ______
8. $\frac{5}{8} = \frac{25}{40}$ ______

Solve for the unknown variable.

9. $\frac{10}{6} = \frac{n}{36}$
10. $\frac{4}{x} = \frac{16}{24}$
11. $\frac{13}{26} = \frac{y}{78}$
12. $\frac{11}{m} = \frac{132}{60}$
13. $\frac{18}{28} = \frac{n}{42}$
14. $\frac{x}{19} = \frac{15}{57}$
15. $\frac{x}{52} = \frac{58}{104}$
16. $\frac{18}{15} = \frac{n}{10}$

Name ______________________________

Proportions and Cross-Multiplying (cont.)

17. A team of 5 players scored 486 points over 6 games. What is the average number of points per player in each game?

____

18. If a 12-pack of soda costs $5.50 and a 6-pack costs $3.55, which has the best price per soda?

____

19. The exchange rate between U.S. dollars and Euros is 0.86 Euros per U.S. dollar. How many Euros is $286 U.S. dollars?

____

20. Bags of chips are $0.79 each, which is $0.85 with tax. If Evelyn has $7.50, how many bags of chips can she buy?

____

Name ____________________

Rates

A **rate** is a fixed ratio between two things. It is solved exactly like a proportion problem.

Example: Maria drives at a rate of 65 miles per hour. How many hours does it take her to drive 195 miles?

Step 1: Express the proportion problem using two ratios. In this problem, let's use *h* for the unknown number of hours.

$$\frac{1 \text{ hour}}{65 \text{ miles}} = \frac{h \text{ hours}}{195 \text{ miles}}$$

Step 2: Cross-multiply.

$195 = 65 \times h$

Step 3: Divide each side by 65 to solve for *h*:

$h = \frac{195}{65}$

$h = 3$

So it will take Maria 3 hours to drive 195 miles!

Exercises SOLVE

1. George likes to sweeten his ice tea. When he is drinking a 20-ounce ice tea, he adds two teaspoons of sugar. If he makes a gallon of ice tea, how many teaspoons of sugar should he add (there are 128 ounces in a gallon)?

   ____

2. Peter wants to make scrambled eggs for the customers at the diner. His recipe calls for 12 eggs and is enough for 5 people. How many eggs will he need if he has to feed 75 customers?

   ____

3. A person needs to drink 3 quarts of water for every hour of running time. If a runner plans to complete a marathon in 5 hours, how many quarts of water should she drink during the race?

   ____

4. Diane's car uses 5 gallons of gasoline to travel 125 miles. How far will Diane be able to travel on 20 gallons of gasoline?

   ____

5. When Frank goes on a 4-day vacation with his family, he packs 4 t-shirts and 3 pairs of shorts. If he is going on an extended vacation for 12 days, how many t-shirts and shorts will he need to pack?

   ____

6. There were 90 customers at the restaurant on Friday, 60 of whom ordered the vegetarian meal. If there are 195 customers on Sunday, how many vegetarian meals would you expect to sell?

   ____

Name ____________________

Rates (cont.)

7. Cheri's car goes 27 miles per gallon. If she has 12.25 gallons of gas, how many miles can she go?

   ____

8. If Rilee can unload 90 boxes from a truck in 1 hour at her warehouse job, how long will it take her to unload a truck full of 360 boxes at the same rate?

   ____

9. It takes Bradley 20 minutes to drive to his office, which is 12 miles away. What is his average speed in miles per hour?

   ____

10. It takes Molly 38 minutes to decorate 24 cupcakes, but it only takes Jenna 32 minutes. How long will it take them to decorate 24 cupcakes if they work together?

    ____

11. Randy launched his website this year. During the first three months of operation, his site recorded 835,884 hits. If he maintains that same monthly average, how many hits should he expect by the end of the fifteenth month?

    ____

12. Vivian volunteered to register voters for an upcoming election. She was able to sign up 374 new voters in just 1 voting precinct. If there are 11 precincts in the town, and Vivian expects to have the same success rate in each precinct, how many new voters will she sign up before the election?

    ____

13. In a bicycle race, it took Sydney 2.3 hours to complete the first half of the course, which is a mostly flat 40 miles. The second half of the course was over hilly terrain, and it took him twice as long. What was his rate for the second half of the course?

    ____

14. If Aaron types 72 words per minute, how many minutes will it take him to type a 1500-word document?

    ____

Name ___________________________________

Proportions and Percent

What if you wanted to answer the question, "What percent of 80 is 48?"

Remember that the word **percent** means "per 100." Think of percent as a proportion where the denominator is always 100. So if you wanted to know what percent 48 is of 80, then you would set the problem up as a proportion.

Examples: What percent of 80 is 48?

Step 1: Express the problem using two ratios. Use x for the unknown. "48 is to 80 as x is to 100" or $\frac{48}{80} = \frac{x}{100}$

Step 2: Cross multiply: $4800 = 80x$

Step 3: Divide each side by 80 to solve for x:
$4800 \div 80 = 60$
$x = 60$
So 48 is 60% of 80.

What if you wanted to know what number is 50% of 90? Just like the first example, you would solve the problem using two ratios.

Step 1: Set up the problem using two ratios. Remember that percent is just a ratio with 100 as the denominator: $\frac{x}{90} = \frac{50}{100}$

Step 2: Cross-multiply: $100x = 4500$

Step 3: Divide each side by 100: $4500 \div 100 = 45$
$x = 45$
So 45 is 50% of 90.

Exercises CALCULATE USING PROPORTIONS

1. 40% of 50 is __________
2. 72 is 18% of __________
3. 14 is ________% of 35
4. 12% of 85 is __________
5. 50 is 40% of __________
6. 18 is ________% of 270
7. For a dance competition, 70 people auditioned and 70% of them qualified for the second round of competition. How many people were eliminated? ____________________
8. Mom set out a tray of cookies for the party and then went to change clothes. When she came back, she saw that 21 of the cookies were missing. She yelled, "You kids ate 30% of the cookies!" How many cookies had been on the tray originally? ____________________
9. Bruce used 1.5 inches of a piece of rope that had been 75 inches long. What percent of the rope did he use? ____________________

Name ______________________________

Percent Change, Mark-up, and Discount

When calculating **percent change**, you are determining the percentage change from a starting point. If you want to determine the percent your height has changed, say from 65 inches to 70 inches, you want to know how much it has changed relative to your starting height of 65 inches. Simple subtraction tells us your height has changed 5 inches, but to calculate the percent change, you must set up an equation: $\frac{\text{Change}}{\text{Starting point}} = \frac{x}{100}$

Example:

Starting height = 65 inches
Change in height = (70 in. − 65 in.) = 5 inches

Step 1: Set up your equation: $\frac{5}{65} = \frac{x}{100}$

Step 2: Calculate: $500 = 65x \quad 7.69 = x$
Your height has increased approximately 7.69%

Mark-up is an amount that you want to add to something you sell. Say your store's headquarters has determined that you should sell all your products at cost plus 25%; the 25% is called the mark-up. One way to calculate mark-up is to take the cost, calculate 25% of the cost, and add it to the cost. This is your selling price. If you have a product that costs $200, what is the mark-up and selling price? To calculate the mark-up you must set up a proportion.

Example:

Step 1: Set up your equation: $\frac{x}{200} = \frac{25}{100}$

Step 2: Calculate: $100x = 5000 \quad x = 50$
Your mark-up is $50, so you would sell the product for $200 + $50 = $250

Discount is much like a mark-up, but instead of increasing the price, you are reducing the price of an item. You are at a sale and the sign states to take 30% off all items. You see an MP3 player that has a price of $150. How much is it after the discount?

Example:

Step 1: Set up your equation: $\frac{x}{150} = \frac{30}{100}$

Step 2: Calculate: $100x = 4500 \quad x = 45$
The discount is $45, so the sale price would be $150 − $45 = $105

Exercises SOLVE

1. What is the selling price for an item that costs $50 and has a mark-up of 40%?

____

2. What is the mark-up amount for an item that costs $125 and has a mark-up of 35%?

____

3. What is the selling price for an item that costs $70 and has a discount of 40%?

____

4. What is the discount amount for an item that costs $160 and has a discount of 45%?

____

Name ______________________________

Percents and Fractions

Can you express percents in ways other than as a decimal? Yes, you can change percents into fractions. The denominator of a percent is *always* 100, and the numerator will be the number of the percent.

Example: 30% of 50 = ?

Step 1: Convert the percent to a fraction:
$30\% = \frac{30}{100}$

Step 2: Simplify the fraction if you can:
$\frac{30}{100} = \frac{3}{10}$

Step 3: Multiply: $\frac{3}{10} \times 50 = \frac{150}{10}$

Step 4: Simplify the product: $\frac{150}{10} = 15$
So 30% of 50 = 15

Some fractions can be turned into simple percents. If the denominator of the fraction can divide evenly into 100, find the quotient. Then multiply the numerator by the quotient, and add the percent sign. If the denominator of the fraction cannot divide evenly into 100, the fraction *cannot* be converted into a simple percent.

Example: $\frac{2}{5}$ = ?%

Step 1: Divide 100 by the denominator:
$100 \div 5 = 20$

Step 2 Multiply the numerator by the product:
$2 \times 20 = 40$

Step 3: Add the percent sign. 40%
So $\frac{2}{5}$ = 40%

Exercises CALCULATE USING MULTIPLICATION

1. 18 is ________% of 60
2. 20% of 85 is ________
3. $\frac{42}{70}$ = ________%
4. 30% of 90 is ________
5. $\frac{16}{128}$ = ________%
6. $\frac{12}{48}$ = ________%
7. 15% of 60 is ________
8. $\frac{24}{160}$ = ________%
9. 35% of 220 is ________
10. If $\frac{1}{5}$ of the class became sick from the flu, what percent of the class is that? ________
11. In a school of 250 students, 75 are eighth graders. What percent of the students are eighth graders? ________
12. Vicki divided her box of crayons into 3 equal piles to share with her friends. What percent does each person get? ________

Name ______________________________

Multiplying Percents and Fractions

Can you multiply percents and fractions? Of course! You've learned that percents can be expressed as fractions. So just convert the percent to a fraction and multiply the two fractions. But remember these two important points:

- If you find a percent of a fraction, the product will be a fraction.
- If you find a fraction of a percent, the product will be a percent.

Example: What is $\frac{1}{6}$ of 96%?

Step 1: Convert the percent to a fraction:

$$96\% = \frac{96}{100}$$

Step 2: Multiply the fractions:

$$\frac{1}{6} \times \frac{96}{100} = \frac{96}{600} = \frac{16}{100}$$

Step 3: Convert back to a percent:

$$\frac{16}{100} = 16\%$$

Example: What is 50% of $\frac{2}{3}$?

Step 1: Convert the percent to a fraction:

$$50\% = \frac{1}{2}$$

Step 2: Multiply the fractions: $\frac{1}{2} \times \frac{2}{3} = \frac{1}{3}$

50% of $\frac{2}{3}$ is $\frac{1}{3}$

Another way to find a fraction of a percent is to multiply the percent, *as if it were a whole number*, by the fraction. The product will almost always be an improper fraction. Change that fraction into a mixed number and add the percent sign.

Exercises CALCULATE

1. $\frac{5}{12} \times 60\% =$ __________
2. $\frac{3}{5} \times 82\% =$ __________
3. $\frac{6}{5} \times 55\% =$ __________
4. $\frac{8}{25} \times 125\% =$ __________
5. $\frac{4}{15} \times 75\% =$ __________
6. 25% of $\frac{4}{5} =$ __________
7. 20% of $\frac{5}{6} =$ __________
8. 40% of $\frac{15}{16} =$ __________
9. 75% of $\frac{112}{150} =$ __________
10. 60% of $\frac{40}{75} =$ __________
11. $\frac{7}{12} \times 72\% =$ __________
12. $\frac{5}{4} \times 42\% =$ __________

Name ___________________________

Percents and Decimals

How can you convert decimals with thousandths, ten thousandths, and even smaller places into percents? Just move the decimal point two places to the right and then add the percent sign.

Example: Rename 0.46072 as a percent.

0.46072 = 46.072%

Exercises CONVERT

Convert to a percent.

1. 0.7612 ________
2. 0.01543 ________
3. 1.59 ________
4. 0.5721 ________
5. 0.0012 ________
6. 0.000134 ________
7. 10.45 ________
8. 1.89 ________
9. 0.569 ________
10. 0.9999 ________
11. 0.0011 ________
12. 3.1345 ________
13. 99.99 ________
14. 0.175555578 ________
15. 0.187 ________
16. 0.87 ________

Name ______________________________

Simple and Compound Interest

SIMPLE INTEREST What does *simple interest* mean when you're talking about a loan or a bank account? How do you calculate it? The amount you borrow or put into the bank is called the **principal**. Simple interest is a percent of the principal that has to be paid, by you, if you borrow money, or by the bank, to you, if you deposited money. The **interest** is money that is *added* to the principal.

Example: Principal = \$500
Rate of Interest for one year = 4%

Step 1: Interest (i) =
Principal (p) × Rate of Interest (r):
\$500 × 4% = i

Step 2: Convert the Rate of Interest to a fraction:
$4\% = \frac{4}{100}$

Step 3: Calculate: $\$500 \times \frac{4}{100} = \$20.00$

If you wanted to pay the loan back at the end of the year, you would have to pay both the principal and the interest.

$p + i$ = \$500 (the principal) + \$20 (the interest)
= \$520

If you deposited this money into a savings account, the bank would have to add \$20.00 interest to your deposit at the end of a year.

Exercises CALCULATE

1. How much interest would you earn if you put \$500 in a bank for 15 years and received simple interest of 8%?

____

2. Calculate the simple interest on a bank account where you deposit \$500 and earn 12% a year for 5 years.

____

3. Calculate the ending balance of your savings account if you deposit \$400 and earn simple interest of 7% for 5 years.

____

4. Calculate the ending balance of your savings account if you deposited \$1000 and earned simple interest of 6% for 6 years.

____

Name ____________________

Simple and Compound Interest (cont.)

COMPOUND INTEREST What is the difference between compound and simple interest? Compound interest pays interest on the principal *and* the interest, while simple interest pays interest only on the principal.

Examples:

Let's look at an example where you put $100 in Bank A that pays compound interest of 10% each year, and $100 in Bank B that pays simple interest of 10% each year. We will examine what happens over 3 years.

	Bank A	Bank B
Starting Balance	$100	$100
Interest Earned Year 1	$10	$10
Ending Balance Year 1	$110	$110
Interest Earned Year 2	$11 ($110 × 10%)	$10 ($100 × 10%)
Ending Balance Year 2	$121	$120
Interest Earned Year 3	$12.10 ($121 × 10%)	$10 ($100 × 10%)
Ending Balance Year 3	$133.10	$130

The difference in balances is due to compound interest. If you want to calculate the balance you will have after *n* years, the formula is:

Starting Balance × (1 + interest rate as a decimal)[to the *n*th power]

Calculate the balance at Bank A after 3 years at a compounded interest rate of 10%.

Step 1: Convert the interest rate to a decimal: 10% = 0.1

Step 2: Set up an equation: $\$100 \times (1 + 0.1)^3 = x$

Step 3: Calculate: $\$100 \times (1 + 0.1)^3 = \$133.10$
The balance at Bank A after 3 years is $133.10

Exercises CALCULATE

5 Calculate the interest earned over a 5-year period when you deposit $2000 and earn compound interest of 8% per year.

____

6 How much interest would you earn if you put $500 in a bank for 20 years and received a compound interest rate of 4%?

____

7 How much money would you owe if you borrowed $2000 for 5 years, with a compound interest rate of 28%, and did not make any payments during that period?

____

8 Is it better to receive compounded interest for 7 years at 12% on your balance of $500, or to receive the same rate of simple interest for 9 years on that same balance?

____

Name ____________________

Determine if the following proportions are equal. (Write Yes or No.)

1. $\frac{5}{4} = \frac{24}{26}$ ______
2. $\frac{21}{12} = \frac{7}{36}$ ______
3. $\frac{12}{19} = \frac{38}{48}$ ______
4. $\frac{1}{4} = \frac{6}{24}$ ______

Solve for *x*.

5. $\frac{x}{10} = \frac{30}{20}$
6. $\frac{20}{x} = \frac{40}{100}$
7. $\frac{36}{90} = \frac{12}{x}$

Solve.

8. Walter looked at the list of nutrients in the fruit juice he bought. He noticed that there were a total of 4 grams of carbohydrates and 3 grams of sugar in every bottle of juice. Compare the amount of sugar to carbohydrates in the fruit juice.

____

9. Will rides his unicycle at an average speed of 8 miles per hour. How far will he travel in $2\frac{1}{2}$ hours? ______________________________

10. Jack makes 22 muffins for every 3 batches he bakes. How many batches of muffins will he need to bake in order to sell 242 muffins?

____

11. Priscilla drinks an average of $\frac{2}{3}$ quart of water for each mile she walks. How many quarts of water will she drink if she walks $\frac{2}{3}$ miles?

____

12. Jenny changes the oil in her car every 2,250 miles. How many times will she need to change the oil in her car if she takes a trip that is 9000 miles in length?

____

Name ____________________

13 30% of $1\frac{2}{5}$

14 40% of 440

15 $\frac{1}{4}$ of 48%

16 $\frac{2}{5}$ of 70%

17 $\frac{3}{8}$ of 340%

18 43% of 0.705

19 84% of 1.906

20 $\frac{3}{4}$ of 160%

21 Pete's Pet Emporium is having a sale on birdcages. Pete is selling his $50 cages at a 20% discount, his $75 cages at $\frac{1}{3}$ off, and his $100 cages at 60% off the original price. What are the new sale prices for the 3 cages?

$50 cage __________ $75 cage __________ $100 cage __________

22 Tom is selling wristbands for $4.50. He has to charge sales tax of 6% on each wristband. What is the cost to the customer, including sales tax, for one wristband?

____

23 Ursula put $200 into a money market account that pays 3% simple interest. How much will she have in her account at the end of 1 year if she does not deposit any more money in the account?

____

How much will she have at the end of 2 years?

____

24 Pam put $400 into a savings account that pays 2.5% in compound interest. How much will she have in the account at the end of 2 years, if she does not deposit any more money in the account?

____

How much will she have at the end of 5 years?

____

Name ______________________

25 Val has 175 stamps in her stamp collection, Chris has 133 stamps in his collection, and their son Kai has 212 stamps in his. If Val and Chris combine their stamp collections, what will be the ratio of their stamps to Kai's?

____

26 Carolyn's cell phone plan allows for 1200 minutes of free usage every month. During the month of March (March has 31 days), how many minutes per day can Carolyn talk on average without exceeding her monthly limit?

____

27 Cassie is counting the number of bricks she needs to build a retaining wall for her herb garden. She calculates that she will need 485 bricks to complete the project. If the bricks come in stacks of 24, how many stacks will she need to complete the project?

____

28 Preston's piggy bank contains only nickels, dimes, and quarters in a ratio of 5:3:2. If the bank contains 210 coins, how many are dimes?

____

Name ______________________________

Answers and Explanations

1. No $\frac{24}{26}=\frac{12}{13}$

2. No $\frac{21}{12}=\frac{7}{4}$

3. No $\frac{38}{48}=\frac{19}{24}$

4. Yes $\frac{6}{24}=\frac{1}{4}$

5. $x=15$ $(x)(20)=(10)(30);20x=300;x=15$

6. $x=50$ $(20)(100)=(x)(40);2000=40x;x=50$

7. $x=30$ $(36)(x)=(90)(12);36x=1080;x=30$

8. $\frac{3}{4}$ grams $3:4=\frac{3}{4}$

9. 20 miles $\frac{8\text{ miles}}{1\text{ hour}}=\frac{x\text{ miles}}{2.5\text{ hours}}$; $(8)(2.5)=(1)(x)$; $20=x$

10. 33 batches $\frac{22\text{ muffins}}{3\text{ batches}}=\frac{242\text{ muffins}}{x\text{ batches}}$; $(22)(x)=(3)(242)$; $22x=726$; $x=33$

11. $\frac{4}{9}$ quarts $\frac{\frac{2}{3}\text{ quart}}{1\text{ mile}}=\frac{x\text{ quarts}}{\frac{2}{3}\text{ mile}}$; $\left(\frac{2}{3}\right)\left(\frac{2}{3}\right)=(1)(x)$; $\frac{4}{9}=x$

12. 4 times $\frac{2250\text{ miles}}{1\text{ oil change}}=\frac{9000\text{ miles}}{x\text{ oil changes}}$; $(2250)(x)=(1)(9000)$; $2250x=9000$; $x=4$

13. $\frac{21}{50}$ $\frac{30}{100}\times\frac{7}{5}=\frac{3}{10}\times\frac{7}{5}=\frac{21}{50}$

14. 176 $\frac{40}{100}=\frac{2}{5}$; $\frac{2}{5}\times 440=\frac{880}{5}=176$

15. 12% $\frac{1}{4}\times 48=12$

16. 28% $\frac{2}{5}\times 70=\frac{140}{5}=28$

17. 127.5% $\frac{3}{8}\times 340=\frac{3}{2}\times 85=\frac{255}{2}=127.5$

18. 0.3032 $\frac{43}{100}\times 0.705=\frac{30.315}{100}=0.3032$

19. 1.601 $\frac{84}{100}\times 1.906=\frac{160.104}{100}=1.601$

20. 120% $\frac{3}{4}\times 160=\frac{3}{1}\times 40=120$

21. \$40, \$50, \$40 $\frac{20}{100}\times 50=\frac{1}{5}\times 50=10;50-10=40$; $\frac{1}{3}\times 75=25;75-25=50$; $\frac{60}{100}\times 100=60;100-60=40$

22. \$4.77 $4.5\times 0.06=0.27$; $4.5+0.27=4.77$

23. $206.00, $212.00 — $200 \times 0.03 = 6; 200 + 6 = 206; 6 \times 2 = 12; 200 + 12 = 212$

24. $420.25; $452.56 — $400 \times (1 + 0.025)^2 = 420.25;\ 400 \times (1 + 0.025)^5 = 452.56$

25. 77:53 — $175 + 133 = 308;\ \frac{308}{212} = \frac{77}{53}$

26. 38 minutes — $1200 \div 31 = 38.71$

27. 21 stacks — $485 \div 24 = 20.21$

28. 63 dimes — Divide the total number of coins by the total number of ratio parts to find the multiplier.

	ratio	multiplier	actual
nickels	5		
dimes	3	21	63
quarters	2		
total	10	21	210

Name ______________________________

Multiplying and Dividing Exponents

What if you want to multiply $3 \times 3 \times 3$? Or $5 \times 5 \times 5 \times 5$? Is there a simple way you can write that?

Yes, you can use an **exponent**. The number you keep multiplying by itself is called the **base**. The exponent (written as a small number next to and slightly above the base) tells how many times you multiply the base by itself.

Example: exponent

2^4 3^5 9^2 10^3

$2^4 = 2 \times 2 \times 2 \times 2 = 16$

$3^5 = 3 \times 3 \times 3 \times 3 \times 3 = 243$

$9^2 = 9 \times 9 = 81$

$10^3 = 10 \times 10 \times 10 = 1000$

Exponents are also called **powers**. So 10^3 is 10 to the third power. Any number can be a base. For example, 64 is 4 to the third power.

Often, when a base is raised to the second power, we use the word "squared." 25^2 can be expressed as "25 to the second power," or "25 squared." When a base is raised to the third power, we often use the word "cubed." So 12^3 can be expressed as "12 cubed."

Is there a simple way to multiply and divide bases that have exponents?

Yes. Can you figure out how to do that by looking at the following information?

$3^2 \times 3^3 = 3^5$ $2^4 \times 2^7 = 2^{11}$

$4^6 \div 4^4 = 4^2$ $10^7 \div 10^3 = 10^4$

Can you see how to do it?

To multiply a base raised to a power by the *same* base raised to a power, simply add the exponents. To divide a base raised to a power by the same base raised to a power, simply subtract the exponents.

Exercises CALCULATE

Express your answer using a base and an exponent.

1. $4^5 \times 4^5$
2. $7^5 \div 7^3$
3. $3^{16} \div 3^4$
4. $12^{22} \times 12^5$
5. $11^7 \times 11^5$
6. $12^{32} \div 12^{10}$
7. $10^5 \times 10^4$
8. $23^7 \div 23^6$
9. $16^{16} \div 16^2$
10. $15^5 \div 15^3$
11. $11^{11} \div 11^2$
12. $4^4 \times 4^7$

Name ______________________

Powers

What if you have a problem with 2 exponents separated by parentheses? Is there a rule for how to calculate that expression? Yes, let's take a look at the example.

Example: $(5^3)^3$

This expression means 5^3 multiplied by itself 3 times.

$(5 \times 5 \times 5) \times (5 \times 5 \times 5) \times (5 \times 5 \times 5) = 5^9$

The rule for this type of exponential expression is:
$(A^m)^n = A^{m \times n}$

What about an expression that looks like $(A^m)^n$, except the parentheses are left out: A^{m^n}?

In this case, the order of operations says that you calculate exponents first, so it would be A raised to the m^n power.

So $53^{3^3} = 53^{27}$

Exercises CALCULATE

Express your answer using a base and an exponent.

1. $(5^4)^3$
2. $(8^7)^5$
3. $(14^{10})^7$
4. $(3^{20})^8$
5. 7^{6^4}
6. 8^{2^4}
7. 19^{8^3}
8. 15^{9^3}
9. $(8^3)^8$
10. $(2^5)^6$
11. $(7^4)^{15}$
12. $(13^5)^3$
13. 18^{2^8}
14. 277^{6^4}
15. $(33^3)^{15}$
16. $(3^4)^5$

Name ____________________

More about Exponents

All the work that you have done with exponents has been with a positive number as the exponent, but there are also negative exponents.

What number does 5^{-3} represent? If we multiply $5^3 \times 5^{-3}$ and use the properties of exponents that you already learned, then $5^3 \times 5^{-3} = 5^{3+(-3)} = 5^0 = 1$

5^{-3} is the multiplicative inverse of 5^3, so $5^{-3} = \frac{1}{5^3} = \frac{1}{125}$

When you encounter a negative exponent, you simply apply the same rules of exponents you already know:

$A^m \times A^{-n} = A^{m-n}$

Exercises CALCULATE

Convert to a fraction.

1. 4^{-3}
2. 3^{-3}
3. 6^{-4}
4. 5^{-5}
5. 7^{-2}
6. 4^{-1}
7. 9^{-5}
8. 2^{-8}

Convert to exponential form.

9. $\frac{1}{64}$
10. $\frac{1}{81}$
11. $\frac{1}{9}$
12. $\frac{1}{25}$

Multiply.

13. $4^4 \times 4^{-2}$
14. $5^7 \times 5^{-4}$
15. $7^{12} \times 7^{-6}$
16. $14^{24} \times 14^{-20}$

Name ______________________

Squares and Square Roots

To square a number means that you take the number and multiply it by itself. If you square 6, the result is 36. This would be written as $6^2 = 36$.

Numbers that result from squaring an integer are called **perfect squares**. The numbers that are perfect squares and less than 200 are: 1, 4, 9, 16, 25, 36, 49, 64, 81, 100, 121, 144, 169, 196.

The **square root** of a number is the number that, when multiplied by itself, is equal to that number. The square root of 196, written as $\sqrt{196} = 14$ as $14^2 = 196$. The $\sqrt{\ }$ is called the **radical sign**.

Exercises CALCULATE

Identify the square root.

1. $\sqrt{49}$
2. $\sqrt{121}$
3. $\sqrt{225}$
4. $\sqrt{81}$
5. $\sqrt{144}$
6. $\sqrt{4}$
7. $\sqrt{1}$
8. $\sqrt{169}$
9. $\sqrt{16}$
10. $\sqrt{36}$
11. $\sqrt{100}$
12. $\sqrt{64}$

Square these numbers.

13. 1^2
14. 2^2
15. 3^2
16. 4^2
17. 5^2
18. 6^2
19. 7^2
20. 8^2
21. 9^2
22. 10^2
23. 11^2
24. 12^2

Name ______________________________

Irrational Numbers

An **irrational number** is any number that belongs to the set of real numbers, but cannot be written as a fraction made by dividing two integers. Unlike rational numbers that can be written as decimals that end or eventually repeat, irrational numbers are decimals that go on and on forever without ever repeating.

Example:

π is irrational because it equals a decimal that does not end or repeat: 3.14159265359…

What about the integers that are between the perfect squares? We know that their square roots are not integers. The number 45 is not a perfect square, but you know that its square root must be greater than 6 and less than 7 but closer to 7 as $6^2 = 36$ and $7^2 = 49$. The square root of a number that is not a perfect square is an irrational number.

$\sqrt{2}$ is irrational because it equals a decimal that does not end or repeat: 1.41421356237…

Exercises CALCULATE

Estimate the square root of a number.

1. $\sqrt{89}$ is between _______ and _______ but closer to _______ .

2. $\sqrt{44}$ is between _______ and _______ but closer to _______ .

3. $\sqrt{5}$ is between _______ and _______ but closer to _______ .

4. $\sqrt{50}$ is between _______ and _______ but closer to _______ .

5. $\sqrt{97}$ is between _______ and _______ but closer to _______ .

6. $\sqrt{23}$ is between _______ and _______ but closer to _______ .

7. Noah's garden is a square with an area of 73 square feet. The length of each side is between which two whole numbers? _______________

8. Isabella wants to add a wallpaper border along one wall of her room. If her room is a square with an area of 154 square feet, and the wallpaper border is sold only in whole numbers of feet, how many feet of border should she purchase? _______________

Name ______________________________

Understanding Scientific Notation

Is it difficult to write and read long numbers like 4,500,000,000 or 61,020,000? Is there a simpler way to express long numbers? Yes, you could use **scientific notation**, a way to express any number as a product of 10 and a decimal greater than 1.

Examples:

4,500,000,000 = 4.5×10^9

61,020,000 = 6.102×10^7

When you use scientific notation, notice that the decimal is always *greater than 1*, but *less than 10*. You might think the difficult part is figuring out which power of 10 to use. However, that is not so hard. Look at the number in standard, or regular, notation. If the number does not have a decimal point, put one at the far right of the number. You want to move the decimal point left or right until you create a number that is greater than 1 but less than 10. Count the number of places you had to move the decimal point to do that. If you moved the decimal point to the left, the power will be positive. If you moved the decimal point to the right, the power will be negative.

Exercises CONVERT

Write each number using scientific notation.

1. 0.0013 ____________
2. 810.114 ____________
3. 4.0095 ____________
4. 0.00005 ____________
5. 0.5851 ____________
6. 220.467 ____________
7. 426.7 ____________
8. 11901.55 ____________
9. 0.0606544 ____________
10. 0.8852 ____________
11. 1488.951 ____________
12. 200001.990 ____________
13. 0.0006660 ____________
14. 0.002679 ____________
15. 1.1110 ____________
16. 3007.5 ____________

Write each number in standard form.

17. 2.6699×10^5 ____________
18. 1.4455×10^3 ____________
19. 9.6603171×10^6 ____________
20. 3.0302×10^4 ____________
21. 2.77×10^{-3} ____________
22. 3.919181×10^5 ____________
23. 1.588×10^3 ____________
24. 1.0801×10^{-2} ____________

Name ______________________________

Estimation and Comparison

Scientific notation can be very useful to estimate the size of very large or very small things.

Example:

A grain of sand measures 0.00212 inches in diameter. We can convert this to scientific notation by writing 2.12×10^{-3}. We can estimate the value to be 2×10^{-3}.

You can also use scientific notation to compare the size of things. You can perform operations on numbers in scientific notation just as you would with numbers in standard notation. To find out how many times larger one number is than another, we divide. We can say that 8 is 2 times larger than 4 because $8 \div 4 = 2$. The same can be done with numbers in scientific notation.

Example:

6×10^5 is how many times larger than 2×10^3?

Set it up as a division problem.

$$\frac{6 \times 10^5}{2 \times 10^3}$$

The first part is easy: $\frac{6}{2} = 3$

To divide exponents, you can just subtract the exponents if they have the same base. Expanded out, we have: $\frac{100000}{1000} = 100$. That's the same as subtracting the exponents: $10^{5-3} = 10^2$, so $\frac{10^5}{10^3} = 10^2$.

The full answer then is 3×10^2 or 300. 6×10^5 is 300 times larger than 2×10^3.

Exercises

Use this chart to answer the questions.

Planet	Distance from the Sun (in miles)	Write the distance in scientific notation
Mercury	35,980,000	
Venus	65,240,000	
Earth	92,960,000	
Mars	141,600,000	
Jupiter	483,800,000	
Saturn	888,200,000	
Uranus	1,784,000,000	
Neptune	2,795,000,000	

1. Write each distance in the chart in scientific notation.

2. How many times larger is Uranus than Saturn?

2. How many times larger is Jupiter than Earth?

4. Estimate the distance from the Earth to the Sun in scientific notation.

Name ___

Restate in exponential form, then calculate.

1. $4 \times 4 \times 4 + 3 \times 3 \times 3$

2. $3 \times 3 \times 2 \times 2 - 3 \times 3 \times 3$

3. $4 \times 4 \times 4 \times 2 \times 2 + 4 \times 4 + 6 \times 6 - 3 \times 3$

Restate using scientific notation.

4. 13,224,714.066
5. 25,354.011
6. 0.180705
7. 22,294,698,171.7
8. 866.0506
9. Estimate 118.6591

Calculate.

10. 4^3
11. 6^3
12. $2^5 \times 2^{-3}$
13. $10^9 \div 10^7$
14. $12^{11} \times 12^{-11}$
15. $\sqrt{64}$
16. $\sqrt{144}$
17. $\sqrt{625}$
18. $\sqrt{196}$
19. $\sqrt{2.25}$
20. $\sqrt{1.69}$
21. Estimate $\sqrt{8200}$

Name ______________________________

22 How many times larger is the total U.S. federal budget of $\$4 \times 10^9$ than the budget for education of $\$8 \times 10^7$?

____

23 The speed of light is approximately 3×10^8 meters per second. How far does light travel in one minute? ______________

____

24 The half-life of uranium-238 is approximately 4.5×10^9 years. The half-life of uranium-233 is approximately 1.6×10^5 years. How many times longer is the half-life of uranium-238?

____

25 Britt wants to build a square deck with a total area of 155 square feet. The sides are between ______ and ______ feet.

Name ______________________

Answers and Explanations

1. $4^3 + 3^3 = 91$
2. $3^2 \times 2^2 - 3^3 = 9$
3. $4^3 \times 2^2 + 4^2 + 6^2 - 3^2 = 299$
4. 1.3224714066×10^7
5. 2.5354011×10^4
6. 1.80705×10^{-1}
7. $2.22946981717 \times 10^{10}$
8. 8.660506×10^2
9. 1×10^2
10. 64
11. 216
12. 4
13. 100
14. 1
15. 8
16. 12
17. 25
18. 14
19. 1.5
20. 1.3
21. 90
22. 50

$$\frac{4\times10^9}{8\times10^7} = \frac{4}{8}\times\frac{10^9}{10^7} = \frac{1}{2}\times10^2 = \frac{1}{2}\times100 = 50$$

23. 1.8×10^{10}

$$\frac{3\times10^8 \text{ meters}}{1 \text{ second}} = \frac{x \text{ meters}}{60 \text{ seconds}};$$
$(3\times10^8 \text{ meters})(60) = (1)(x);$

$180\times10^8 \text{ meters} = x;$

$x = 1.8\times10^{10}$

24. 2.8125×10^4 or 28,125 times as long

$$\frac{4.5\times10^9}{1.6\times10^5} = \frac{4.5}{1.6}\times\frac{10^9}{10^5} = 2.8125\times10^4 = 28,125$$

25. 12 and 13

$\sqrt{144} < \sqrt{155} < \sqrt{169}$ so $12 < \sqrt{155} < 13$

Name ______________________________

Understanding Variable Expressions

Sometimes you want to solve a problem to find an unknown number. The unknown number is called a **variable**. A variable is a letter that represents a number. A common variable used in algebra is x. But you will see any letter used as a variable (a, b, c, d, etc.). An **algebraic expression** is a letter, a number, or a combination of the two, connected by some mathematical operation such as addition, subtraction, multiplication, or division.

When you have a variable in a multiplication expression, you don't need to use the multiplication symbol. So $12 \times m$ is usually written as $12m$. The 12 is called a **coefficient**, which is a number that multiplies a variable.

Some algebraic expressions:

$n + 19$ $\quad (p - 72) \times 3 \quad \frac{b}{3}$

$(36 \div g) + 9 \quad 12 \times m$

Sometimes you will need to translate algebraic expressions into words. Other times you will translate a phrase into an algebraic expression. This will help you understand the algebra exercise.

Examples:

$x + 9$ the sum of a number and nine

$7x$ the product of 7 and a number

Six less than four times a number $4x - 6$

A number divided by five plus 10 $\frac{n}{5} + 10$

Remember...

A variable is a letter that represents a number. A common variable is x but can be any letter in the alphabet. The fact that a letter is used in a mathematical exercise should not confuse you. Since the letter represents a number, you treat it like a number when you complete exercises involving variables.

Exercises EXPLAIN

Write in words what each expression is describing.

1. $\frac{a}{2} + 22$ ______________________________

2. $y + 4$ ______________________________

3. $4b + 3$ ______________________________

4. $0.9q - 9$ ______________________________

5. $(x - 4) \div 20$ ______________________________

6. $(3g + 7) - 8 + 33$ ______________________________

7. $3n - 9$ ______________________________

8. $\frac{5}{h}$ ______________________________

Name ______________________

Solving Equations with Addition and Subtraction

You learned the Equality Properties of Addition and Subtraction, which say that if you add or subtract a number from one side of an equation, you must add or subtract the same number from the other side of the equation. This rule is important when you are solving equations that use addition and subtraction.

Example:

Problem: $z - 32 = 51$. Find z.

Can you add 32 to the left side of the equation to leave z by itself? You can do that, but you also have to add 32 to the right side of the equation.

Step 1: Add the same number to both sides of the equation: $z = 51 + 32$

Step 2: Add: $51 + 32 = 83$
So $z = 83$

Example:

Problem: $d + 9 = 21$. Find d.

This time, you can subtract 9 from the left side of the equation to leave d by itself. But you have to subtract 9 from the right side of the equation, too.

Step 1: Subtract the same number from both sides of the equation: $d = 21 - 9$

Step 2: Subtract: $21 - 9 = 12$
So $d = 12$

Exercises SOLVE

1. $x + 9 = 17$
2. $17 = s + 8$
3. $14 + z = 49$
4. $17 - f = 14$
5. $m - 30 = 35$
6. $c - 22 = 22$
7. $y + 11 = 42$
8. $107 = 17 + l$
9. $k + 28 = 64$
10. $28 + u = 43$
11. $59 - t = 42$
12. $13 - a = 4$
13. $24 + b = 54$
14. $54 - e = 22$
15. $15 + d = 39$

Name ______________________________

Solving Equations with Multiplication and Division

Division is the "opposite" of multiplication, and multiplication is the "opposite" of division. If you multiply an original number by a second number, and then divide the product by the second number, you are left with the original number.

For example: $3 \times 5 \div 5 = 3$

If you divide an original number by a second number, and then multiply the quotient by the second number, you will are left with the original number.

For example: $6 \div 3 \times 3 = 6$

If you have a fraction with the same number in the numerator and denominator, the fraction is equal to 1. So $\frac{5}{5} = 1$, $\frac{3}{3} = 1$, and $\frac{w}{w} = 1$. (You do not even need to know the value of w!)

Remember...

In an equation, you need to treat both sides in the same way. Whatever you do to one side, you must also do to the other side.

Examples:

$\frac{k}{5} = 12$. Solve for k.

Since $\frac{k}{5} = k \times \frac{1}{5}$, you multiply the left side of the equation by 5. Then you would have $k \times 1$, which is equal to k alone. You can multiply the left side by 5 *only* if you *also* multiply the right side by 5.

Step 1: Multiply both sides by the same number: $k = 12 \times 5$

Step 2: Multiply: $12 \times 5 = 60$
So $k = 60$

$7u = 56$. Solve for u.

Now, you divide the left side by 7 to get u. Of course, you must *also* divide the right side by 7.

Step 1: $u = 56 \div 7$

Step 2: Divide: $56 \div 7 = 8$
So $u = 8$

Exercises SOLVE

1. $7n = 49$
2. $\frac{q}{5} = 9$
3. $12f = 84$
4. $\frac{42}{b} = 14$
5. $3k = 39$
6. $55 \div s = 11$
7. $\frac{m}{30} = 4$
8. $16h = 112$
9. $\frac{x}{15} = 6$
10. $4n = 56$
11. $18m = 72$
12. $11d = 143$

Name ______________________

Solving 2-Step Equations

Sometimes when solving an equation the process can take more than one step. When you cannot simply add or subtract a number or multiply the coefficient in front of the variable by its multiplicative inverse, you may need to take two steps to solve for the variable. After combining like terms you need to get the variable on one side (traditionally the left) and the number on the right. Once you have done this, you multiply both sides of the equation by the multiplicative inverse of the coefficient of the variable.

Example: $3x + 7 = 12$

Step 1: Subtract 7 from both sides: $3x = 12 - 7$

Step 2: Divide both sides by 3: $x = \frac{5}{3}$

So $x = \frac{5}{3}$

Exercises SOLVE

1. $10x - 7 = 23$ ______________________

2. $14 = 12 + 2x$ ______________________

3. $21 + 4x = 28$ ______________________

4. $200 + 15x = 425$ ______________________

5. $5x + 39 = 41$ ______________________

6. $10z + 17 = 77$ ______________________

7. $65 = 41 + 3x$ ______________________

8. $107 = 75 + 16r$ ______________________

9. $49 + 18d = 37$ ______________________

10. $15b + 18 = 30$ ______________________

11. $5q = 10q + 60$ ______________________

12. $2f + 4f + 18 = 32$ ______________________

13. $3j = 5j - 14$ ______________________

14. $23 + 18r = 6r + 47$ ______________________

15. $13k + 14k + 10 = 13$ ______________________

16. $14v = 10v - 5$ ______________________

Name ______________________

Solving 2-Step Equations (cont.)

17 326 people visited a local park between 9:00 a.m. and noon on Saturday. From noon to 4:00 p.m., $2\frac{1}{2}$ times that many people visited the park. If a total of 1618 people visited the park on Saturday, how many of them were after 4:00 p.m.?

____

18 The U.S. Forest Service estimated that last year Bethesda Canyon was home to 325,000 deciduous trees. This season an insect infestation killed many of the trees. If there were 125,889 trees left after the infestation, how many were killed?

____

19 During a recent hurricane, 1385 of Lakeville Island's inhabitants evacuated the island. If there are 3034 inhabitants, how many of them did not evacuate?

____

20 Sadie spent x minutes on Monday painting. She painted for $2x$ minutes on Tuesday, and $1.5x$ minutes on Wednesday. If she painted for a total of 144 minutes, how many minutes did she paint on Monday?

____

How many minutes on Tuesday?

____

How many minutes on Wednesday?

____

21 The average-size baby rhinoceros weighs 143 pounds at birth. Fully grown, the average weight of a rhinoceros is 3950 pounds. How much weight will the average rhinoceros gain in its lifetime?

____

22 Laura has 210 pieces of candy she wants to share with her class at school. There are 22 students in her class. Write an equation that shows x as the number of pieces of candy each person will receive.

____

Name ____________________

Equations with Infinite or No Solutions

Some linear equations may have an infinite number of solutions; in other words, any number you substitute for the variable will make the equation true. Some equations may have no solution at all. You cannot always tell just by looking at an equation that it has only one solution. You may need to start solving the equation to see that you are going to end up with infinite solutions or no solution at all.

Examples:

Solve this equation: $7x - 7x = 0$.

You can add $7x$ to both sides to get $7x = 7x$, then divide to get $x = x$, but that doesn't tell you anything. No matter what number you substitute for x, the equation is true. This equation has infinite solutions.

Solve this equation: $x - x = 3$.

You can add x to both sides to get $x = 3 + x$, then subtract x from both sides to get $0 = 3$, but that isn't true. This equation has no solutions.

Exercises SOLVE

Write "infinite" if the equation has an infinite number of solutions. Write "No solution" if the equation cannot be solved.

1. $0 = -2x + 2x$ ____________________

2. $4x - 7 = 21$ ____________________

3. $6 = x + 2 - x$ ____________________

4. $3x + 2 - 3x = 7$ ____________________

5. $5x + 4 - 5x = 4$ ____________________

6. $8x - 24 = 0$ ____________________

Name ____________________________

Understanding Inequalities

An inequality is similar to an equation, except instead of an equal sign, an inequality uses a sign to show that the expressions are *not* or *may not be* equal. These signs include:

- $>$ greater than
- $\geq$ greater than or equal to
- $<$ less than
- $\leq$ less than or equal to

Examples:

The inequality $x < 5$ means that a number is less than 5. Any real number less than 5 could be the value of x.

The inequality $2x \geq 12$ means that 2 times a number is greater than or equal to 12.

Exercises EXPLAIN

Write an inequality that expresses the description given.

1. A number squared is greater than or equal to twenty-five.

   ____

2. A number divided by five is less than sixty-three.

   ____

3. A number plus nine is less than twelve.

   ____

4. Six hundred forty-three is less than the sum of two numbers.

   ____

5. A number plus two is less than or equal to fifteen.

   ____

6. Four times a number is greater than seventeen.

   ____

7. One minus a number is greater than or equal to negative sixty-three.

   ____

8. Three times a number is less than or equal to four times another number.

   ____

9. 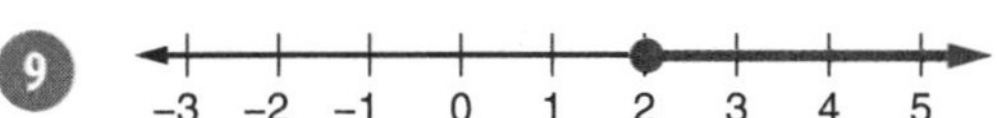

10. 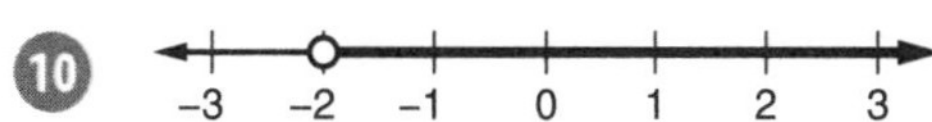

Name ______________________________

Solving Inequalities by Addition and Subtraction

You can solve an inequality by addition or subtraction in exactly the same way you solve an equation by addition or subtraction. Just treat the inequality sign as if it were an equals sign.

Examples:

Solve $75 + x > 36$ for x.

Subtract 75 from both sides:

$$75 + x - 75 > 36 - 75$$

$$x > -39$$

Solve $y - 16.78 \leq 42.5$ for y.

Add 16.78 to both sides:

$$y - 16.78 + 16.78 \leq 42.5 + 16.78$$

$$y \leq 59.28$$

Exercises SOLVE

Solve for the variable shown in the expression.

1. $x + 6 < 17$ ______________________
2. $25 > 23 + x$ ______________________
3. $7.35 + x \leq 10.8$ ______________________
4. $0.9 \geq x + 0.22$ ______________________
5. $x - 4.5 < 26.74$ ______________________
6. $5{,}047 > 98 - x$ ______________________
7. $7 - x \leq 49$ ______________________
8. $1.8 \geq x - 16.63$ ______________________

Write an inequality to express the situation, then solve for the variable.

9. Marisa had $20 to spend at the mall. She spent $14.50 on a shirt. She wants to get a bracelet to go with the shirt. What is the most she can spend on a bracelet?

____

10. John passes out 15 pencils from a box and then realizes he needs at least 23 pencils to give everyone in the class one pencil. What is the minimum number of pencils he must have left in the box in order for everyone to get a pencil?

____

Name ____________________

Solving Inequalities by Multiplication and Division

Solving an inequality by multiplication or division is basically the same way you would solve an equation by multiplication or division, with one really important difference: if you multiply or divide an inequality by a negative number, you have to reverse the direction of the inequality sign.

Examples:

Solve $-3x > -6$ for x.

To solve for x, you must divide both sides of the inequality by -3. Watch what happens:

$$\frac{-3x}{-3} > \frac{-6}{-3}$$

$$x > 2$$

Is this a true statement? Let's test the solution. Let $x = 3$. $-3(3) > -6$.

Is $-9 > -6$? No. $-9 < -6$. That's why you have to reverse the direction of the sign when you multiply or divide by a negative. The correct answer is $x < 2$.

Solve $\frac{x}{-3} \leq 15$ for x.

Here, you have to multiply both sides of the inequality by -3, so you should also reverse the direction of the inequality sign.

$$\frac{x}{-3}(-3) \geq 15(-3)$$

$$x \geq -45$$

Remember...

You *only* have to reverse the direction of the sign if you multiply or divide by a negative number.

Exercises SOLVE

Solve for the variable shown in the expression.

1. $2x + 15 > 25$ ____________________
2. $5 + 5x < 70$ ____________________
3. $8x + 8 > 220$ ____________________
4. $17 + \frac{x}{-3} \leq 45$ ____________________
5. $34 \geq 10 - 4x$ ____________________
6. $42 > 7 + \frac{x}{5}$ ____________________
7. $232 \leq 8 + 8x$ ____________________
8. $63 < 3 - 4x$ ____________________
9. $12 \geq -\frac{x}{9}$ ____________________
10. $3x + 5 > 51.5$ ____________________

Write an inequality to express the situation, then solve for the variable.

11. Erlene has to volunteer at a local clinic least 4 hours per week for her nursing class. If she volunteered 45 weeks during the class, what is the minimum number of hours she volunteered? Last year?

____

12. Amee has saved up $100 to use as her summer vacation spending money. If her vacation lasts 6 days, what is the maximum amount she can spend per day on average?

____

Name ______________________________

Describe in words the following expressions.

1. $2x + 15$

____

2. $5y - 12$

____

Solve for *x*.

3. $x + 4 = 7$ ________

4. $x + 8 = 124$ ________

5. $x + 2 = 7$ ________

6. $x + 9 = 14$ ________

7. $x - 6 = 4$ ________

8. $11x - 2 - 11x = -2$ ________

9. $x - 2 = 13$ ________

10. $x - 5 = 9$ ________

Solve for *y*.

11. $3y - 5 = 7$ ________

12. $2y + 3 = 11$ ________

13. $4y - 3 = 13$ ________

14. $2y - 7 = 9 + 2y$ ________

15. $6y - 6 = 18$ ________

16. $7y - 14 = 28$ ________

17. $16y + 24 = 56$ ________

18. $12y - 24 = 48$ ________

Name ______________________________

Solve for *z*.

19. $z + 26.9 > 58.4$ ____________

20. $14 - z < -12$ ____________

21. $8.2z \leq 95$ ____________

22. $\frac{z}{3} \geq 6.9$ ____________

23. $-3z \leq 72$ ____________

24. $\frac{z}{-4} > \frac{1}{2}$ ____________

25. $2z + 42 - 5z \leq 72$ ____________

26. $80 - \frac{z}{7} < 164$ ____________

27. Kalee started her collection of shells with 6 shells. She has added 2 new shells every week and she now has 28 shells in her collection. How many weeks has she been collecting?

____

28. A new accountant processed x reports yesterday. Today, she processed 20 more than she did yesterday. If she processed 300 reports today, how many did she process yesterday?

____

29. There are two major grades in Nick's biology class: the midterm exam and the final exam. If Nick got 87 points on his midterm exam, what is the minimum number of points he needs to get on the final exam to have a total of 250 points?

____

30. Last year, Lynda was three times as old as Sydney was. If Sydney is now 12 years old, how old is Lynda?

____

Name ____________________

Answers and Explanations

1. Two times a number plus fifteen
2. A number times five less twelve
3. $x = 3$ $\quad x+4-4=7-4;\ x=3$
4. $x = 116$ $\quad x+8-8=124-8;\ x=116$
5. $x = 5$ $\quad x+2-2=7-2;\ x=5$
6. $x = 5$ $\quad x+9-9=14-9;\ x=5$
7. $x = 10$ $\quad x-6+6=4+6;\ x=10$
8. Infinite $\quad -2=-2$
9. $x = 15$ $\quad x-2+2=13+2;\ x=15$
10. $x = 14$ $\quad x-5+5=9+5;\ x=14$
11. $y = 4$ $\quad 3y-5+5=7+5;\ 3y=12;\ \frac{3y}{3}=\frac{12}{3};\ y=4$
12. $y = 4$ $\quad 2y+3-3=11-3;\ 2y=8;\ \frac{2y}{2}=\frac{8}{2};\ y=4$
13. $y = 4$ $\quad 4y-3+3=13+3;\ 4y=16;\ \frac{4y}{4}=\frac{16}{4};\ y=4$
14. No solution $\quad 2y-7+7=9+2y+7;\ 2y=2y+16;\ 2y-2y=2y+16-2y;\ 0\neq 16$
15. $y = 4$ $\quad 6y-6+6=18+6;\ 6y=24;\ \frac{6y}{6}=\frac{24}{6};\ y=4$
16. $y = 6$ $\quad 7y-14+14=28+14;\ 7y=42;\ \frac{7y}{7}=\frac{42}{7};\ y=6$
17. $y = 2$ $\quad 16y+24-24=56-24;\ 16y=32;\ \frac{16y}{16}=\frac{32}{16};\ y=2$
18. $y = 6$ $\quad 12y-24+24=48+24;\ 12y=72;\ \frac{12y}{12}=\frac{72}{12};\ y=6$
19. $z > 31.5$ $\quad z+26.9-26.9>58.4-26.9;\ z>31.5$
20. $z > 26$ $\quad 14-z-14<-12-14;\ -z<-26;\ \frac{-z}{-1}>\frac{-26}{-1};\ z>26$
21. $z \le 11.59$ $\quad \frac{8.2z}{8.2}\le\frac{95}{8.2};\ z\le 11.59$
22. $z \ge 20.7$ $\quad \frac{z}{3}(3)\ge 6.9(3);\ z\ge 20.7$
23. $z \ge -24$ $\quad -3z\le 72;\ \frac{-3z}{-3}\ge\frac{72}{-3};\ z\ge -24$
24. $z < -2$ $\quad \frac{z}{-4}>\frac{1}{2};\ \frac{z}{-4}(-4)<\frac{1}{2}(-4);\ z<-2$
25. $z \ge -10$ $\quad -3z+42\le 72;\ -3z+42-42\le 72-42;\ -3z\le 30;\ \frac{-3z}{-3}\ge\frac{30}{-3};\ z\ge -10$
26. $z > -588$ $\quad 80-\frac{z}{7}-80<164-80;\ -\frac{z}{7}<84;\ -\frac{z}{7}(-7)>84(-7);\ z>-588$

Name ____

27. 11 weeks $6+2w=28$; $6+2w-6=28-6$; $2w=22$; $\frac{2w}{2}=\frac{22}{2}$; $w=11$

28. 280 reports $x+20=300$; $x+20-20=300-20$; $x=280$

29. 163 points $87+x\geq 250$; $87+x-87\geq 250-87$; $x\geq 163$

30. 34 years old $x-1=3(12-1)$; $x-1=33$; $x=34$

Name ______________________________

Plotting Ordered Pairs

All points on a grid can be expressed, or identified, by using two numbers.

Example:

Find the first number by looking along the *x*-axis (the horizontal line). Put your finger on that spot. If you move your finger up and down in a vertical line, you will still be at the same *x* number. To find the exact point you want, look at the second number. This second number tells you where to move your finger along the vertical line. In the diagram, Point A is written as (2, 4). Point B is written as (3, 1).

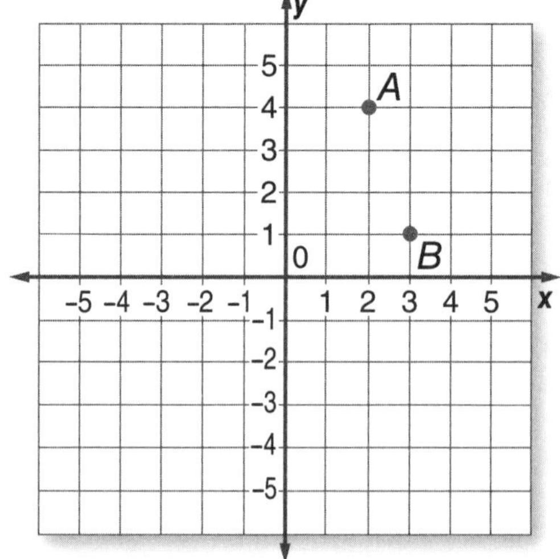

Exercises **GRAPH**

Graph #1

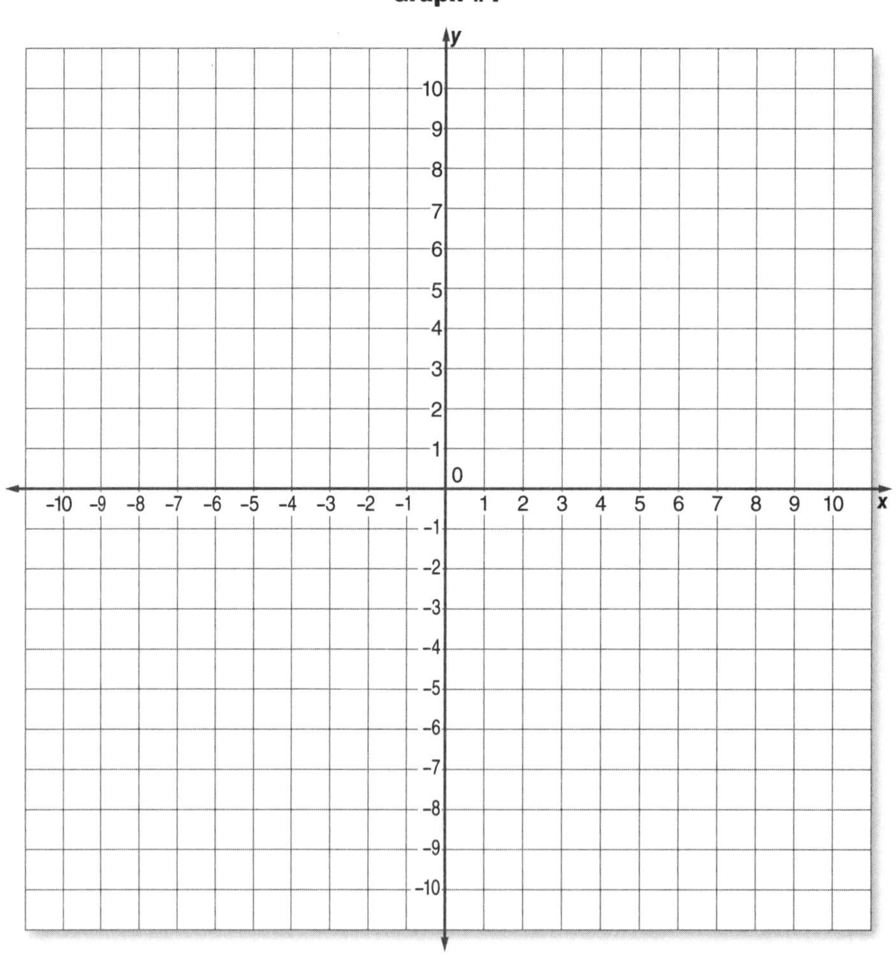

1. Plot the following ordered pairs on the graph:

   A (4, 2)

   B (6, −6)

   C (−8, −8)

   D (−4, 4)

   E (5, 5)

   F (2, 9)

   G (3, 4)

   H (−4, −3)

   I (−5, −5)

   J (6, −1)

   K (−3, −3)

Name ______________________________

Graph #2

2 Give the coordinates for each point on the graph:

A ____________

B ____________

C ____________

D ____________

E ____________

F ____________

G ____________

H ____________

I ____________

J ____________

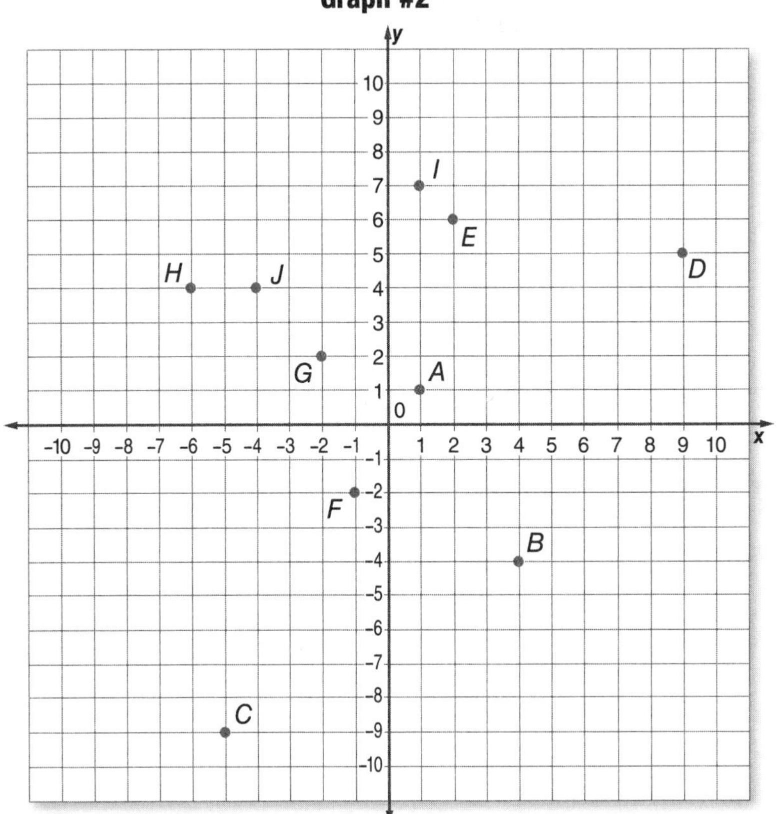

Graph #3

3 Give the coordinates for each point on the graph:

A ____________

B ____________

C ____________

D ____________

E ____________

F ____________

G ____________

H ____________

I ____________

J ____________

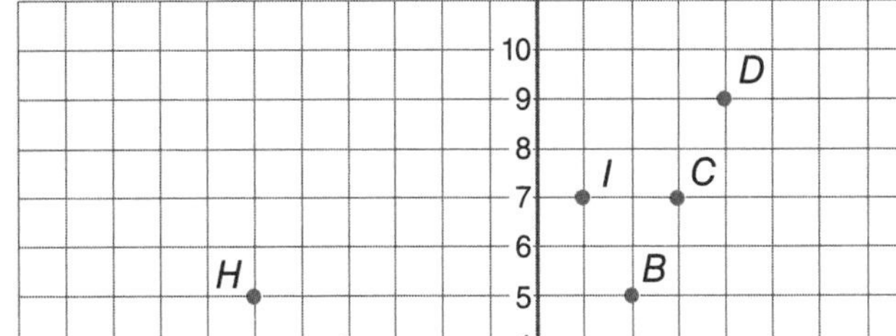

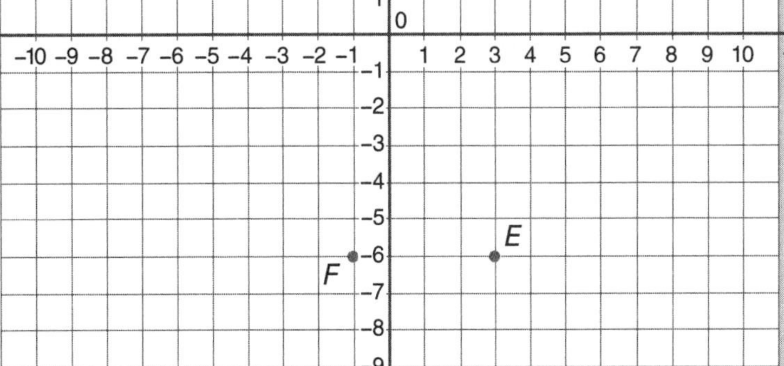

Name ____________________

Function Tables

Can you make a graph of an equation? Yes, you can draw a function such as $y = 3x + 2$ on a graph, you just need a number of order pairs (x, y) to plot on the coordinate plane. The easiest way to do this is to make a **function table.**

To generate a function table, you substitute a number of values of x in the equation, and then complete the equation to determine the value of y. The function table allows you to make a record of these ordered pairs so that you can quickly plot the points. When choosing values of x to substitute in the equation, it is good to use whole numbers that will likely generate whole-number values for y. These are easier to plot.

Using $x = 0$ is always a good value. Also, when the function has an exponent, make sure that you use some negative numbers.

Exercises CALCULATE

Fill in the corresponding values of *y* for the given *x* value in the function table.

1. $y = x + 1$

x	y
0	
1	
2	
3	
4	
5	

2. $y = 2x + 2$

x	y
−2	
−1	
0	
1	
2	
3	

3. $y = x - 4$

x	y
0	
1	
4	
6	
8	
10	

4. $y = 2x - 3$

x	y
−1	
0	
1	
2	
3	
5	

Name ______________________________

5 $y = 2x + 1$

x	y
−2	
1	
0	
2	
4	
6	

6 $y = \frac{1}{2}x + 1$

x	y
−4	
−2	
0	
2	
4	
6	

Identify the function by looking at the ordered pairs (*x*, *y*) in the function table.

7 ______________________

x	y
0	2
1	3
2	4
3	5
4	6
5	7

8 ______________________

x	y
−2	5
−1	7
0	9
2	13
4	17
5	19

9 ______________________

x	y
−4	18
−2	6
0	2
2	6
3	11
4	18

10 ______________________

x	y
−3	−27
−2	−8
0	0
1	1
2	8
3	27

Name ______________________

Complete the function table and then graph the function.

11 $y = 3x - 3$

x	y
−2	
−1	
0	
1	
2	
3	

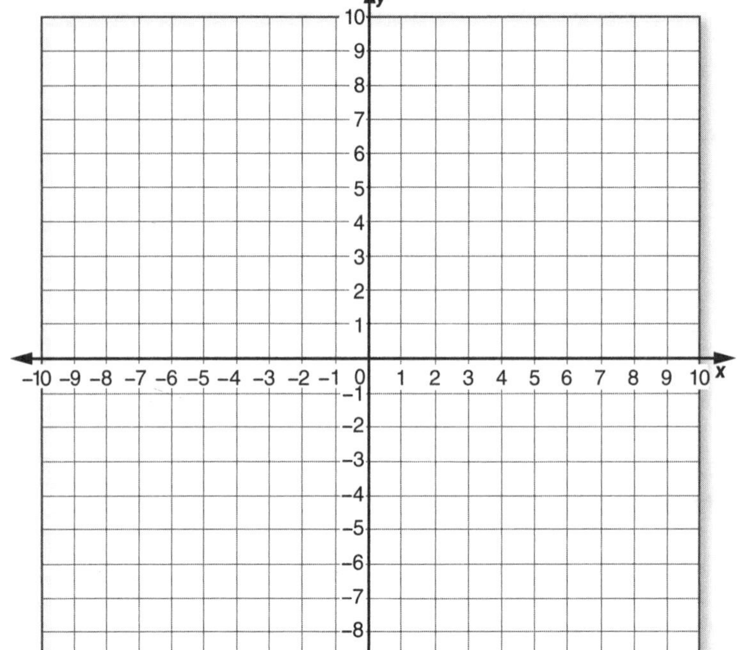

12 $y = x^2$

x	y
−3	
−2	
−1	
0	
1	
2	
3	

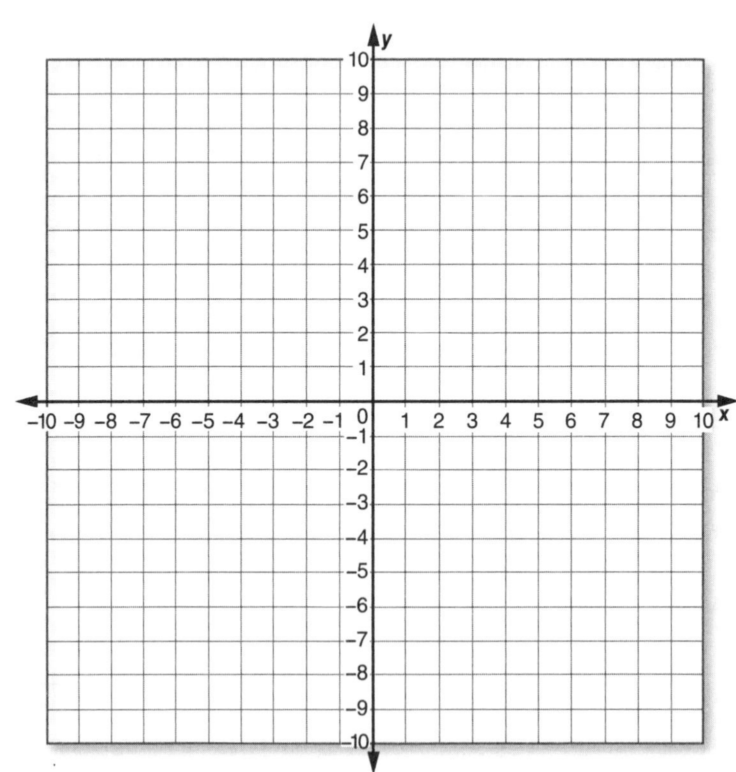

Name ______________________________

Solve Equations by Graphing

One way to determine the point of intersection of two lines is to graph the lines and see where they meet. The process takes three steps:

1. Create function tables for each line.
2. Plot the two lines on a coordinate plane.
3. Visually assess the lines to determine the point of intersection.

This method will enable you to make a good estimation of the point of intersection of the lines. Sometimes the two lines will meet at a point where the ordered pair (x, y) has integer values for both x and y, but many times they will not. So, you will have to make an estimation of the coordinates of the point of intersection.

Exercises GRAPH

Determine the point of intersection of the two lines.

1 $y = x + 3$

x	y

$y = 2x + 1$

x	y

Name ______________________________

2 $y = x - 4$

x	y

$y = -x + 2$

x	y

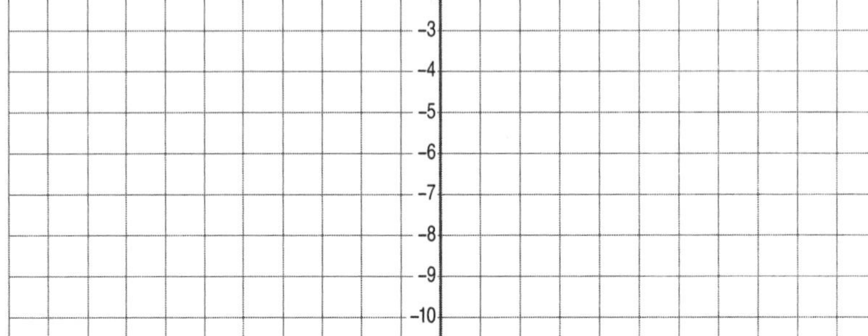

3 $y = 4x - 3$

x	y

$y = x$

x	y

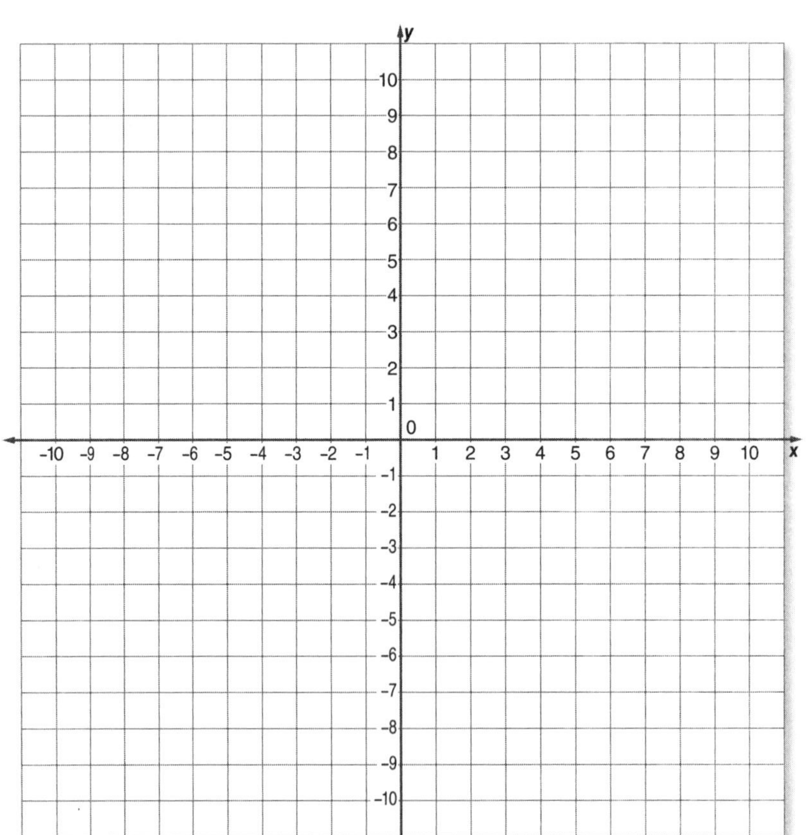

Name ______________________________

Slope

Slope refers to the amount by which a line rises or falls as you read a coordinate grid from left to right.

POSITIVE SLOPE A line that rises as it goes across the coordinate grid from left to right has a positive slope.

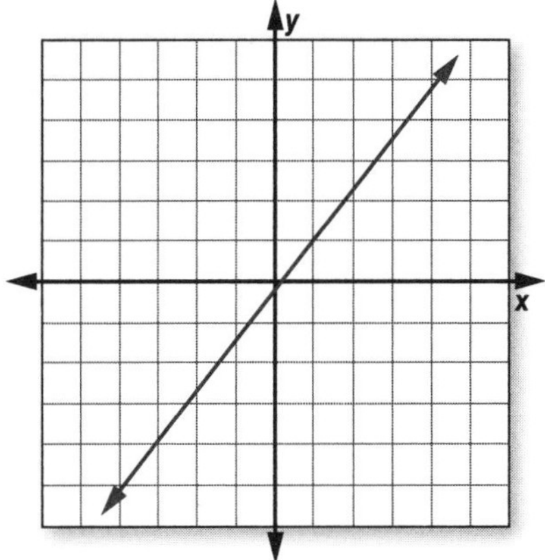

NEGATIVE SLOPE A line that falls as it goes across the coordinate grid from left to right has a negative slope.

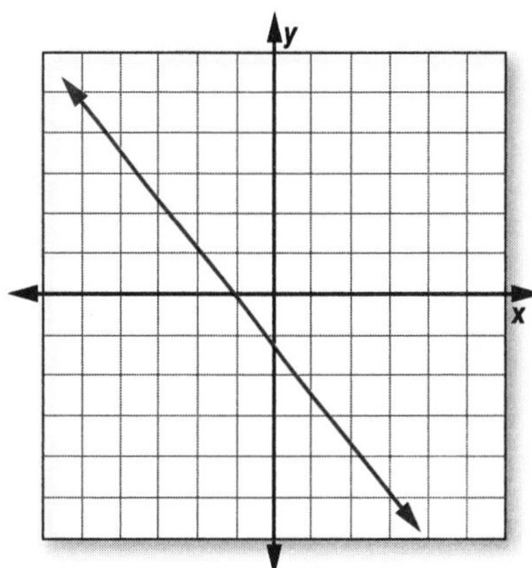

ZERO SLOPE A flat line that neither rises nor falls as it goes across the coordinate grid from left to right has a zero slope.

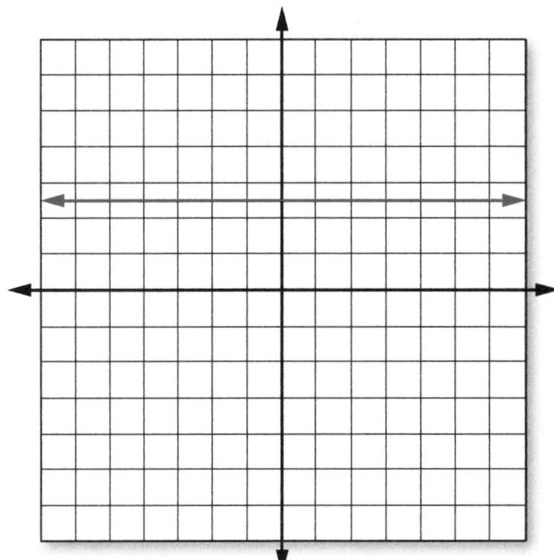

UNDEFINED SLOPE We say that a vertical line has an "undefined" slope.

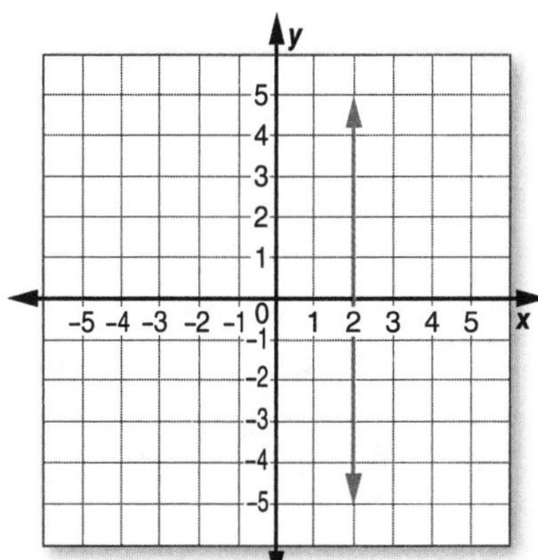

Name ______________________________

Slope (cont.)

There are a number of ways to calculate the slope of a line. Picture a series of similar right triangles forming a line with positive slope. Measure the base and height of one of the triangles in the graph.

The base = 3 and the height = 4. One way to calculate slope is to count the **rise**, or the height of the triangle we made, over the **run**, or the length of the base of our triangle.

$$\text{Slope} = \frac{\text{rise}}{\text{run}}$$

For this line, the slope is $\frac{\text{rise} = 4}{\text{run} = 3} = \frac{4}{3}$.

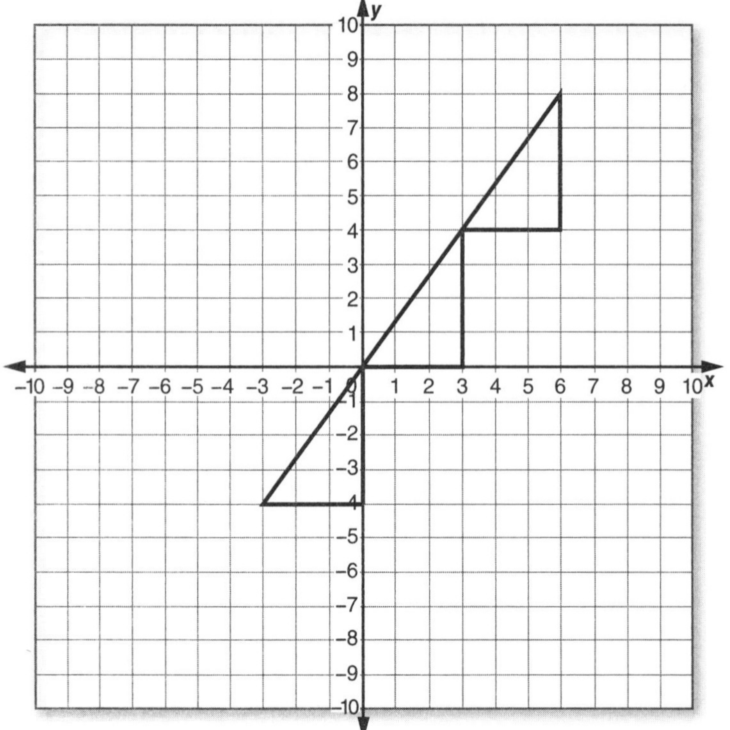

Example:

Find the slope of the line shown on the graph.

Step 1: Picture a right triangle forming part of the line. Measure the base and height.

Step 2: Set the rise (height) over the run (base). Remember, if the line is going down from left to right, the slope is negative. In other words, it falls rather than rises.

$$\text{Slope} = \frac{\text{rise}}{\text{run}} = \frac{-3}{3} = -1$$

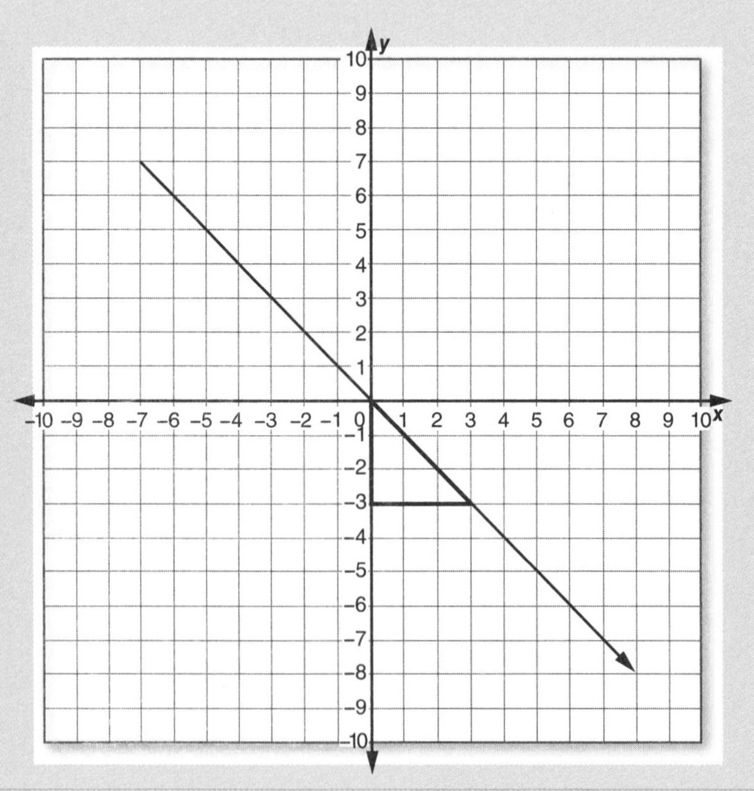

Name ____________________

Slope (cont.)

You can also find the slope of a line by using the equation for a line in the form $y = mx + b$ where x and y are the coordinates of a point on the line, b is the point at which the line intercepts the y-axis, and m is the slope. For example, the line $y = 2x + 1$ has a slope of 2 because the number 2 is in the place of m in the equation of the line. You also know that this line intercepts the y-axis at (0, 1) because the number 1 is in the place of b in the equation of the line. If you see an equation for a line that does not have a b value, then b equals 0, and there is no y-intercept. That means that the line goes through the origin. Simply by knowing the equation of the line, you can create a graph of the line.

Example:

Find the slope of the line $y - 3 = \frac{1}{2}x$.

Step 1: Put the equation of the line in the form $y = mx + b$.

Add 3 to both sides: $y - 3 + 3 = \frac{1}{2}x + 3$ and you get $y = \frac{1}{2}x + 3$.

Step 2: Identify the number in the m position: $m = \frac{1}{2}$.

Slope $= \frac{1}{2}$

Graph the line.

Step 1: Identify the slope and y-intercept. You found slope $= \frac{1}{2}$. Look at the equation in the form $y = mx + b$ and identify the number in the b position. $y = \frac{1}{2}x + 3$ has a y-intercept of 3.

Step 2: Graph the y-intercept. Then draw a line with a rise of 1 and a run of 2. Starting at the y-intercept of (0, 3), go up 1 and over 2. This will put you at (2, 4). Do it again to move to (4, 5). This should be enough for you to draw a straight line through the points.

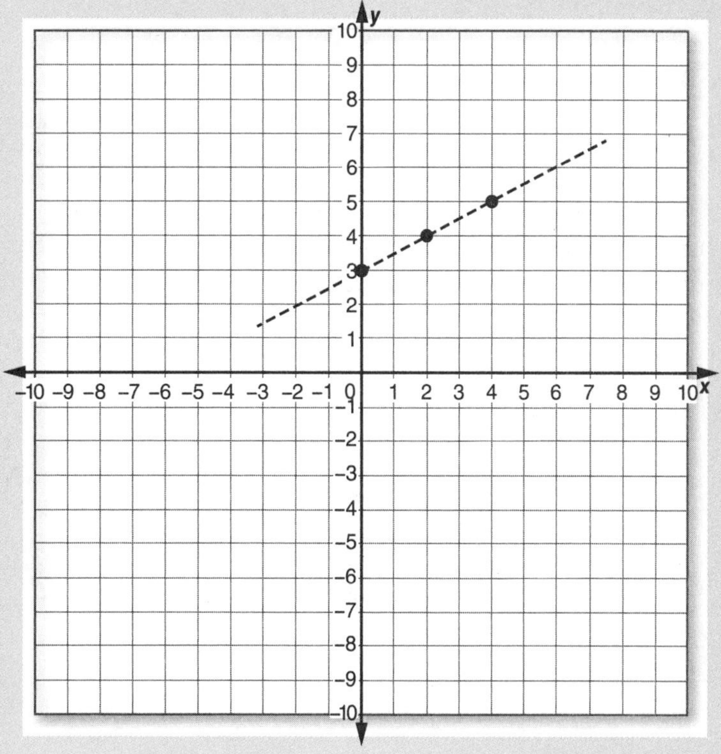

Name ______________________________

Exercises FIND THE SLOPE

1

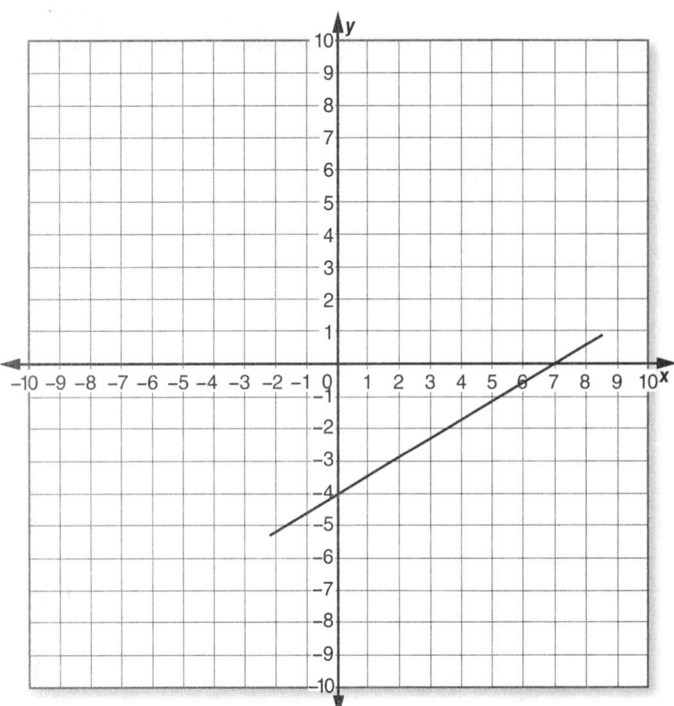

2

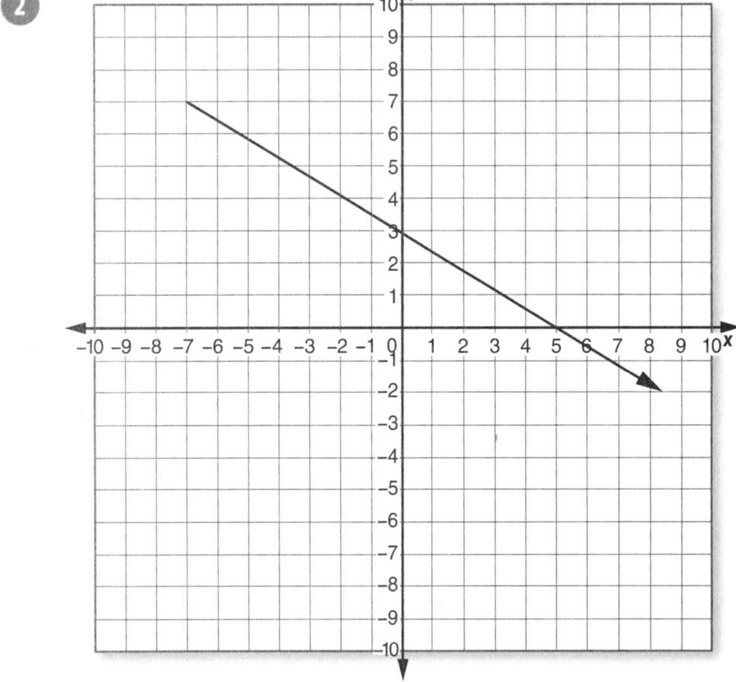

3 $y = 6x - 2$

4 $y - x = 4$

5 $-3 = \frac{2}{3}x - y$

6 $x + y = -5$

Name ______________________________

Graphing Relationships

There are a number of ways to describe the relationships you see on graphs. A **linear function** shows the graph as a straight line. In the lesson on slope, all the graphs were linear functions. That means that you could find the slope of the line and use the equation of a line $y = mx + b$.

A **nonlinear function** is a graph that is not a straight line. You can calculate the slope between two specific points on the line, but the graph does not show a consistent slope over the length of the function.

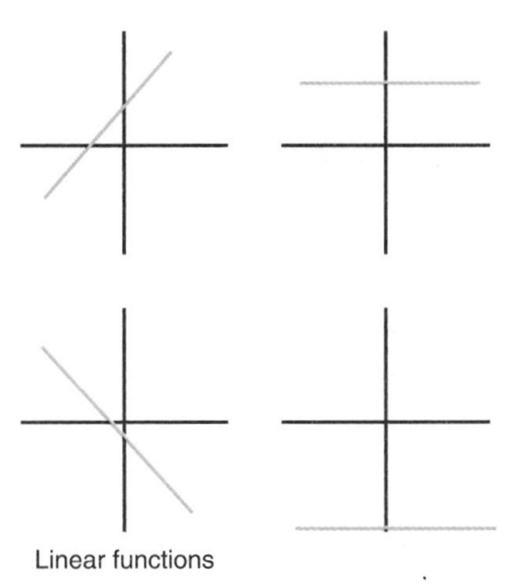

Linear functions

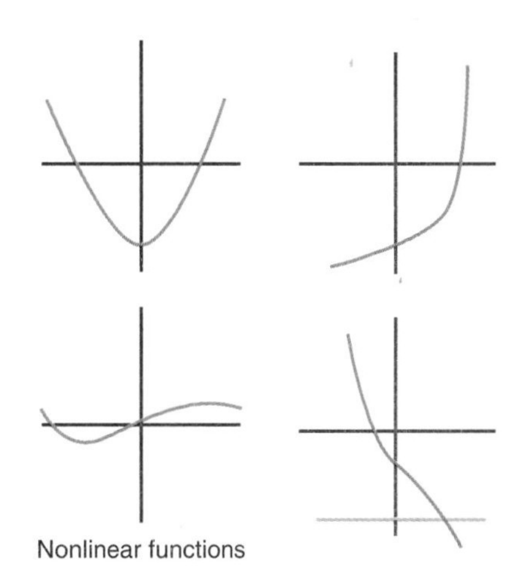

Nonlinear functions

We can describe the function as positive or negative based on the graph of the function. A function is **positive** where the line is above the x-axis. A function is **negative** where the line is below the x-axis.

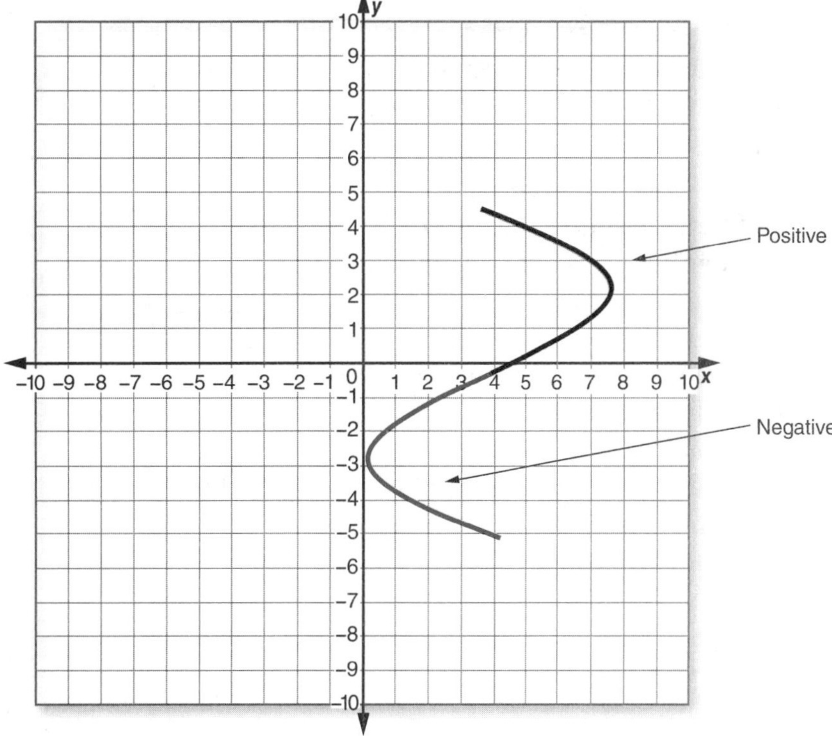

Graphing Relationships (cont.)

We can also describe the function as increasing or decreasing based on the graph of the function. A function is **increasing** when the slope is positive. As the *x* values increase, the *y* values also increase. A function is **decreasing** when the slope is negative. As the *x* values increase, the *y* values decrease.

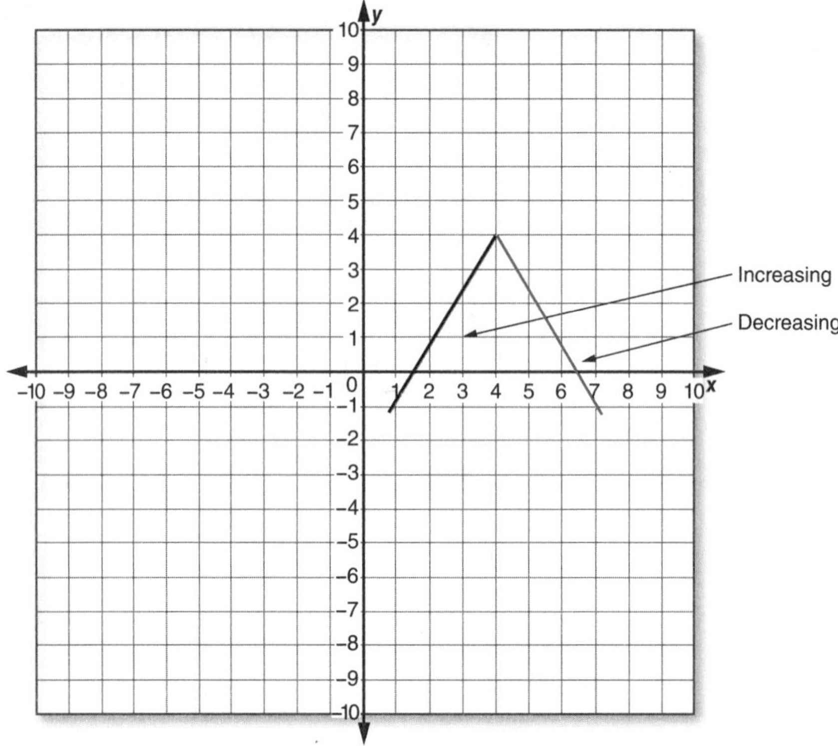

A graph can make it easy to see the relationship between two or more quantities. You can see how a quantity changes in response to a variable such as distance or price or time.

For a linear function graph, the slope of the line shows the unit rate for the quantity. Remember, a **unit rate** is the ratio of two measurements when the second term is a 1. For example, miles per hour or price per dollar is a unit rate. You can find the unit rate for something by looking at a graph of the rate. This graph shows the price per pound of apples.

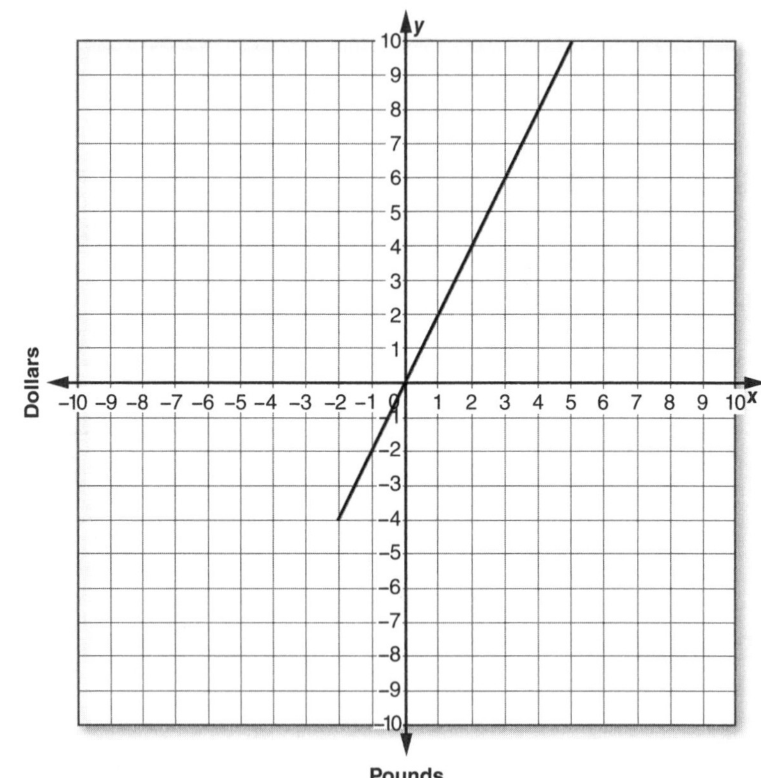

Name ______________________________

Graphing Relationships (cont.)

There are two ways you can find the unit rate:

1) Look for the value of y when $x = 1$. Here, that value is 2, so the unit rate is 2 dollars per pound.

2) Find the slope of the line. Find two points on the line. Let's use (1, 2) and (5, 10). The rise is 8 and the run is 4. The slope is 2, so the unit rate is 2 dollars per pound.

Example:

Look at this graph of meat prices over time.

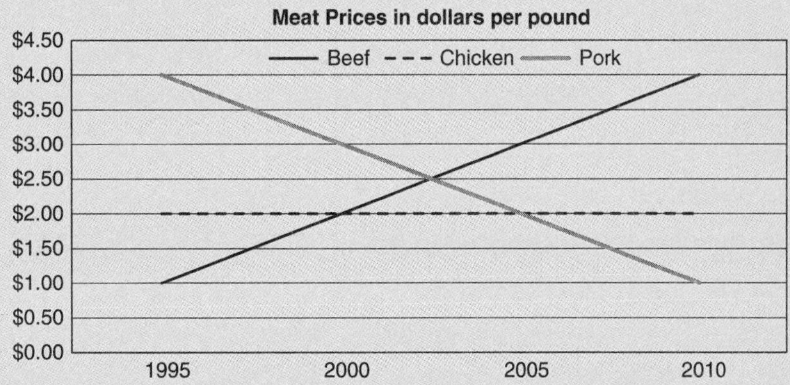

You can quickly see that the price of beef rose over this period, the price of chicken was stable, and the price of pork dropped. The slopes of these lines show you the unit rate, dollars per pound, over time. This will help you make comparisons about the prices of these meats.

When did the unit rate for beef exceed that of pork? Find the spot on the graph where the line for beef increases past the line for pork. It was approximately 2003.

Which was the least expensive meat in 2002? Find the approximate place on the graph for 2002 and see which line is the lowest. Chicken was least expensive in 2002.

Is the function for pork prices increasing or decreasing? Since the graph shows a line with negative slope, the function is decreasing.

Exercises

Noah and Kim are making blue frosting for cupcakes. Kim adds 6 drops of blue food coloring to 1 cup of frosting and stirs until it is completely mixed. Noah adds 12 drops of blue food coloring to 2 cups of frosting and stirs until it is completely mixed. When they compare their two bowls, Noah is surprised to see that both frostings are the same shade of blue; he had expected his to be darker since he used more blue food coloring.

1. Explain why the two bowls of frosting are the same shade of blue.

____

2. What is the ratio (unit rate) of drops of food coloring to cups of frosting?

____

Name ______________________________

3 Fill in the rest of the function table below for that ratio.

Cups of frosting (y)	Drops of food coloring (x)
	3
1	6
	9
2	12

4 Plot the ordered pairs from the function table on the grid.

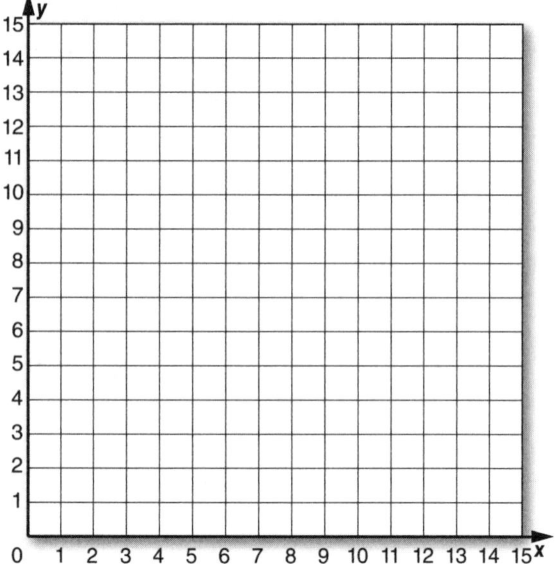

5 What is the slope of the line created?

The chart below shows the speed of two cars in miles per hour.

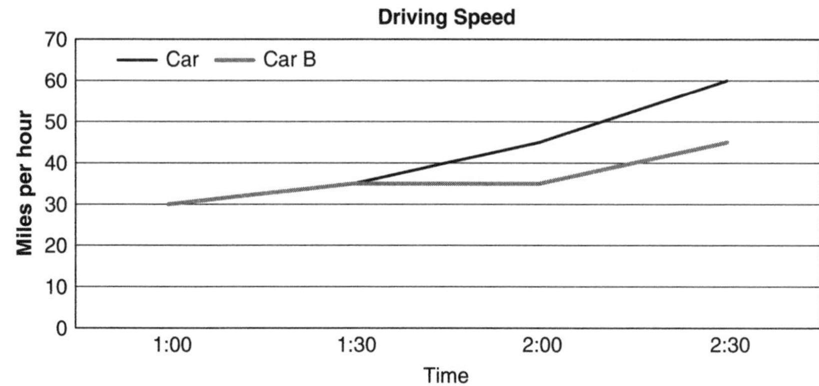

6 Which car increased in speed more between 1:30 and 2:00? How do you know?

____

7 At what time do the cars begin to go different speeds?

____

8 Which car is going faster at 2:30?

____

Name ______________________________

9 Find the unit rate for the graph below.

____

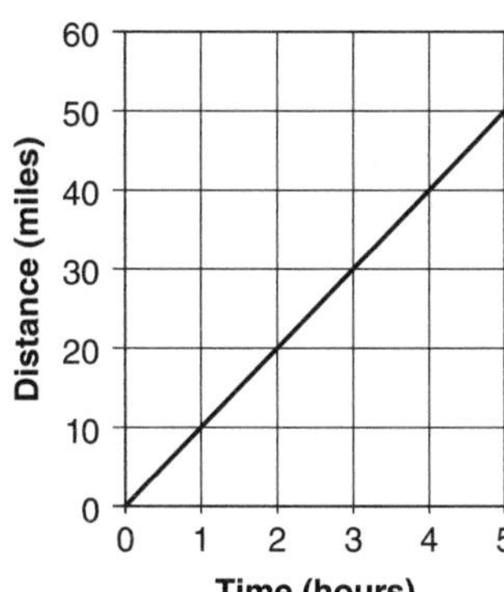

10 Is the function above increasing or decreasing? ______________________________

____

11 Sketch a graph of a linear function that is negative and decreasing.

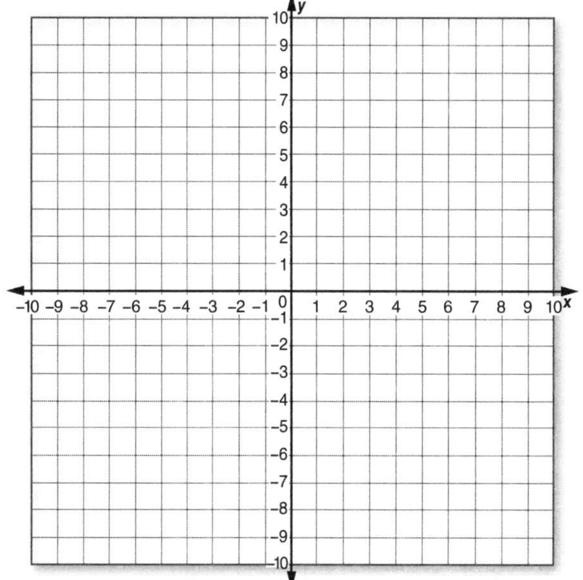

12 Is this function linear or nonlinear?

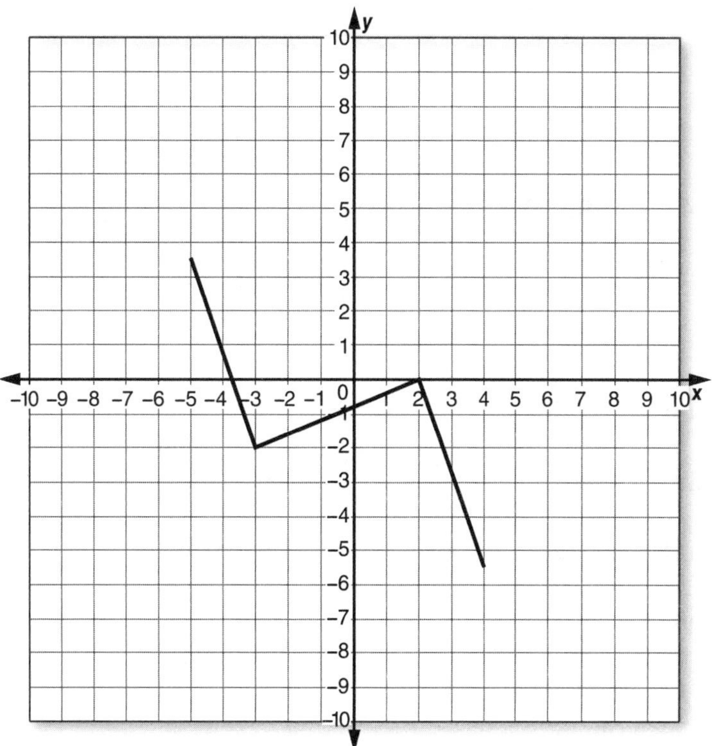

Name ______________________________

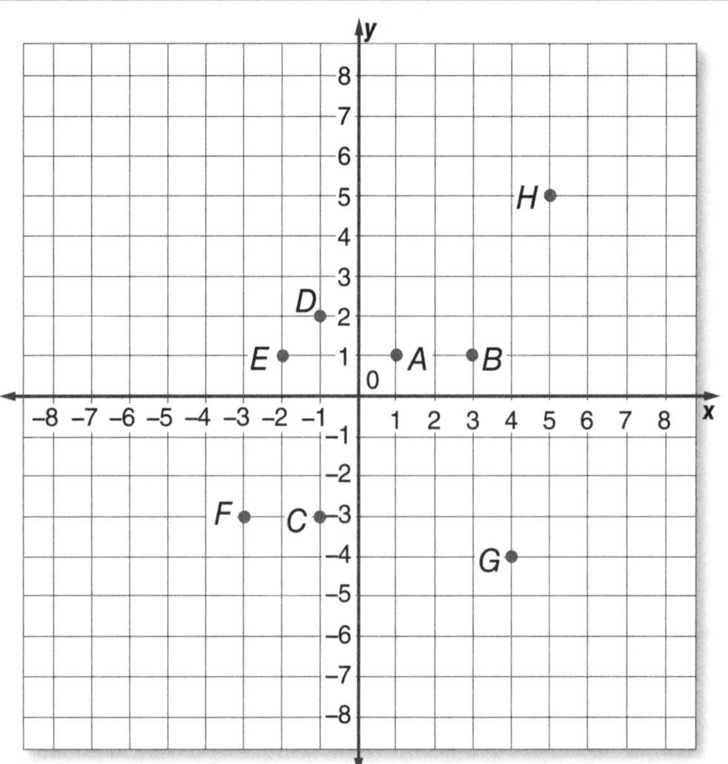

Give the coordinates for each point.

1. A ____________
2. B ____________
3. C ____________
4. D ____________
5. E ____________
6. F ____________
7. G ____________
8. H ____________

Plot the following points on the grid.

9. Point A (6, 6)

   Point B (−3, −3)

   Point C (−1, 2)

   Point D (3, −2)

   Point E (4, −2)

   Point F (−4, 2)

   Point G (−6, −6)

   Point H (−1, 3)

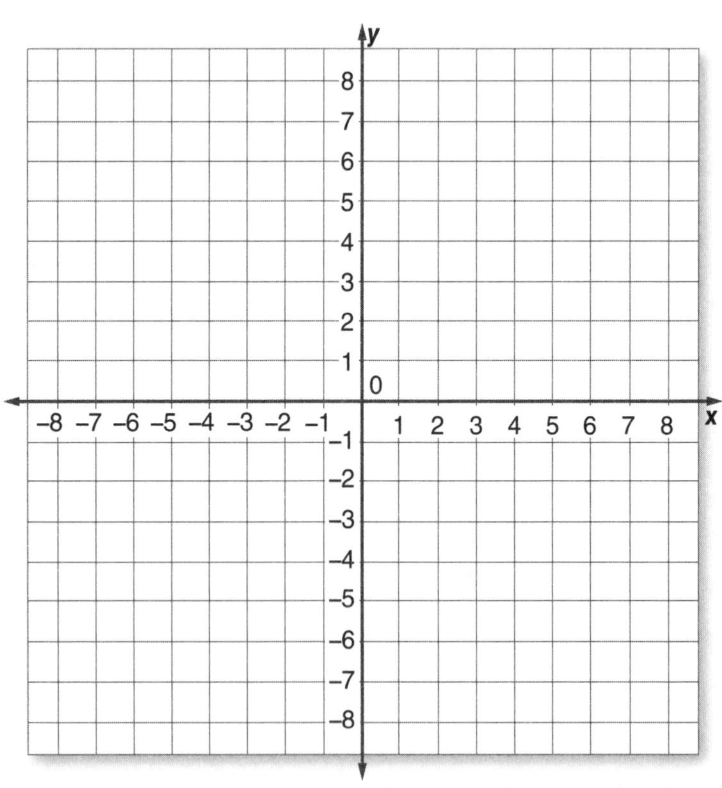

Name ___________________________

Create a function table for $2x + 1$ and plot the ordered pairs on the grid.

10 $2x + 1$

x	y

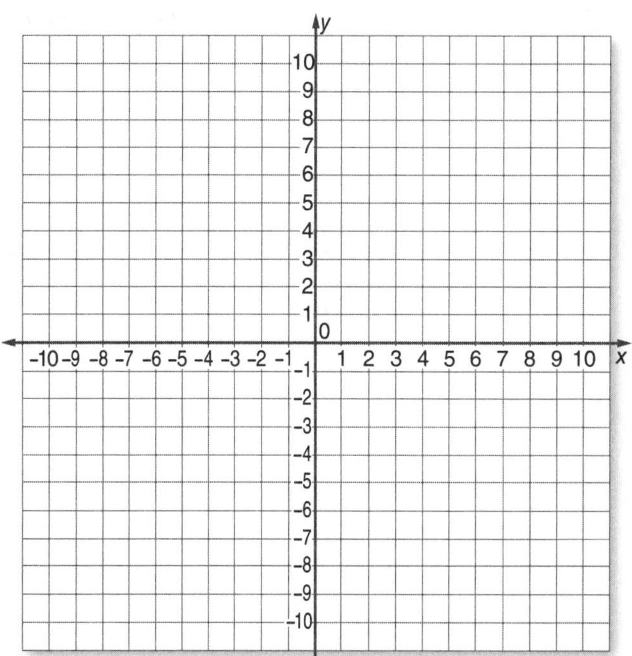

11 What is the slope of the line created?

12 If the function table above (for question 10) were changed to $2x + 3$, what would happen to the slope of the line?

Create function tables for $2x - 1$ and $x + 3$. Plot the ordered pairs and determine the value of x where the equation $2x - 1 = x + 3$ is true.

13 $2x - 1$

x	y

$x + 3$

x	y

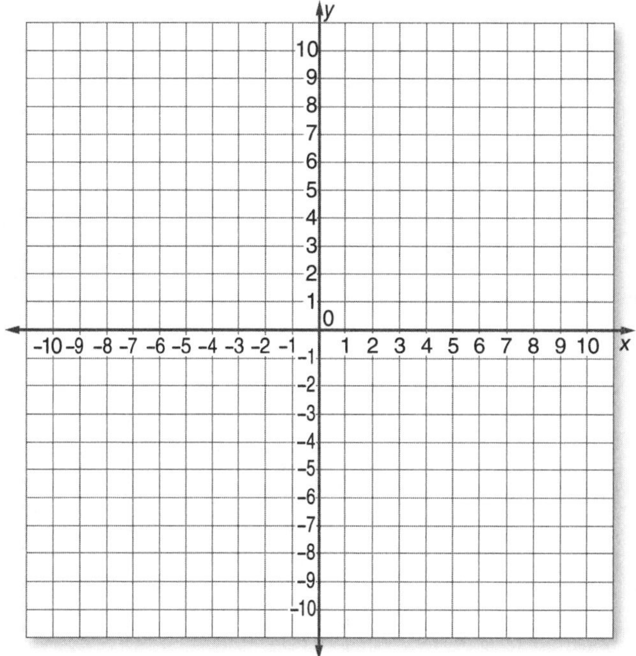

Name ____________________

Wendy made a graph to show the prices of some baked goods at a local bakery. The bakery offers discounts for buying more than one bagel, but no discount for muffins.

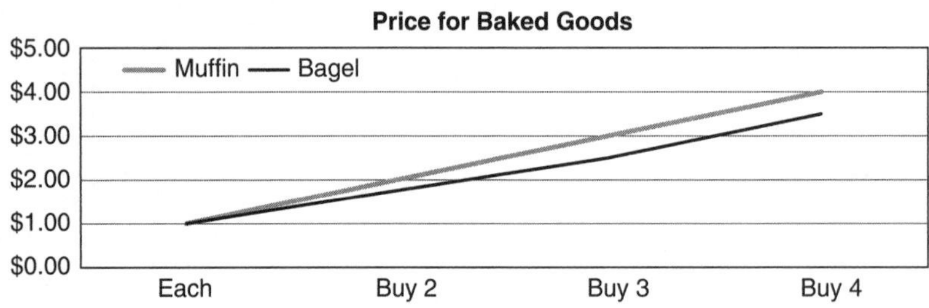

14. If Wendy wants to buy 2 of an item, which one is cheaper?

15. What is the unit rate for muffins?

16. If there were no discount for buying multiple bagels, what would 3 bagels cost?

Val made a graph of how much money she made and borrowed during a month.

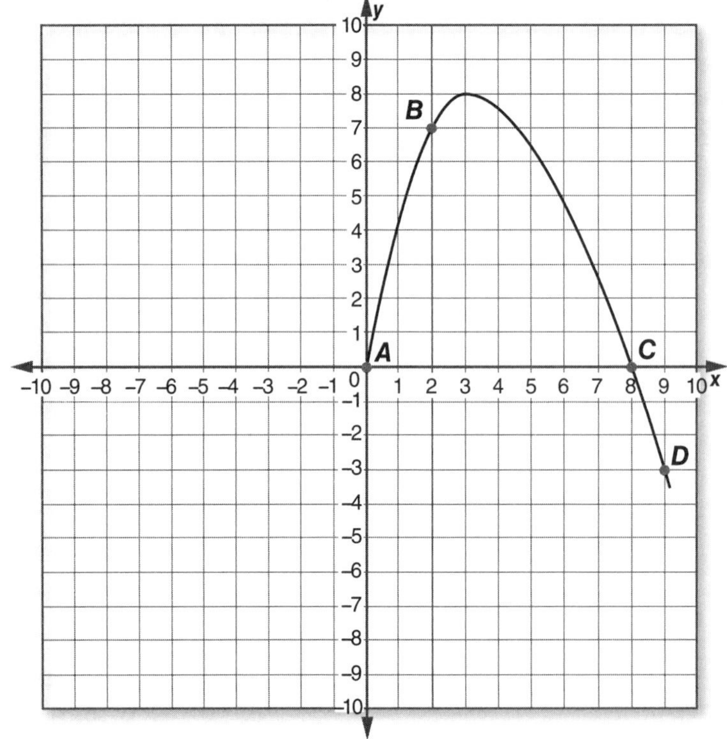

17. Between which points on the graph is the function negative?

18. Between which points on the graph is the function increasing?

19. At which labeled point is the function positive?

20. Is this a linear function?

Name ___________________________

Answers and Explanations

1. A (1, 1)
2. B (3, 1)
3. C (−1, −3)
4. D (−1, 2)
5. E (−2, 1)
6. F (−3, −3)
7. G (4, −4)
8. H (5, 5)
9. 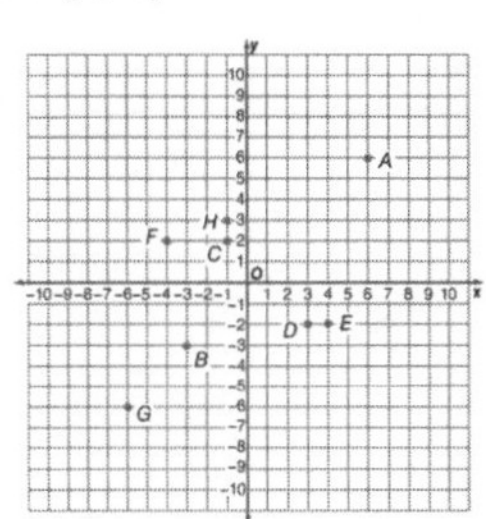

10. 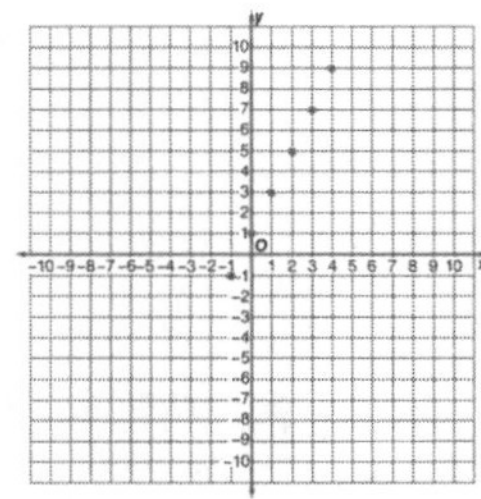

11. The slope is 2.
12. The line shifts, but the slope is still 2.
13. 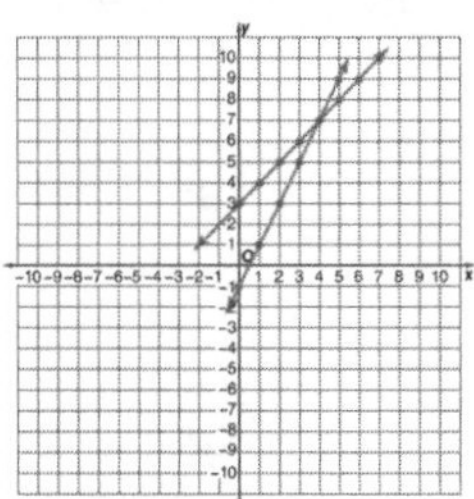

    Answer (4,7)

14. the bagel
15. $1.00 per muffin
16. $3.00
17. C and D
18. A and B
19. B
20. No

Name ______________________________

Customary Units of Length

The **customary units of length** are inches (in.), feet (ft), yards (yd), and miles (mi). You can compare them to each other, and even convert one to another by using simple calculations.

1 foot = 12 in.

1 yard = 3 ft

1 mile = 1760 yd or 5280 ft

Remember...

You do *not* need to add the plural *s* when you abbreviate units of measure.

Exercises CONVERT

1. 72 in. = ________ ft
2. 12 ft = ________ in.
3. 3 ft 8 in. = ________ in.
4. 192 in. = ________ ft
5. 7920 ft = ________ mi
6. 16 ft 6 in. = ________ yd
7. 4 ft 9 in. = ________ in.
8. 1056 ft = ________ mi
9. $\frac{4}{5}$ mi = ________ in.
10. 66 in. = ________ ft
11. 648 in. = ________ yd
12. $7\frac{1}{2}$ yd = ________ ft = ________ in.
13. 35 ft = ________ yd
14. 16 yd 2 ft = ________ in.
15. 2 mi 303 yd = ________ ft
16. 34 yd 2 ft = ________ in.
17. The river is 768 yards wide where the city plans to build a new bridge. How many 32-foot sections of bridge will the city engineers need in order to build the bridge?

    ____

18. Patty wants to know how far she can throw a softball. After throwing, she estimates that the ball traveled 1764 inches.

    How many yards is that? ________

    How many feet? ________

Name ____

Customary Units of Liquid Volume

When you buy a bottle of juice, or when you add a liquid to a recipe, you will often measure in units of **liquid volume**. Liquid volume is the amount of liquid a container can hold. Liquid volume is measured in cups (c), pints (pt), quarts (qt), and gallons (gal). Just like units of length, you can compare these units to each other, and change one to another by using simple calculations.

1 pint = 2 cups   1 quart = 2 pints

1 gallon = 4 quarts

Example:

How many cups are in a gallon?

Step 1: You know that there are 4 quarts in a gallon, and there are 2 pints in a quart. So multiply the number of quarts × 2 to find out how many pints are in a gallon.

Step 2: 4 × 2 = 8 pints in a gallon.

Step 3: You know that there are 2 cups in a pint. So multiply the number of pints × 2.

Step 4: 8 × 2 = 16 cups in a gallon.

Exercises CONVERT

1. 72 c = ________ qt
2. 12 qt = ________ c
3. 3 qt 1 pt = ________ c
4. 192 gal = ________ qt
5. 328 qt = ________ gal
6. 2 gal 1 qt = ________ c
7. 6 qt 1 c = ________ c
8. 52 c = ________ qt
9. $\frac{3}{4}$ gal = ________ c
10. 66 pt = ________ gal
11. 4 qt 1 c = ________ c
12. $7\frac{1}{2}$ qt = ________ gal = ________ c
13. 35 qt 3 c = ________ gal
14. 256 c = ________ gal
15. 132 c = ________ pt = ________ qt
16. 34 gal 1 qt = ________ pt
17. Allison's aquarium holds 25 gallons of water. One quart of water evaporated from the aquarium. How much water is left in the aquarium?

    ____
18. Bobby drinks 1 quart and 1 cup of water for every 3 miles he runs. If he runs 9 miles, how much water should he drink?

    ____

Name ______________________________

Customary Units of Weight

Can you name the **customary units of weight**? Weight is customarily measured in ounces (oz), pounds (lb), and tons (T). As with units of length and liquid volume, you can compare units of weight to each other, and change one to another by using simple calculations.

1 pound = 16 oz

1 ton = 2000 lb

Example:

How many ounces are in three pounds?

Step 1: You know that there are 16 oz in one pound. So multiply the number of ounces in one pound by three.

Step 2: $16 \times 3 = 48$ ounces in three pounds.

Exercises **CONVERT**

1. 86 oz = ________ lb
2. 8 lb 5 oz = ________ oz
3. 10 T = ________ lb
4. 2400 lb = ________ T
5. 166 oz = ________ lb
6. 13 lb 6 oz = ________ oz
7. $\frac{1}{4}$ T = ________ lb
8. $\frac{2}{5}$ T = ________ lb
9. 2 lb 12 oz + 2 lb 5 oz = ________ oz
10. 104 oz = ________ lb
11. Barton's backpack weighs 498 ounces. How many pounds does the backpack weigh?

    ____
12. If Jason weighed 167 lb and he lost 112 oz during the summer, how much does he weigh after losing the weight?

    ____
13. Kathleen weighed her two cats. The first cat weighed 7 lb 12 oz and the second weighed 11 lb 15 oz. How much did the two cats weigh in total?

    ____
14. Freddie's camping gear weighs 70 lb in total. He adds an extra pair of shoes which weighs 2 lb 4 oz and removes tent stakes that weigh 6 lb 8 oz. How much does the gear weigh now?

    ____

Name ________________________________

Perimeter with Customary Units

Imagine that you want to find the length around a figure. How can you measure that? You want to find the figure's **perimeter**, or the distance around it. To find the perimeter of a figure, add the lengths of all of its sides.

Example:

The perimeter of this triangle is 3 + 4 + 5 = 12 in.

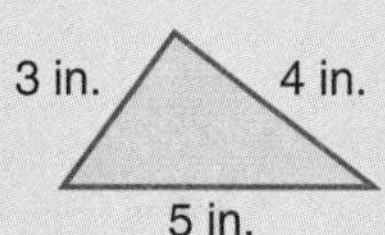

You could change this total number into feet by dividing the number of inches by 12.

$\frac{12}{12} = 1$ ft

The perimeter of this rectangle is
8 + 4 + 8 + 4 = 24 ft

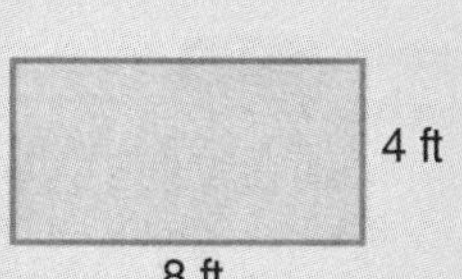

You could change this total into inches by multiplying by 12.

24 × 12 = 288 ft

Exercises CALCULATE

1. What is the perimeter of the figure shown?

____

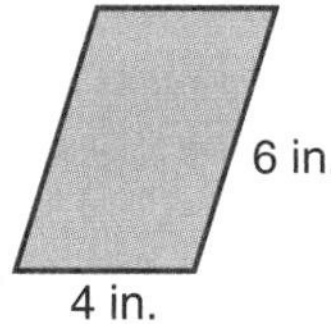

2. What is the perimeter of the figure shown?

____

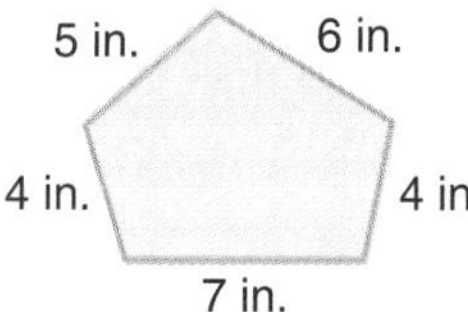

3. What is the perimeter of the triangle?

____

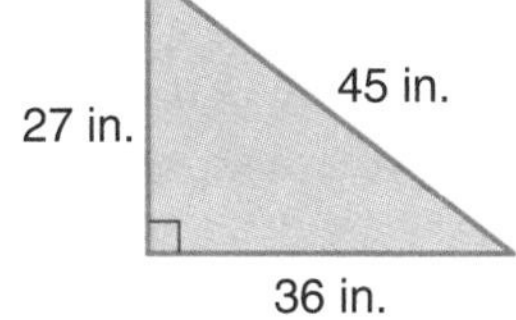

4. What is the perimeter of the figure shown?

____

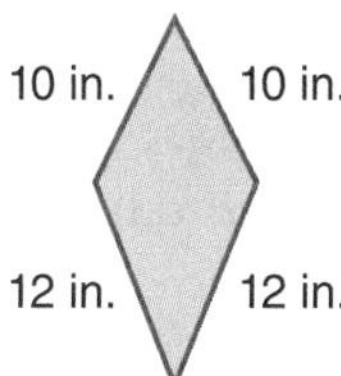

5. What is the perimeter of the figure shown?

____

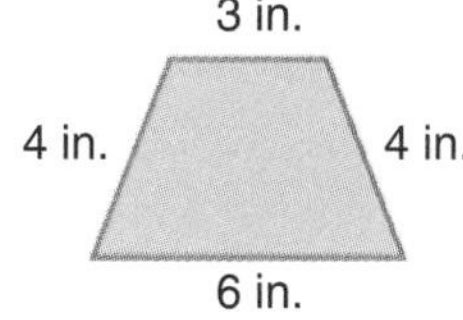

6. What is the perimeter of the figure shown?

____

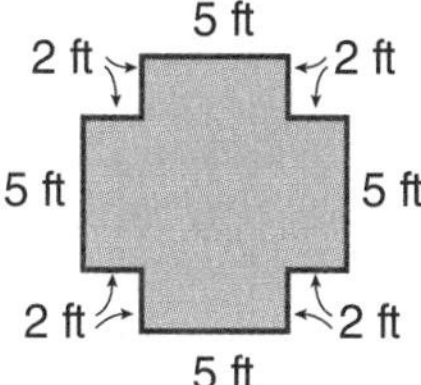

7. Jane created the odd-shaped wheel pictured in the figure. If she were to push the wheel 3 times around, how far would she have pushed the wheel?

____

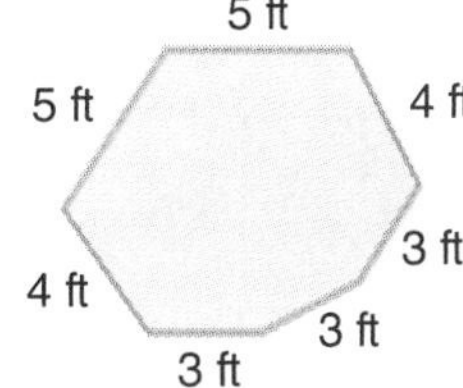

Name ______________________________

Area with Customary Units

Sometimes, you want to know a figure's **area**, or the number of units it would take to fill it. Those units are called square inches, square feet, square yards, or even square miles.

Remember...

Be careful! A square foot *does not equal* 12 square inches. It equals 144 square inches. A square yard *does not equal* 3 square feet. It equals 9 square feet.

Examples:

The area of a *rectangle* is its length (l) × its width (w).

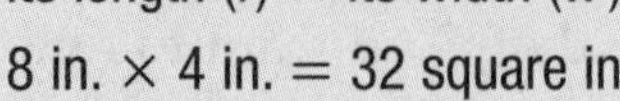

8 in. × 4 in. = 32 square in.

A *square* is a special kind of rectangle, with all of its sides equal in length. You may remember that a number to the second power, or a number multiplied once by itself, is called "squared."

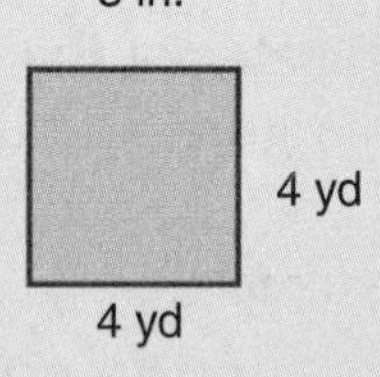

4 yd × 4 yd = 16 square yards

The area of a *triangle* is $\frac{1}{2}$ × *base (b)* × height *(h)*.

$\frac{1}{2}$ × 3 ft × 4 ft = 6 sq ft

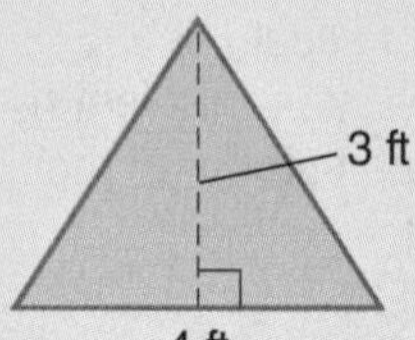

Exercises CALCULATE

1. What is the area of the rectangle?

   ____

2. What is the area of the square?

   ____

3. What is the area of the triangle?

   ____

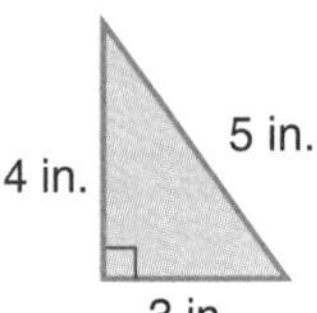

4. What is the area of the square?

   ____

5. What is the area of the rectangle?

   ____

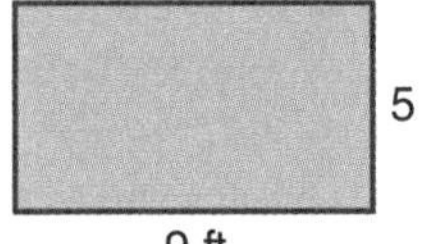

6. What is the area of the triangle?

   ____

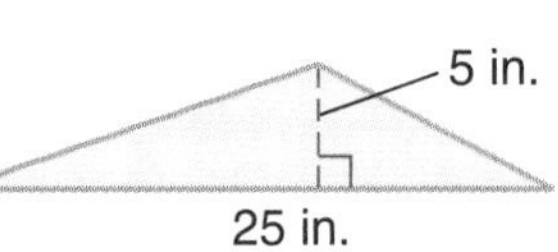

7. What is the area of the square?

   ____

8. What is the area of the rectangle?

   ____

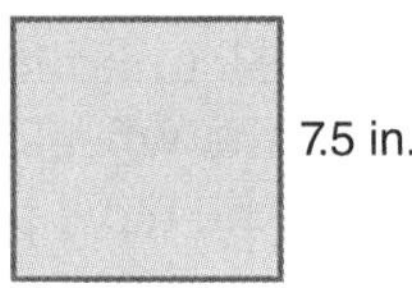

Name ______________________________

Metric Units of Length

You may have heard of metric units. These units are much easier to work with mathematically than customary units. That is because metric units are all based on the **powers of 10**. The **metric units of length** are millimeters (mm), centimeters (cm), meters (m), and kilometers (km).

1 centimeter = 10 mm
1 meter = 100 cm
1 kilometer = 1000 m

Remember...

To make calculations simpler for yourself, learn these prefixes:

milli = thousandth centi = hundredth kilo = thousand

Example:

How many cm = 35 m?

Step 1: Think: 100 cm = 1 m

Step 2: Multiply the number of meters × 100.

You can do this by regular multiplication.

$35 \times 100 = 3500$

However, it is much easier to move the decimal point two places to the right.

35 m = 3500 cm

How many m = 465 mm?

Step 1: Think: 1000 mm = 1 m

Step 2: Divide: $465 \div 1000 = \frac{465}{1000}$

You can also do this calculation by moving the decimal point three places to the left.

456 mm = 0.456 m

Exercises CONVERT

1. 210 m = ________ km
2. 145 mm = ________ cm
3. 573 m = ________ cm
4. 26 m = ________ mm
5. 400 cm = ________ km
6. 400 m = ________ cm
7. 1.6 m = ________ mm
8. 2.5 km = ________ m
9. 116 mm = ________ m
10. 1.557 km = ________ mm
11. 4355 mm = ________ cm
12. 0.4667 km = ________ cm
13. 3.0556 m = ________ mm
14. Terry covered the outside edge of his cousin's monster truck tires with a border of fluorescent yellow paint. If each tire measured 6.25 meters around the outside edge, then how many centimeters of edging did he paint on one tire?

    ____

15. The distance from Mike's house to the school is 0.775 kilometers. How many meters is that?

    ____

Name ______________________________

Metric Units of Liquid Volume

The basic **metric unit of liquid volume** is the **liter** (L). There are also milliliters (mL) and kiloliters (kL).

You can probably figure that:

1 liter = 1000 mL   1 kiloliter = 1000 L

Remember...

All metric units are powers of 10.

Example:

How many milliliters are in 3.5 liters?

Step 1: Think: 1000 mL = 1 liter

Step 2: Multiply 1000 by 3.5 = 3500 mL

Exercises CONVERT

1. 873 mL = ________ L
2. 1455 mL = ________ kL
3. 4.75 L = ________ mL
4. 7945 mL = ________ L
5. 100 mL = ________ kL
6. 2554 mL = ________ L
7. 0.0025 L = ________ mL
8. 0.007 kL = ________ mL
9. Pam's recipe calls for 3.4 L of olive oil. Unfortunately, all she has is a measuring cup that holds 10 mL. How many times will she have to fill her measuring cup with olive oil to complete the recipe?

   ____

10. Ron mixed 4500 milliliters of his favorite paint color. How many 1-liter containers can he fill with the mixture?

    ____

11. Harriet had 5.768 liters of special-liquid cleanser before she gave 554 mL of it to her mother, and 1.4 mL to her younger sister. How much liquid cleanser does she have left?

    ____

12. The science teacher instructs the students to add 256 mL of Liquid A to 1.5 L of Liquid B. How much liquid will there be altogether, assuming nothing evaporates or turns to a solid?

    ____

Name ______________________________

Metric Units of Mass

The basic **metric unit of mass** is the **gram** (g). There are also milligrams (mg), centigrams (cg), and kilograms (kg).

Since you know about metric prefixes, you could probably make the following list yourself!

1 cg = 10 mg   1 g = 100 cg   1 kg = 1000 g

Examples:

How many grams are in an object that has a mass of 4.25 kilograms?

Step 1: Think: 1000 grams = 1 kilogram

Step 2: Multiply: $4.25 \times 1000 = 4250$ grams

Exercises CONVERT

1. 400 g = ________ kg
2. 225 kg = ________ mg
3. 6600 g = ________ kg
4. 4505 mg = ________ g
5. 21.35 kg = ________ mg
6. 530 mg = ________ g
7. 650 mg = ________ g
8. 71 kg = ________ cg
9. 3.721 kg = ________ g
10. 2313 g = ________ kg
11. 546 mg = ________ g
12. 12,305 g = ________ kg
13. 4430 mg = ________ g
14. 12.34 kg = ________ g
15. 2 mg = ________ kg
16. 300 kg = ________ mg
17. 258 mg = ________ cg
18. 65 g = ________ kg
19. Larry has 5,599.4 milligrams of saffron seasoning that he brought back from India. He sells 1.06 grams to a local health food restaurant, and he gives his mother 0.0034 kg. How much saffron does Larry have left?

    ____
20. Richard keeps three bee hives in his backyard. He collected 1,678.616 grams of honey from the first hive, 1.6 kilograms from the second hive, and 1,660,301 milligrams from the third hive. Which hive produced the most honey?

    ____

    How much more honey did it produce than the hive that produced the second most amount of honey?

    ____

Name ______________________________

Calculating Perimeter and Area with Metric Units

You can also use metric units to calculate perimeter and area. You perform exactly the same kinds of calculations as when you are working with customary units of length. The only difference is that when you work with metric units, your answers will be expressed in metric units.

Perimeter is expressed in mm, cm, m, or km.

Area is expressed in sq mm, sq cm, sq m, or sq km.

Remember...

Do not change between metric units.
For example, 1 sq km does not = 1000 sq m

Exercises CALCULATE

1. What is the perimeter of a square with sides of 10 cm?

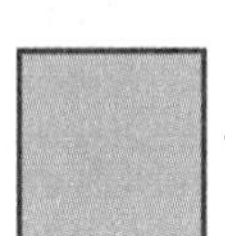

____

What is the area?

____

2. What is the perimeter of the figure?

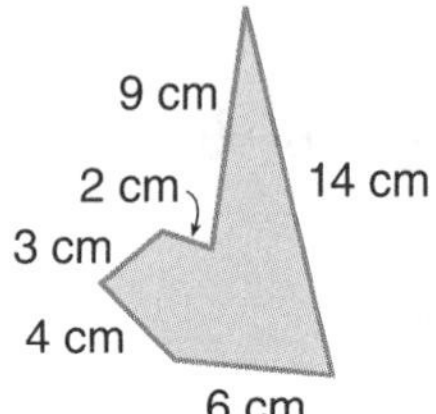

____

3. A rectangle has sides of 4.4 cm and 6 cm. What is the perimeter of the rectangle?

____

What is the area?

____

4. What is the perimeter of a rectangle with 2 sides of 12 meters and 2 sides of 6 meters?

____

What is the area?

____

5. What is the area of the triangle?

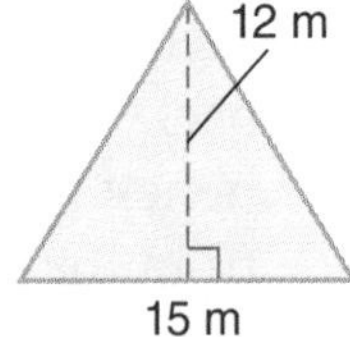

____

6. What is the area of the triangle?

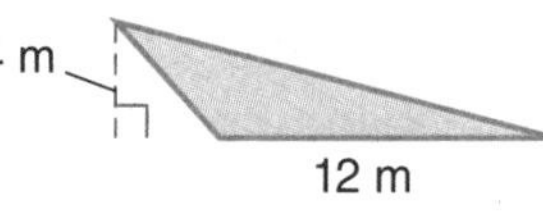

____

7. Ariel is cleaning a rug that is 4.2 meters long and 3 meters wide. If the dry cleaning store charges $18.00 per square meter to clean it, how much will she pay to clean the rug? ______________________

What is the perimeter of the rug? ______________________

Name ___________________________________

Changing from Customary Units to Metric Units

Can you change customary units to metric units? Yes. Here is a chart to guide you. Keep in mind that some of the metric units are not exact, but they are pretty close.

There is one customary unit on the chart that you may not recognize. In some parts of the world, beverages are often measured in **fluid ounces.**

Length	Liquid Volume	Weight or Mass
1 inch = 2.54 centimeters	1 cup = 0.237 liters	1 ounce = 28.35 grams
1 foot = 0.305 meters	1 pint = 0.473 liters	1 pound = 0.454 kilograms
1 yard = 0.914 meters	1 quart = 0.946 liters	1 ton = 907.18 kilograms
1 mile = 1.609 kilometers	1 gallon = 3.785 liters	
	1 fluid ounce = 29.574 milliliters	

Exercises CONVERT

1. 14 in. = ________ cm
2. 15 ft = ________ m
3. 12 yd = ________ m
4. 4 yd = ________ m
5. 3 mi = ________ km
6. 4 c = ________ L
7. 3 pt = ________ L
8. 9 qt = ________ L
9. 3.5 gal = ________ L
10. 11 fl oz = ________ mL
11. 14 oz = ________ g
12. 3 lbs = ________ kg
13. 6 oz = ________ g
14. 2 mi = ________ m
15. 11 c = ________ L
16. Which would be heavier: 4.8 lb or 2000 g of silver? ________
17. About how many meters tall is a 120-ft building?

    ____
18. Farah's cooler holds 8 qt of liquid. About how many mL will it hold?

    ____

Name ______________________________

Changing from Metric Units to Customary Units

Since customary units can be changed to metric units, you can also reverse this process. Again, remember that some of the numbers on the chart below are not exact. However, they are all close.

Length	Liquid Volume	Weight or Mass
1 millimeter = 0.039 inches	1 liter = 1.057 quarts	1 gram = 0.035 ounces
1 centimeter = 0.394 inches	1 kiloliter = 264.2 gallons	1 kilogram = 2.205 pounds
1 meter = 39.37 inches		
1 kilometer = 0.621 miles		

Exercises CONVERT

1. 24 mm = ________ in.
2. 143 cm = ________ in.
3. 3 m = ________ in.
4. 4 km = ________ mi
5. 20 g = ________ oz
6. 6 L = ________ qt
7. 3 kL = ________ gal
8. 4.5 kg = ________ lb
9. 242 mm = ________ in.
10. 13 kg is about how many oz? ________
11. 1100 mm = ________ in.
12. 2 kg + 32 g = ________ oz
13. The average player on the school basketball team is 190 centimeters tall. The average volleyball player is 6 ft 4 inches tall. Which team has a taller average height?

    ____

14. The Booster Club sponsored a 10-km walk to raise money for charity. About how many miles is the length of the walk?

    ____

Name ______________________________

Customary and Metric Units of Temperature

The units used to describe temperature are called **degrees**. Degrees are written with a small circle at the top right of a number: 30 degrees = 30°. Customary degrees are measured on the **Fahrenheit** scale. You must add the word Fahrenheit (or just F), because other temperature scales that are *not* customary are also used to describe temperature.

The metric unit to describe temperature is called the **Celsius** degree (or just C). This is also sometimes referred to as **Centigrade**.

Celsius	Fahrenheit	
0° C	32° F	Freezing point of water
100° C	212° F	Boiling point of water
35° C	95° F	Hot air temperature
37° C	98.6° F	Human body temperature

The Celsius scale is used in scientific work and is easier to use than the Fahrenheit scale. Even though both are expressed in degrees, a Celsius degree *does not* equal a Fahrenheit degree!

You can change Celsius to Fahrenheit temperatures, or Fahrenheit to Celsius temperatures. To do so, you must use the following equations:

$(F - 32) \times \left(\frac{5}{9}\right) = C \qquad C \times \left(\frac{9}{5}\right) + 32 = F$

Example:

Convert 98.6° F to C.

Step 1: Set up the equation:

$(98.6 - 32) \times \left(\frac{5}{9}\right) = C$

Step 2: Calculate: $66.6 \times \frac{5}{9} = 37$

98.6° F = 37° C

Exercises CONVERT

1. 150° C = ________ F
2. 150° F = ________ C
3. 0° C = ________ F
4. 0° F = ________ C
5. 216° F = ________ C
6. 105° C = ________ F
7. 72° F = ________ C
8. 30° C = ________ F
9. −25° F = ________ C
10. 35° F = ________ C
11. 37° C = ________ F
12. 950° C = ________ F
13. The melting point of aluminum is 1,219° F and the melting point of nickel is 2,646° F. What is the temperature difference between the two melting points? Express your answer in degrees Celsius.

    ____
14. Jamie took his temperature with a Celsius thermometer, and it read 38° C. What would his temperature be in degrees Fahrenheit?

    ____

Name ______________________________

1. Manny is going to replace the trim around the windows in his house. The trim for each window measures $10\frac{1}{2}$ feet. If Manny has 15 windows in his house, how many inches of trim does he need to replace?

____

2. Annie's fish tank holds $39\frac{1}{2}$ gallons of water. She is using a 1 quart container to fill the tank. How many full containers will Annie need to fill the tank?

____

3. Florence weighed boxes for the shipping department. The first box weighed 196 ounces. The second box weighed $13\frac{3}{8}$ pounds. Which box weighed more?

____

4. Mandie plans to paint the side of her barn. The side measures 10 meters long and 5.5 meters high. How much area does Mandie need to cover with paint?

______________________________ square meters

5.

What is the area of the rectangle?

____

What is the perimeter of the rectangle?

____

6.

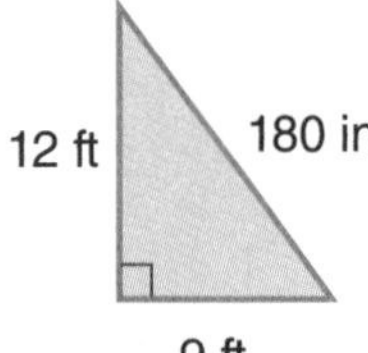

What is the area of the right triangle?

______________________________ square feet

What is the perimeter?

______________________________ inches

7. What is the area of the base of the rectangular box?

______________________________ square feet

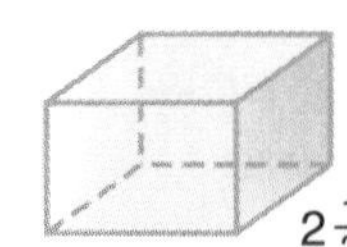

Name ______________________________

8 A spacecraft must travel 24.1 kilometers per second to leave the Earth's atmosphere. How far does the spacecraft travel in a minute?

____

In an hour? ____________________ In a day? ____________________

9 A school banner is 5.5 meters in length and 1,850 millimeters in width. How much fabric was used to make the banner?

______________________________ sq cm

10 Blanche has three cans of paint to mix. One can holds 1957 milliliters of paint, the second can holds 115.6 centiliters of paint, and the third can holds 3.9 liters of paint. How much paint will Blanche mix?

______________________________ liters

11 What is the area of a triangle with sides of 12 cm, a base of 6 cm, and a height of 8 cm?

______________________________ sq cm

What is the perimeter of the triangle?

____

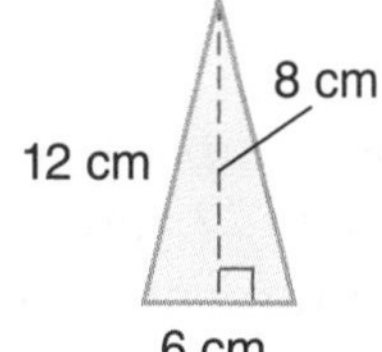

12 Frank walked around the entire rectangular school playground, which measures 126 meters by 6500 centimeters. How far did Frank walk?

______________________________ meters

What is the area of the school playground?

______________________________ square meters

13 What is the area of a rectangle that measures 4.6 meters in width, and 5.5 meters in length?

______________________________ square meters

14 The average player on the soccer team weighs 165 pounds. About how much is that in kilograms?

____

Name ______________________

15 The average pickup truck has a gas tank that holds 95 liters of gasoline. How much is that in quarts and in gallons?

______________ quarts ______________ gallons

16 Pauline was looking for lawn-mowing jobs for the summer. She surveyed the neighborhood and found out that the average lawn measured 60 feet by 45 feet. What is the area in square feet?

______________ sq ft

About how much is the total area in square meters?

______________ sq meters

17 The distance of a flight from Cleveland to New Orleans is about 1250 miles. The average speed of a commercial airliner is about 830 kilometers per hour. About how long will it take to fly from Cleveland to New Orleans?

______________ hours

18 The air-conditioning company suggests that people keep the temperature in their homes between 22 and 28 degrees Celsius during the summer. What is the temperature range in degrees Fahrenheit?

____

19

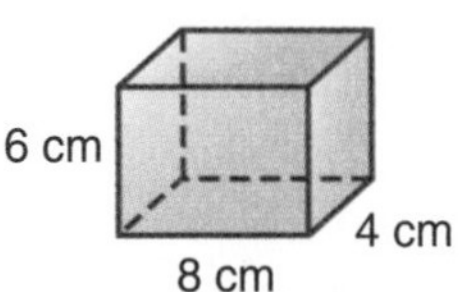

What is the area of the base of the rectangular solid shown?

____

20

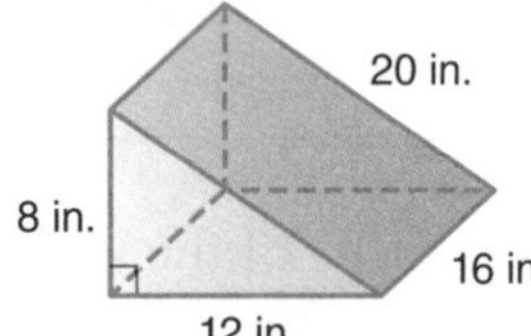

What is the area of the triangular face on the figure shown?

____

21 In track and field, the standard middle distance event is the 5000 meter race. About how many feet is 5000 meters?

______________ feet

22 A body temperature of 103.6° F is considered an extremely high fever. What temperature is that in Celsius?

____

Name ______________________________

Answers and Explanations

1.	1890 in.	$10\frac{1}{2}\text{ ft} \times 12 = 126\text{ in.}; 126 \times 15 = 1890$
2.	158 containers full	$39\frac{1}{2}\text{ gal} \times 4 = 158$
3.	The second box $13\frac{3}{8}$ lb vs. 12.25 lb	$196\text{ oz} \div 16 = 12.25$
4.	55 square meters	$10 \times 5.5 = 55$
5.	Area 132 sq ft, Perimeter 46 ft	$132\text{ in.} \div 12 = 11\text{ ft}; 11 \times 12 = 132; 11 + 11 + 12 + 12 = 46$
6.	Area 54 sq ft, Perimeter 432 inches	$A = \frac{1}{2}bh = \frac{1}{2}(9)(12) = \frac{1}{2}(108) = 54;$ Change sides to inches for perimeter: $12 \times 12 = 144\text{ in.}; 9 \times 12 = 108\text{ in.}; 144 + 108 + 180 = 432$
7.	7.5 sq ft	$36\text{ in.} \div 12 = 3\text{ ft}; 3 \times 2\frac{1}{2} = 7\frac{1}{2}$
8.	1446 km, 86,760 km 2,082,240 km	$24.1 \times 60 = 1,446\frac{\text{km}}{\text{min}}; 1,446 \times 60 = 86,760\frac{\text{km}}{\text{hr}}; 86,760 \times 24 = 2,082,240\frac{\text{km}}{\text{day}}$
9.	101,750 sq cm	$5.5\text{ m} \times 100 = 550\text{ cm}; 1,850\text{ mm} \div 10 = 185\text{ cm}; A = 550 \times 185 = 101,750$
10.	7.013 liters	$1,957\text{ mL} \div 1,000 = 1.957\text{ L}; 115.6\text{ cL} \div 100 = 1.156\text{ L}; 1.957 + 1.156 + 3.9 = 7.013$
11.	24 sq cm; 30 cm	$A = \frac{1}{2}bh = \frac{1}{2}(6)(8) = \frac{1}{2}(48) = 24; 12 + 12 + 6 = 30$
12.	382 meters; 8190 sq m	$6,500\text{ cm} \div 100 = 65\text{ m}; P = 126 + 126 + 65 + 65 = 382; A = 126 \times 65 = 8,190$
13.	25.3 sq m	$4.6 \times 5.5 = 25.3$
14.	75 kg	$165 \times 0.454 = 74.91$
15.	About 100 quarts, 25 gallons	$95 \times 1.057 = 100.415; 100 \div 4 = 25$
16.	2700 sq ft; about 250 sq meters	$60 \times 45 = 2,700; 60 \times 0.305 = 18.3; 45 \times 0.305 = 13.725; 18.3 \times 13.7 = 250.71$
17.	About $2\frac{1}{2}$ hours	$1,250 \times 1.609 = 2,011.25; 2,011 \div 830 = 2.42$
18.	71.6° to 82.4° F	$22°\text{C} \times \frac{9}{5} + 32 = 39.6 + 32 = 71.6°\text{F}; 28°\text{C} \times \frac{9}{5} + 32 = 50.4 + 32 = 82.4°\text{F}$

Name ____________________

19. 32 sq m $8 \times 4 = 32$

20. 48 sq in. $A = \frac{1}{2}bh = \frac{1}{2}(12)(8) = \frac{1}{2}(96) = 48$

21. 16404 ft $5{,}000 \times 39.37 = 196{,}850$ in.; $196{,}850 \div 12 = 16{,}404$ ft

22. 39.8° C $(103.6°F - 32) \times \frac{5}{9} = 71.6 \times \frac{5}{9} = 39.8°C$

Name ______________________________

Points and Lines

You probably used the words "point" and "line" before, but do those terms have special meaning in mathematics?

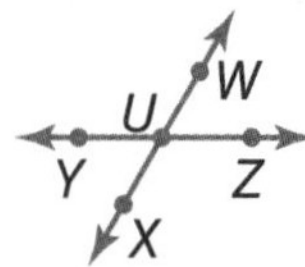

Yes, they do. You may think of a point as a dot, which is what we mean when we use "point" in everyday use. However, a **point** in mathematics is a specific location in space. It has no dimensions. A point is usually labeled with a capital letter.

A **line** is a straight path of points. A line goes in both directions and never ends. When we draw a line, we use a pencil so we can see it. A line drawn with a pencil has width and length.

However, a line in mathematics has only one dimension, length.

Because a line is a path of points, it can be named by *any* two points located *anywhere* on it, and you can use those points in either order. So in our illustration, Line $\overleftrightarrow{YZ}$ = Line $\overleftrightarrow{ZY}$, and Line $\overleftrightarrow{WX}$ = Line $\overleftrightarrow{XW}$.

Intersecting lines cross each other at a specific point. In this example, Lines $\overleftrightarrow{YZ}$ and $\overleftrightarrow{WX}$ cross at Point U.

Remember...

A line extends in *both* directions. It does not end in *either* direction.

Exercises SOLVE

1. Draw the line denoted by $\overleftrightarrow{CD}$.

2. Draw $\overleftrightarrow{QR}$.

3. What would the single letter D indicate?

____

4. What two lines are shown in the figure?

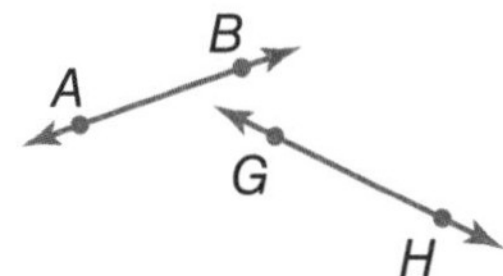

____

____

5. Describe in words what $\overleftrightarrow{JK}$ denotes.

____

____

____

____

6. Which of the following is *not* a line? ____

a. Z Q

b. M N

c.

Name ____________________

Line Segments and Rays

If lines go on forever in both directions, can you describe a line that ends at one or both sides? Yes, and there are some mathematical terms used to describe these.

A **line segment** is a specific part of a line that has ends at two points. It is named by its two end points. So Segment $\overline{ST}$ = Segment $\overline{TS}$. We can write it this way:

$$\overline{ST} = \overline{TS}$$

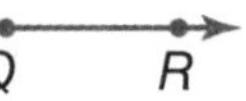

A **ray** is a part of a line that begins at a specific point, called a **vertex**, or **endpoint**. The line extends from that point in one direction without ending. To define a ray, you must use another letter along the line's path. Remember that the second letter is *not* the line's end. The *first* point in naming a ray is its vertex. So ray $\overrightarrow{QR}$ *does not* equal ray $\overrightarrow{RQ}$. Ray $\overrightarrow{QR}$ has a different vertex from ray $\overleftarrow{QR}$, and goes in the opposite direction.

Exercises SOLVE

1. Draw a diagram that illustrates a ray $\overrightarrow{YX}$.

2. Identify two rays and two line segments in the figure.

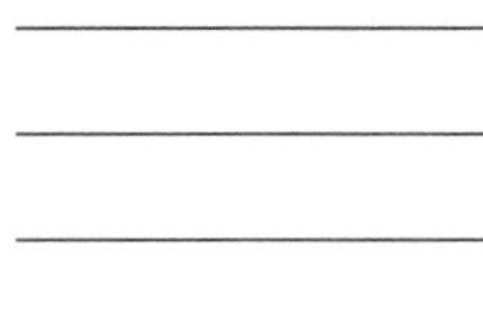

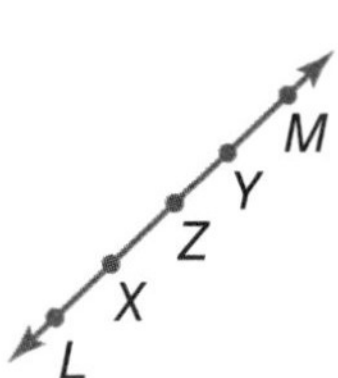

3. Identify three line segments in the diagram.

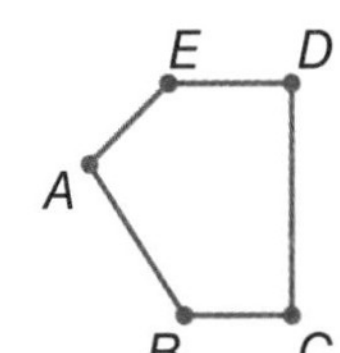

4. Draw two rays $\overrightarrow{AB}$ and $\overrightarrow{AC}$.

5. Identify the two line segments.

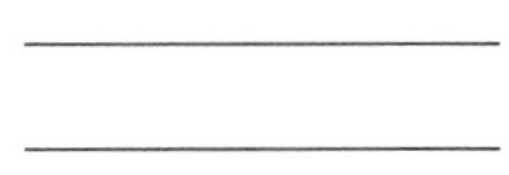

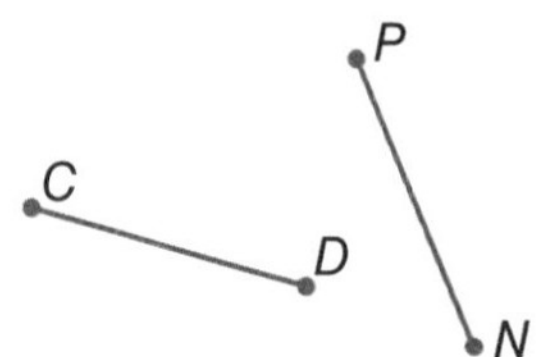

Name ______________________________

Measuring and Naming Angles

Do you think that rays from two intersecting lines can meet at the same point, or vertex? Yes they can. When they do, they form an **angle**, which is named by both its lines. The vertex is the middle letter of the angle's name.

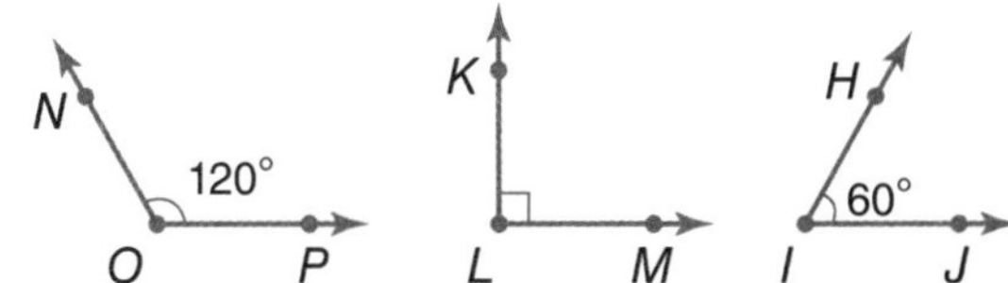

$\overrightarrow{NO}$ and $\overrightarrow{OP}$ intersect at point O, the vertex of each line, to form ∠NOP.

You measure angles in degrees. A straight line is 180°, so angles are always smaller than 180°. If an angle is greater than 90°, it is an **obtuse angle**. If it is less than 90°, it is an **acute angle**. If it is *exactly* 90°, it is a **right angle**. Right angles are often shown with a small square inside the angle.

∠NOP is an obtuse angle. ∠HIJ is an acute angle. ∠KLM is a right angle.

Exercises IDENTIFY

Identify the angle as acute, right, or obtuse.

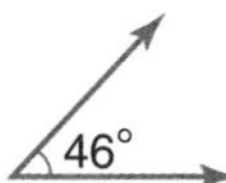

1 ______________________________

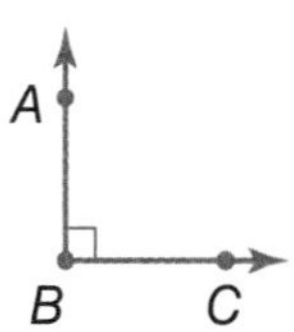

2 ______________________________

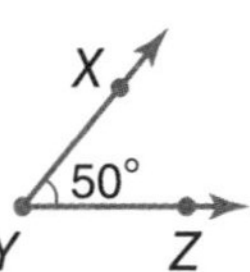

3 ______________________________

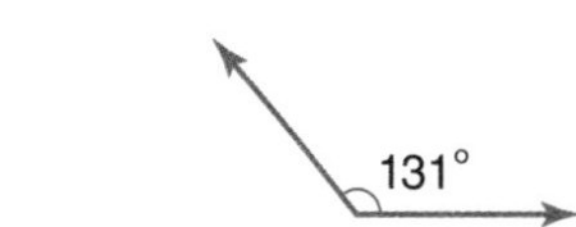

4 ______________________________

5 ______________________________

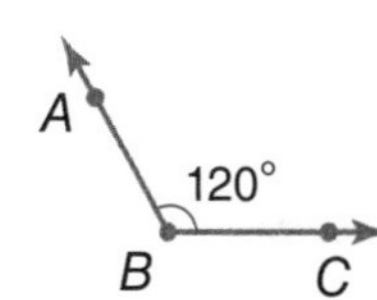

6 ______________________________

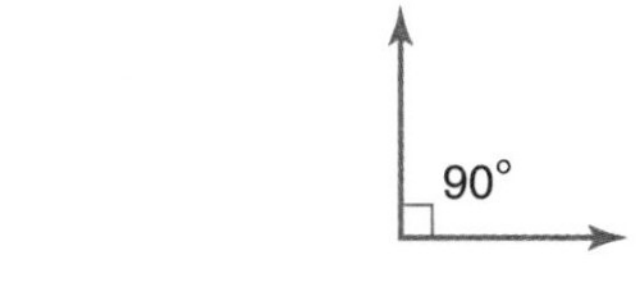

7 ______________________________

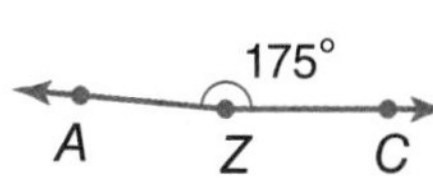

8 ______________________________

Name ______________________

Types of Angles

If angles always measure fewer degrees than a straight line, can two angles be added together to form 180°, or a straight line?

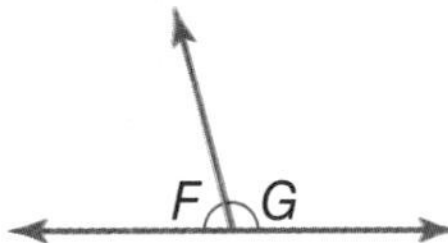

Yes, two angles that form a line are called **supplementary angles**. Their sum will equal 180°. So if you know the measurement of one angle, you can figure out the measure of the other angle. Notice that a single letter placed near the vertex can sometimes be used to identify angles.

If ∠F = 75°, you subtract this value from 180°. 180 − 75 equals angle G. Angle G = 105°.

Angles can have other kinds of relationships with each other. Two acute angles that form a right angle are called **complementary angles**. The sum of these two angles equals 90°.

So if ∠E = 35°, you subtract 35 from 90 to find angle D. Angle D = 55°.

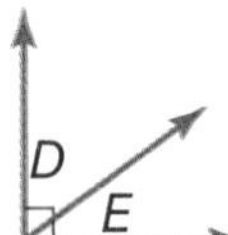

Two intersecting lines always form four angles. The angles opposite each other are called **vertical angles**, and they are equal. ∠A = ∠C. ∠B = ∠D.

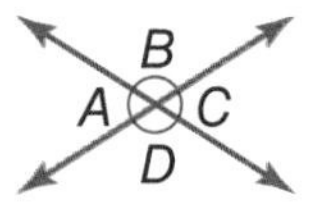

Two different types of angles are created when a line intersects two parallel lines. Look at the figure below. Lines *x* and *y* are parallel and a line, or transversal, intersects, or crosses them. Eight angles are created and are labeled 1 through 8.

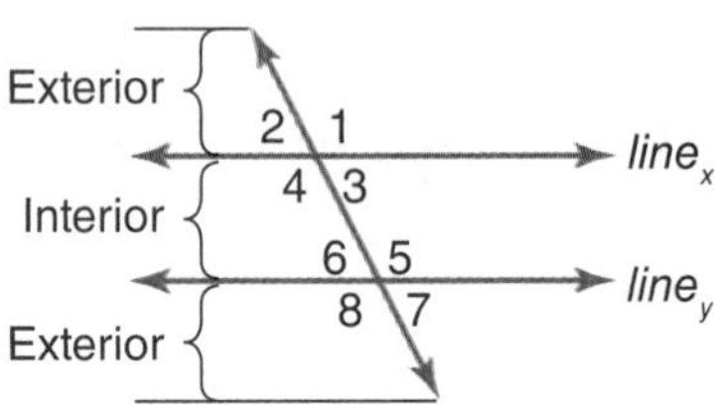

Angles 1, 2, 7, and 8 are **exterior angles** because they are located outside parallel lines *x* and *y*.

Angles 3, 4, 5, and 6 are **interior angles** because they are between parallel lines *x* and *y*.

Remember...

You can prove that vertical angles are equal. In the example at the top of this column, angle A and angle B form a straight line. So angle A = 180° − angle B. Angle C and angle D also form a straight line. Angle C = 180°. So angle A = angle B.

Exercises IDENTIFY

1. From the figure below, give examples of two complementary, two supplementary and two vertical angles.

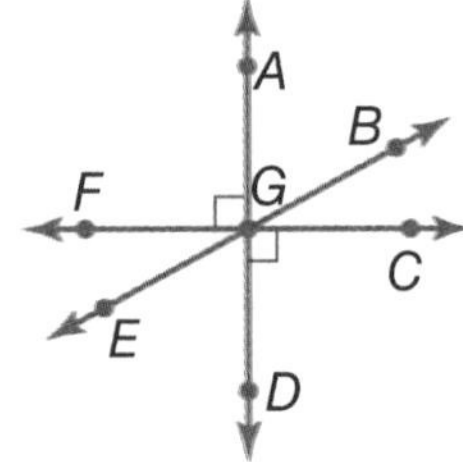

Complementary ______________________

Supplementary ______________________

Vertical ______________________

Name ____________________

Types of Angles (cont.)

2 For the figure below, list all complementary and supplementary angles.

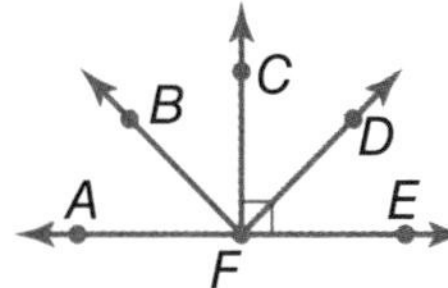

Complementary ____________________

____

Supplementary ____________________

3

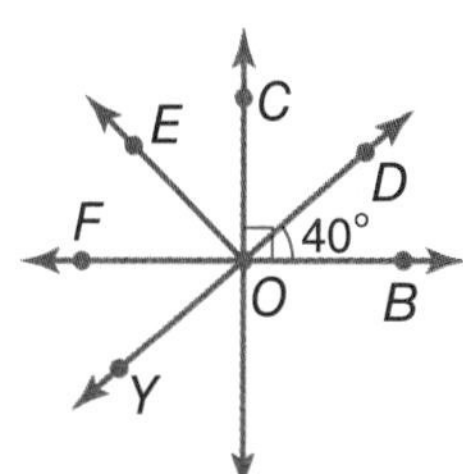

Are angle DOB and angle DOC complementary? ____________________

Explain. ____________________

____

____

4 In the figure below, a line is intersecting two parallel lines. Fill in the missing information:

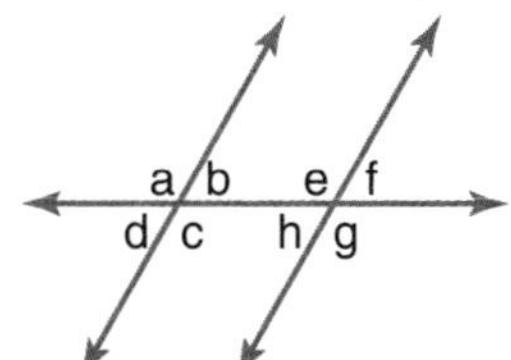

∠a = ∠_____ = ∠_____ = ∠_____

5 In the figure below, a line is intersecting two parallel lines. Fill in the missing angle measurements:

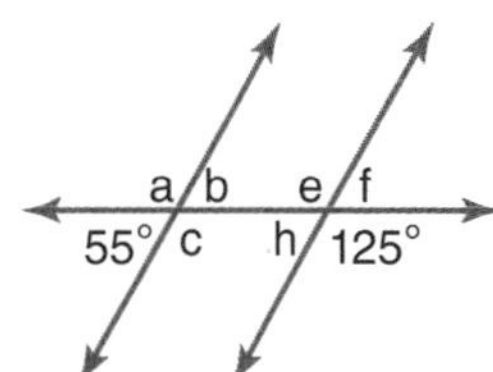

∠a = _____; ∠b = _____; ∠c = _____

∠e = _____; ∠f = _____; ∠h = _____

Name ______________________________

Finding Missing Angle Measurements

Remember, when two parallel lines are intersected by another line, or transversal, eight angles are formed.

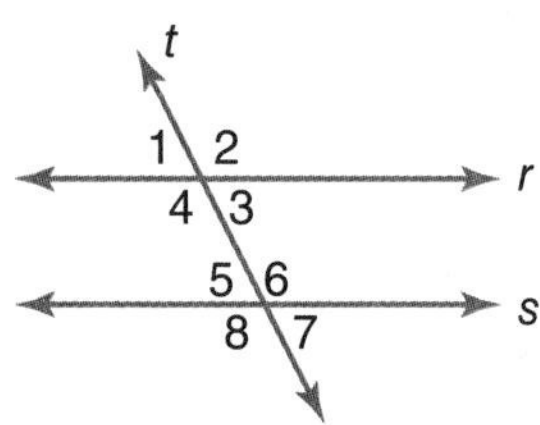

- Adjacent interior angles 4 and 5 and 3 and 6 are supplementary.
- Alternate interior angles 4 and 6 and 3 and 5 are equal.
- Adjacent exterior angles 1 and 8 and 2 and 7 are supplementary.
- Alternate exterior angles 1 and 7 and 2 and 8 are equal.

Exercises SOLVE

1 Fill in the angle measurements for the other seven angles.

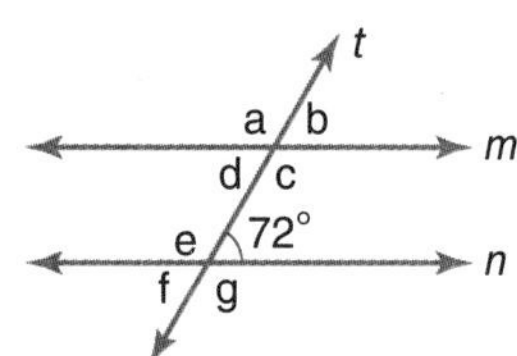

∠a ____________ ∠b ____________

∠c ____________ ∠d ____________

∠e ____________ ∠f ____________

∠g ____________

2 Angle 3 is 48 degrees. List the measurements of the other seven angles.

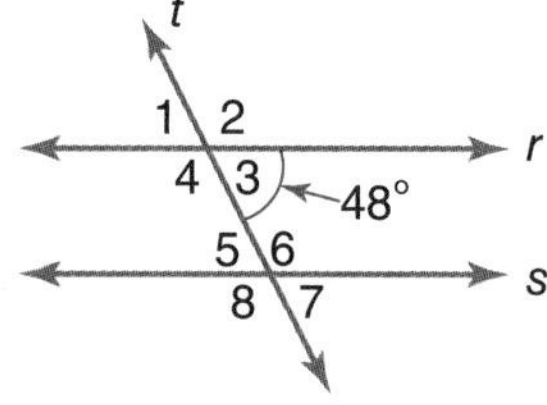

∠1 ____________ ∠2 ____________

∠4 ____________ ∠5 ____________

∠6 ____________ ∠7 ____________

∠8 ____________

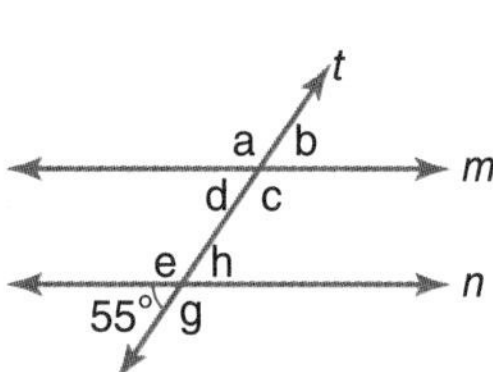

3 Fill in the angle measurements for the other seven angles.

∠a ____________ ∠b ____________

∠c ____________ ∠d ____________

∠e ____________ ∠g ____________

∠h ____________

E
D
F
C
44°
O
G
B
A

4 What is the measurement of ∠FOE? ____________________

What is the measurement of ∠EOC? ____________________

What is the measurement of ∠BOC? ____________________

Name ____________________________________

Types of Triangles

A 2-dimensional figure with three sides is called a **triangle**. The three angles in a triangle always add up to 180°.

acute triangle

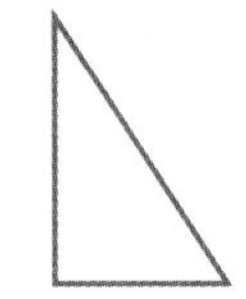
right triangle

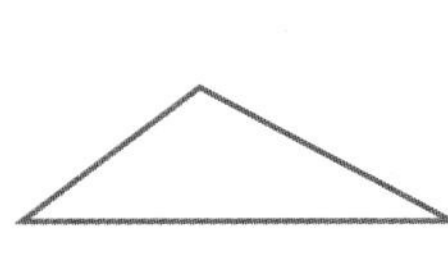
obtuse triangle

All triangles have at least two angles that are acute. In an **acute triangle**, *all* three angles are acute. In a **right triangle**, one of the angles is a right angle. In an **obtuse triangle**, one of the angles is obtuse. Because *all three of its angles add up to 180°*, a triangle can have only one angle that measures 90° or more.

equilateral triangle

isosceles triangle

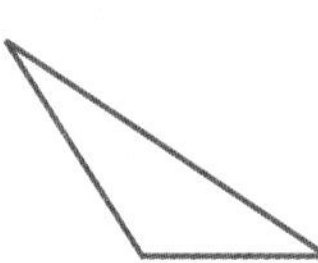
scalene triangle

Another way of looking at triangles is to look at the length of their sides. In an **equilateral triangle**, the three sides are the same length. They are **congruent**, or equal. In an **isosceles triangle**, two sides are congruent, but the third side is not. In a **scalene triangle**, none of the sides is congruent.

Exercises IDENTIFY

Identify as acute, right, or obtuse.

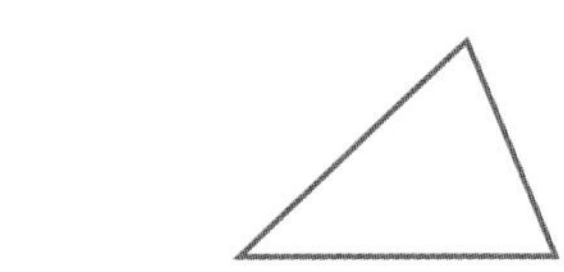
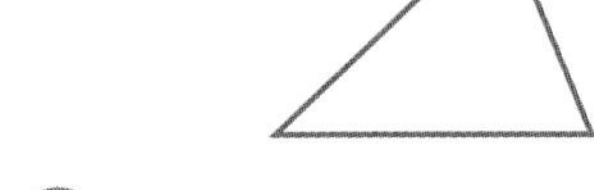
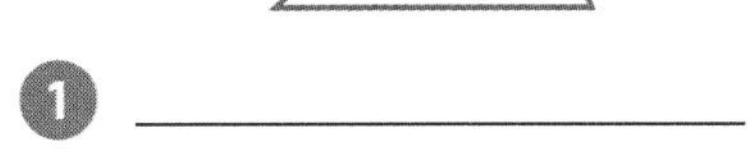

1 ____________________

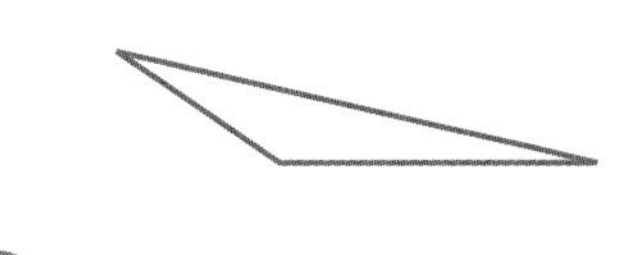
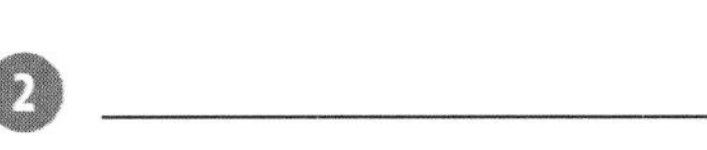

2 ____________________

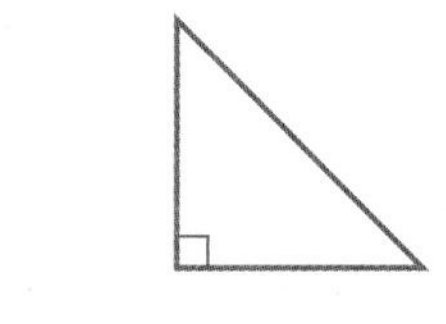

3 ____________________

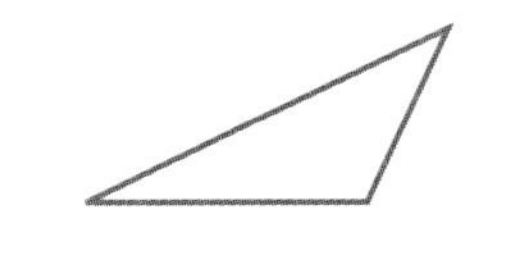

4 ____________________

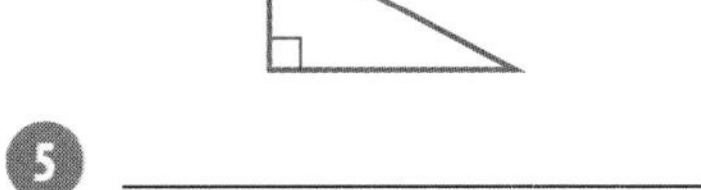

5 ____________________

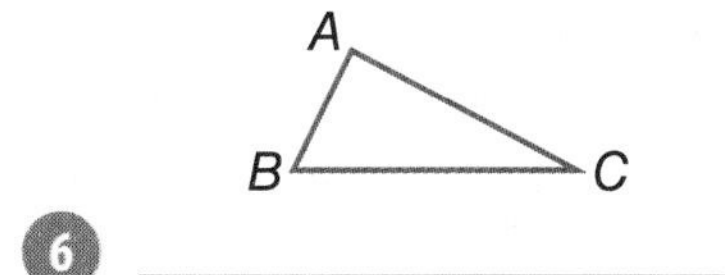

6 ____________________

Identify as isosceles, scalene, or equilateral.

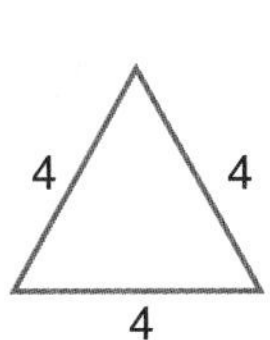

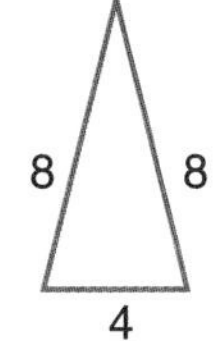

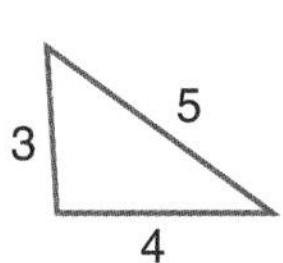

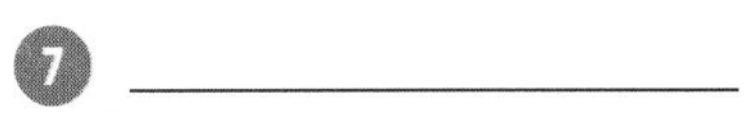

7 ____________________

8 ____________________

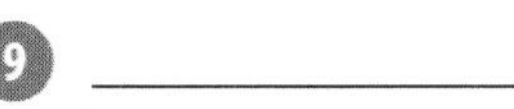

9 ____________________

Name ______________________

Congruent and Similar Triangles

Similar triangles are triangles with the same shape, but with different sizes. Triangles that have the same angles are similar. The best example of this is an equilateral triangle, a triangle whose sides are all of equal length. Equilateral triangles have three equal angles of 60°. However, the sides of equilateral triangles can be different lengths. This is true of all triangles that have equal angles. The triangles look the same, but they can be different sizes.

Congruent triangles have equal sides and equal angles. They are the same, or **congruent**. Obviously, if two triangles are congruent they are also similar.

Exercises IDENTIFY

Identify each set of triangles as similar, congruent, or neither. Explain your answer.

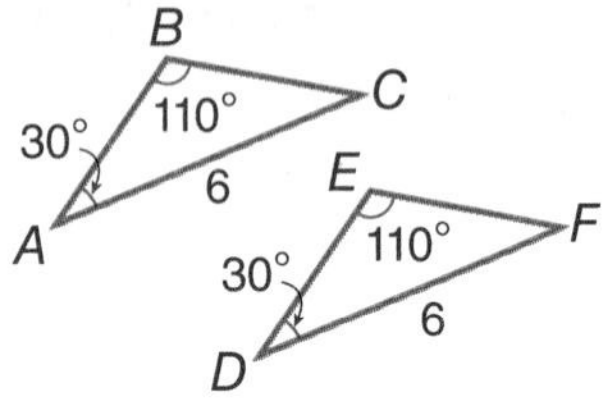

1 ______________________

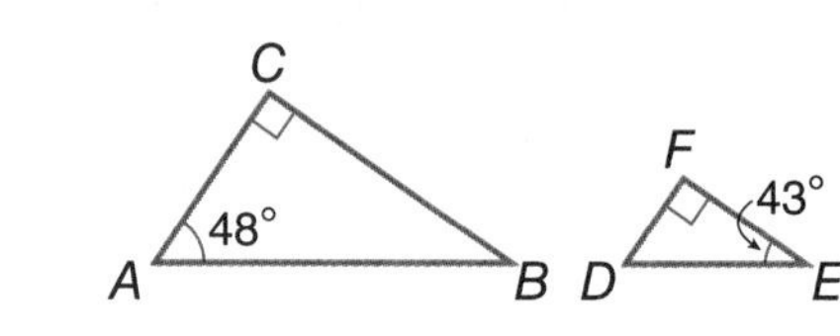

2 ______________________

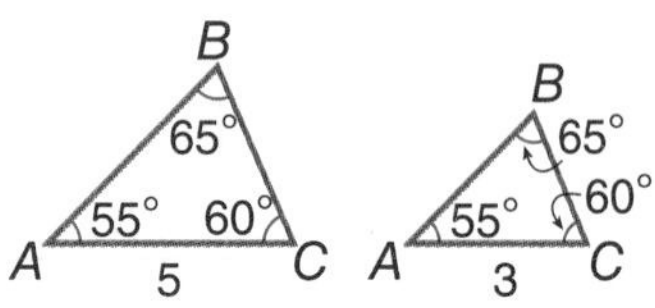

3 ______________________

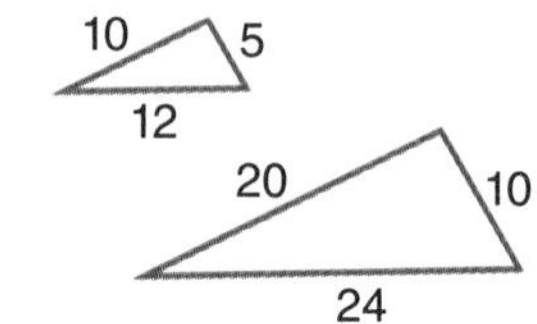

4 ______________________

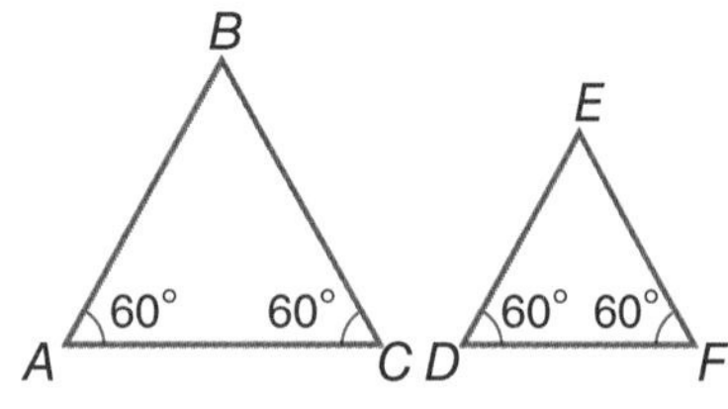

5 ______________________

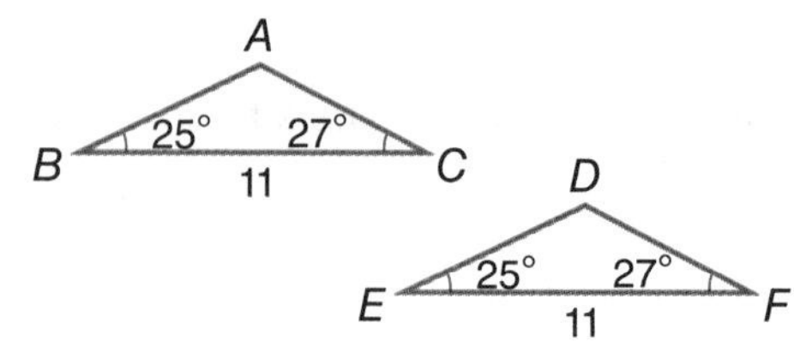

6 ______________________

Name ______________________________

Right Triangles and Pythagorean Theorem

The **Pythagorean Theorem** was developed a long time ago by a Greek mathematician after observing the special characteristics of right triangles. The theorem states that for all right triangles, the square of the length of the hypotenuse (the side opposite the right angle) is equal to the sum of the squares of lengths of the other two sides, or legs as they are also known.

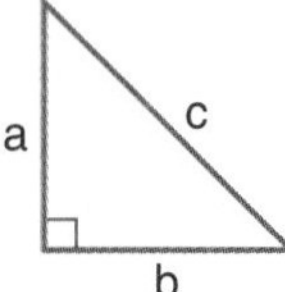

In the figure, side c is the hypotenuse and sides a and b are the legs. So the Pythagorean Theorem states that the square of the hypotenuse equals the sum of the squares of the lengths of the other two sides, or $c^2 = a^2 + b^2$, where c is the hypotenuse and a and b are the legs.

Example: In the right triangle above, suppose the length of $a = 3$ and $b = 4$. What would the length of c equal?

Step1: Set up the equation using the Pythagorean Theorem: $3^2 + 4^2 = c^2$

Step 2: Calculate: $9 + 16 = c^2$

$\sqrt{25} = c$

$c = 5$

Remember...

There are several special cases of right triangle that will help you to solve equations in the future. Look at the chart below for examples.

Side a	Side b	Hypotenuse
1	1	$\sqrt{2}$
3	4	5
6	8	10
5	12	13
9	12	15

Exercises SOLVE

Use the Pythagorean Theorem to determine the length of the missing side.

1. If side A is 6 and side B is 8, then side C (the hypotenuse) is ________

2. If side A is 9 and side B is 9, then side C (the hypotenuse) is ________

3. If side A is 10 and side B is 24, then side C (the hypotenuse) is ________

4. If side A is 9 and side C (the hypotenuse) is 15, then side B is ________

5. If side B is 6 and the hypotenuse is 10, then side A is ________

6. If side A is 12 and side B is 5, then side C (the hypotenuse) is ________

Name ______________________________

Right Triangles and Pythagorean Theorem (cont.)

You can also use the Pythagorean Theorem and the ratio of *similar* triangles to find the unknown lengths of sides.

Example: ABC and DEF are similar. That means the ratios of the sides are equal. You can use the ratios and cross-multiplication to solve for the unknown.

Step1: Set up the equation:

$$\frac{AB}{BC} = \frac{DE}{EF}, \text{ or } \frac{9}{12} = \frac{15}{n}$$

Step 2: Calculate: $9n = 180 \qquad n = 20$

So side EF is 20 and side DF $= \sqrt{15^2 + 20^2}$ $= 25$

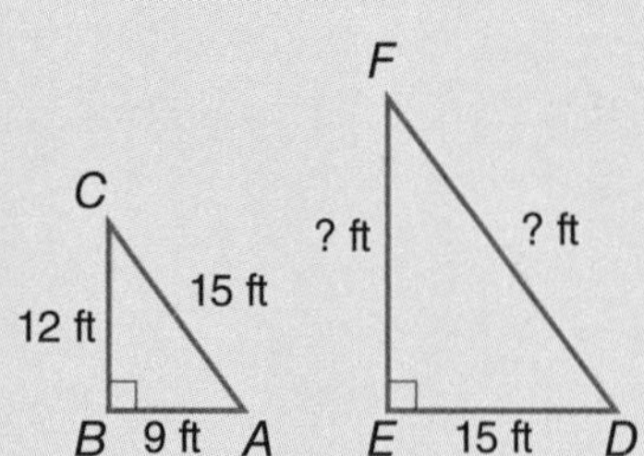

Exercises SOLVE

Find the missing sides of the following pairs of *similar* right triangles:

7. HI = ________ ft

KL = ________ ft

JL = ________ ft

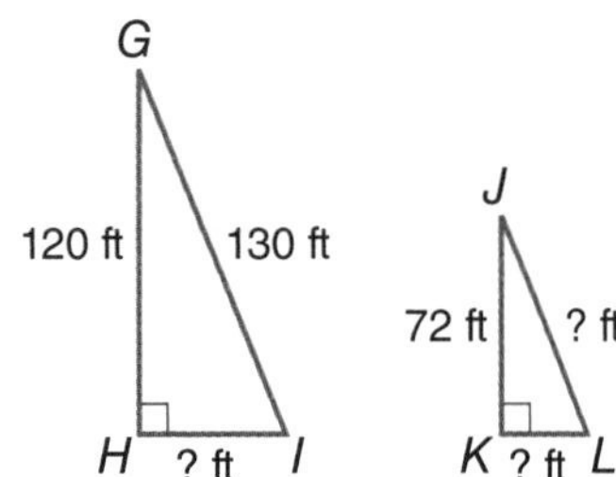

8. LN = ________ m

PQ = ________ m

OQ = ________ m

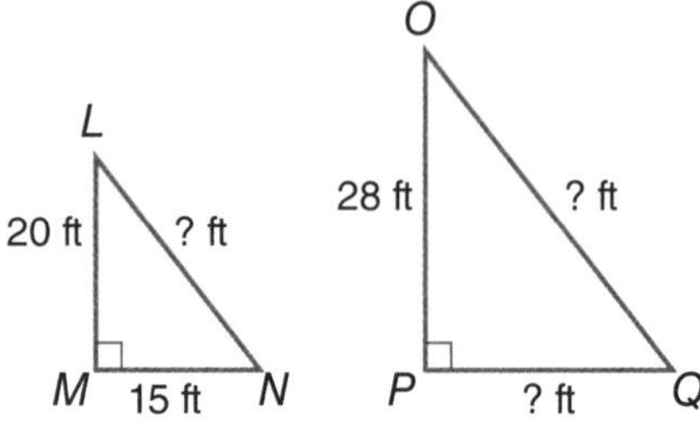

9. RT = ________ in.

VW = ________ in.

UW = ________ in.

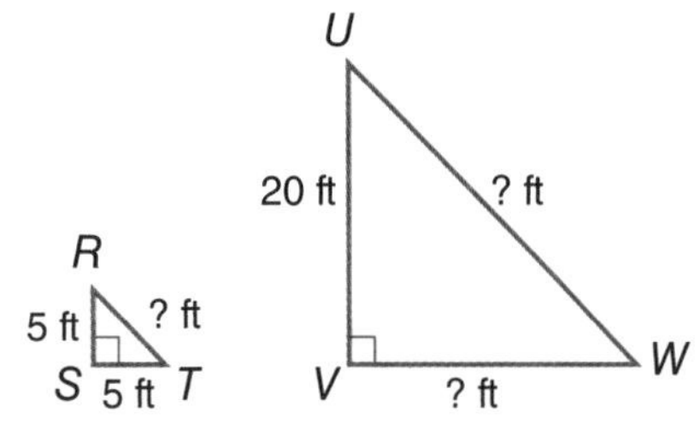

10. If the two triangles are similar, then what is the length of the missing side?

____

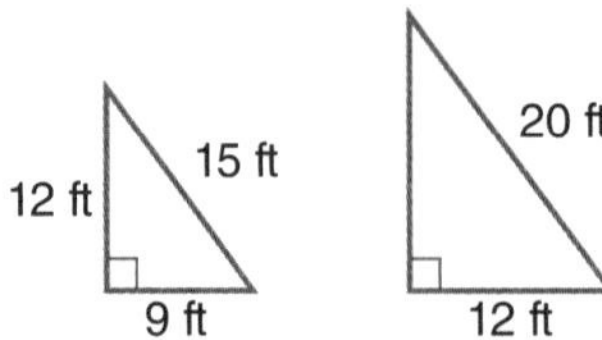

Name ______________________________

Quadrilaterals

A 2-dimensional figure with four angles and four sides is called a **quadrilateral**. You can already recognize a **rectangle**, a 2-dimensional figure with four right angles. The opposite sides of a rectangle are parallel and the same length.

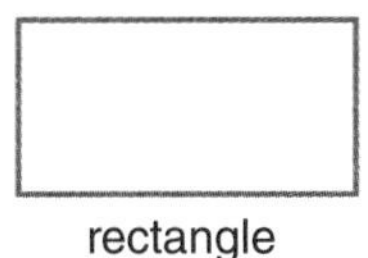
rectangle

If *all* four sides of a rectangle are the same length, it is a **square**.

square

Like a rectangle, the opposite sides of a **rhombus** are parallel and all sides are the same length. However, unlike a rectangle, a rhombus does *not* have four right angles.

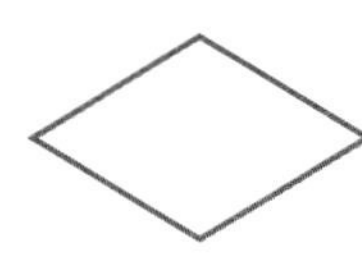
rhombus

A **trapezoid** has two opposite sides that are parallel, but the sides are *not* the same length. The other two sides of a trapezoid are *not* parallel.

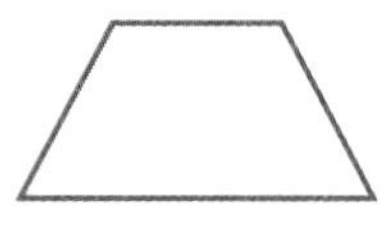
trapezoid

If a quadrilateral looks like a typical toy kite, it is called a **kite**. Two of its angles are equal. Its longer two *touching* sides are equal in length, and so are its shorter two *touching* sides.

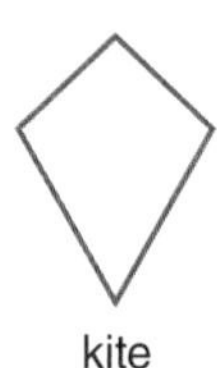
kite

Exercises IDENTIFY

For each figure below, label as a square, rectangle, rhombus, trapezoid, or kite.

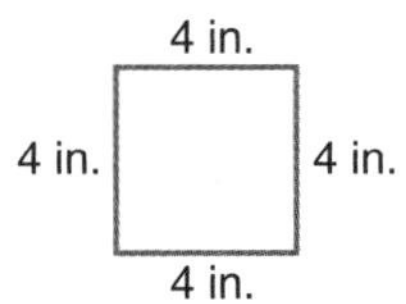

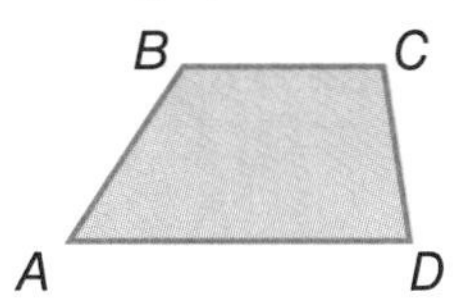

1. ______________

2. ______________

3. ______________

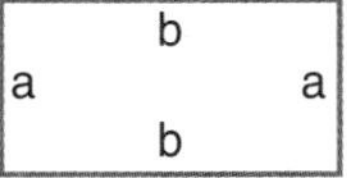

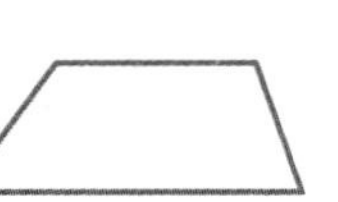

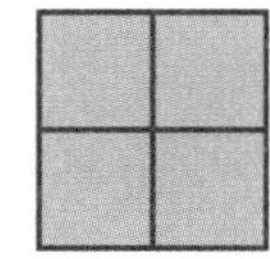

4. ______________

5. ______________

6. ______________

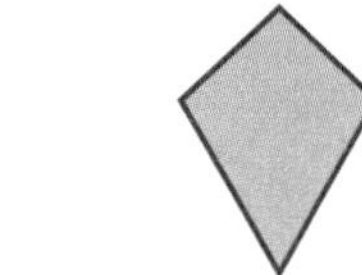

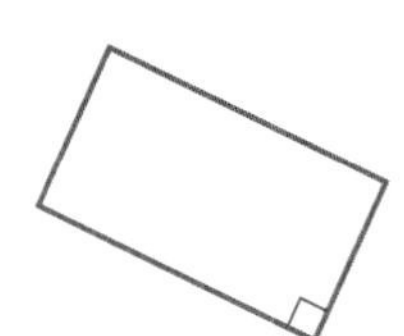

7. ______________

8. ______________

9. ______________

Name ______________________________

Polygons

Have you ever seen a 2-dimensional figure that has more than 4 sides? You have if you have seen a traffic sign. A stop sign is an octagon, an eight-sided **polygon**. A polygon is a closed 2-dimensional figure made up of line segments. In fact, triangles and quadrilaterals are polygons, too. However, mathematicians usually do not call a figure a polygon unless it has more than 3 sides. As you might have guessed, for each side there is also an angle. The most common polygons are named for the number of their sides.

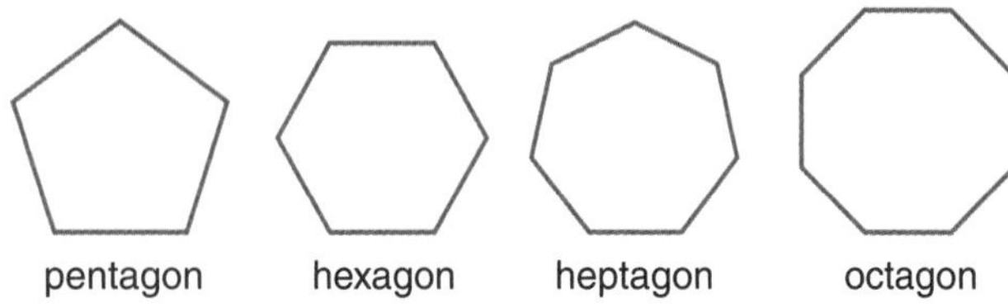

penta = 5, **hexa** = 6, **hepta** = 7, **octa** = 8.

If two polygons have exactly the same shape, size, and angles, then they are congruent. Congruent polygons do *not* have to face in the same direction. So do *not* trust your eyes. The best way to tell if two polygons are congruent is to measure the sides and angles of both.

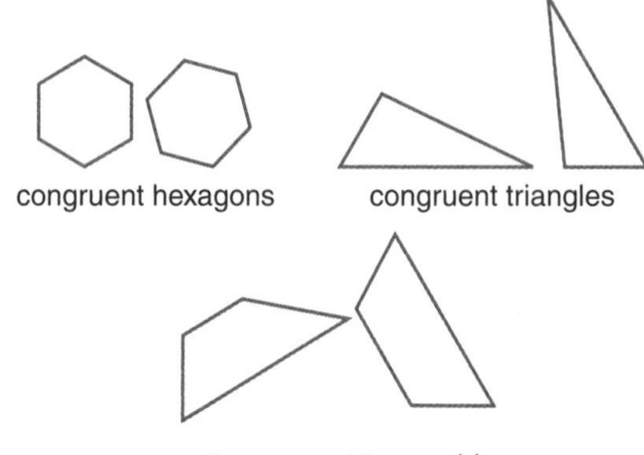

To find the perimeter of a polygon, add the lengths of its sides.

Exercises IDENTIFY

Indicate whether the figure is a polygon. Write "Polygon" or "Not a Polygon."

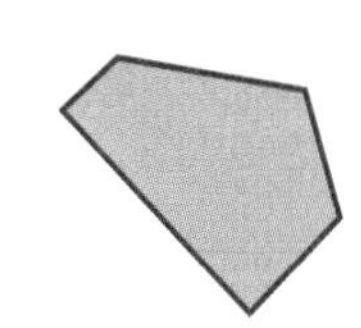

1 ______________________

2 ______________________

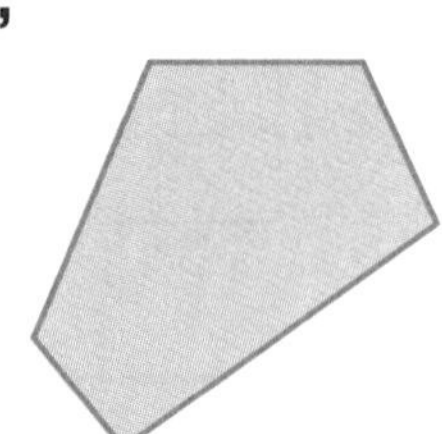

3 ______________________

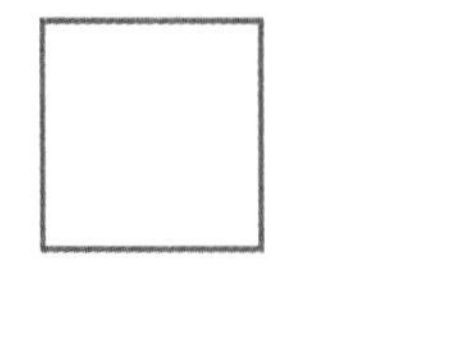

4 ______________________

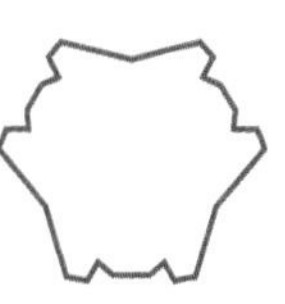

5 ______________________

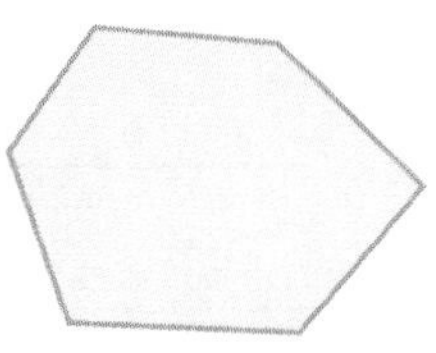

6 ______________________

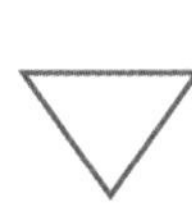

7 ______________________

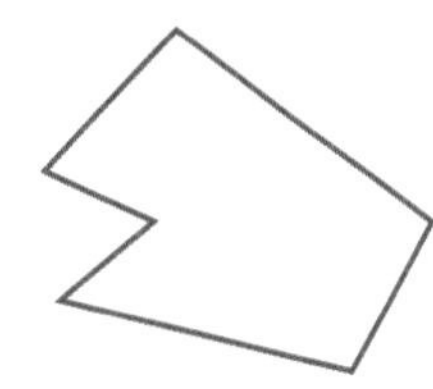

8 ______________________

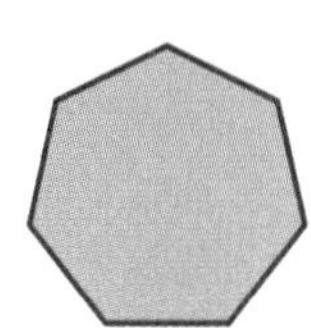

9 ______________________

Name ____________________

Circles

Can you think of a closed 2-dimensional figure that has *no* angles? Did you think of a **circle**?

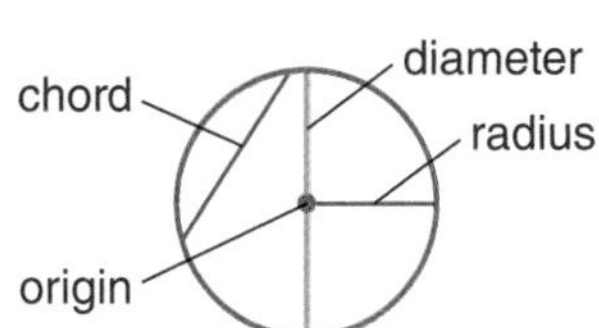

You need to know some special terms to describe circles. A circle's **circumference** is its perimeter, the distance around it. Every point on a circle's circumference is an equal distance from the circle's center point, or **origin**.

A **radius** is a line segment that begins at a circle's origin and extends to its circumference. In a circle, all radii (plural of "radius") are equal in length.

A line segment that has both of its endpoints on the circumference is called a **chord**. If a chord passes through the circle's origin, it is called a **diameter**. The length of a circle's diameter is two times the length of a circle's radius.

Exercises SOLVE

1. What is the diameter of the circle?

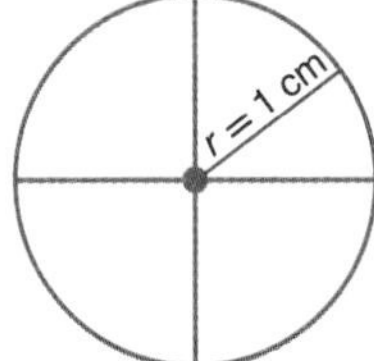

____

2. What is the diameter of the circle?

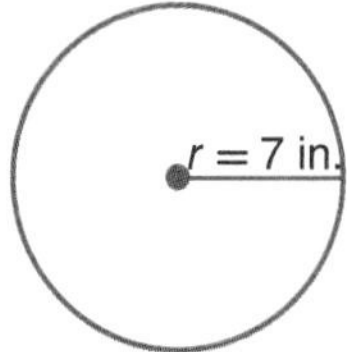

____

3. What is the radius of the circle below?

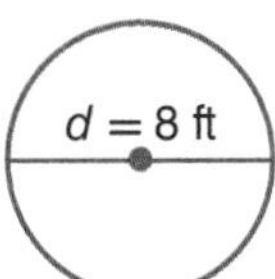

____

4. What is the center of the circle?

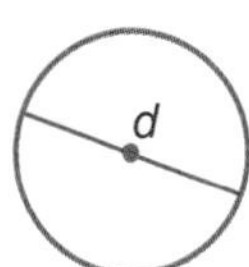

____

5. What is the radius of the circle?

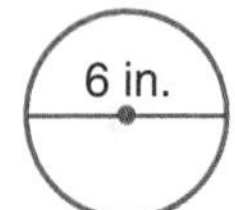

____

6. What are the two radii of the circle?

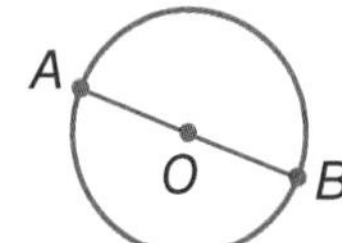

____

Name ______________________________

Circles (cont.)

Imagine that you want to find the length around a figure. Imagine that you want to find the circumference, or perimeter, of a circle, the distance around it. How can you measure that? And how can you find the area of a circle? A circle's circumference and area are calculated by using a special long decimal, written as the Greek letter π, pronounced **pi**. To make calculations easier, pi is often rounded to 3.14.

Pi is the ratio of a circle's diameter to its circumference—a ratio that is exactly the same for every circle.

Calculating the circumference and area of a circle is actually fairly easy to do. A circle's circumference = pi times its diameter (πd). A circle's area = pi times the square of its radius = πr^2.

Exercises SOLVE

7

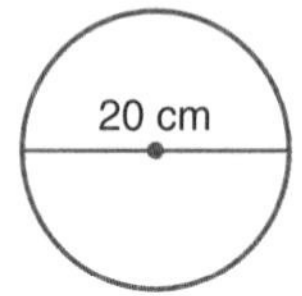

What is the area of the circle? ________

What is the circumference? ________

8

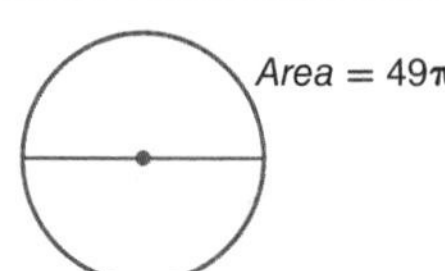

What is the circumference of the circle?

____

What is the radius? ________

9

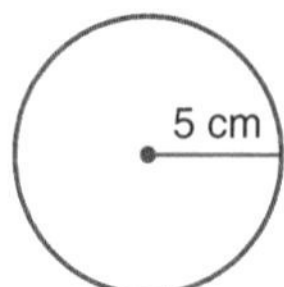

What is the diameter of the circle? ____

What is the area? ________

What is the circumference? ________

10

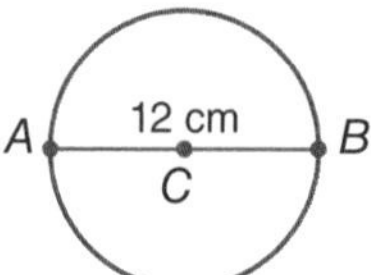

What is the circumference of the circle?

____

What is the area of the circle? ________

11 A bicycle wheel measures 25 inches in diameter. How far would a bike travel if the wheel went completely around 4 times?

________________ inches

12 Brenda walks her dog along two circular routes laid out in the park. How much longer is Route B then route A? (Leave the answer in terms of pi.)

5 km
10 km
Route A
Route B

________________ π km

Name ______________________________

Symmetry and Transformations

SYMMETRY

Symmetry is best illustrated by graphing a figure on a piece of paper, with a line going down the center. If you can fold the paper along that line and one half is identically sitting atop the other, then the figure is symmetrical. Every point on one side of the line has a matching point on the other side.

Some figures have only one line of symmetry, like the heart, and some have many lines of symmetry, like the triangle.

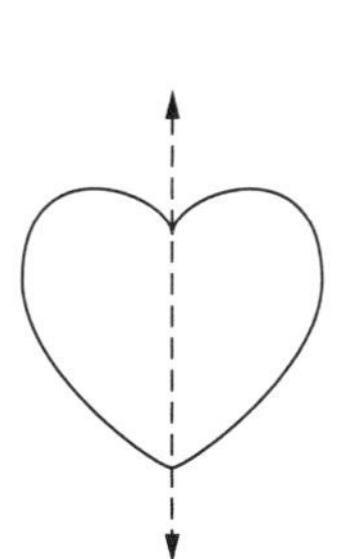

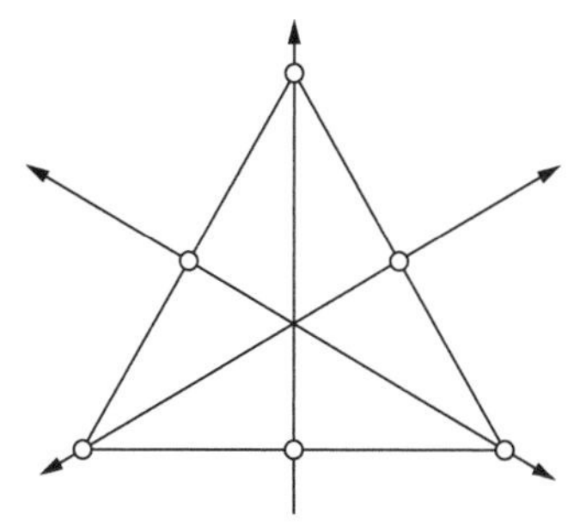

TRANSFORMATIONS

Geometric transformations are the result of changing a shape in one of four ways:

- translation
- rotation
- reflection
- dilation

A **translation** occurs when you take a figure and make an identical duplicate of it. You can move the figure right or left and up or down.

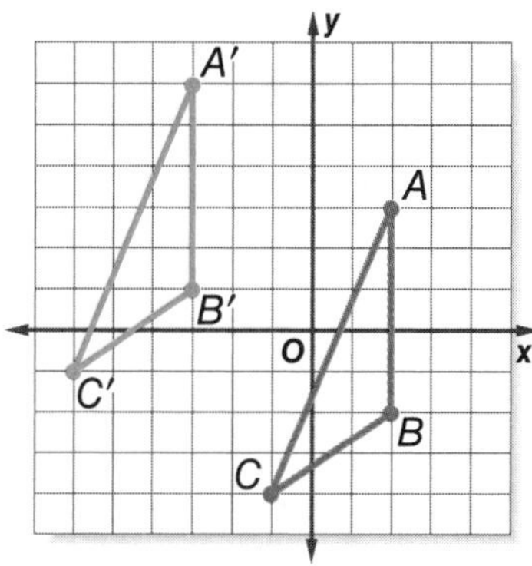

Rotation occurs when you move a figure around a point or a line. The shape remains the same, but its orientation, or the way it faces, changes.

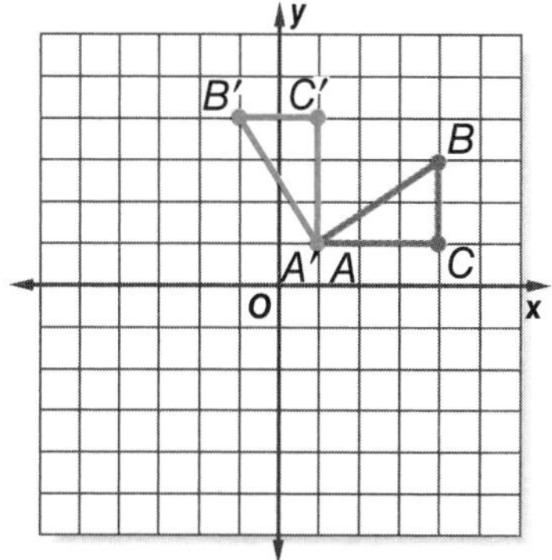

Reflection occurs when you create a mirror image of the original. To do this, pretend you are flipping the figure over an imaginary line called a line of reflection. Each point of the new image is the same distance from the line as the original image was, just on the opposite side of the line.

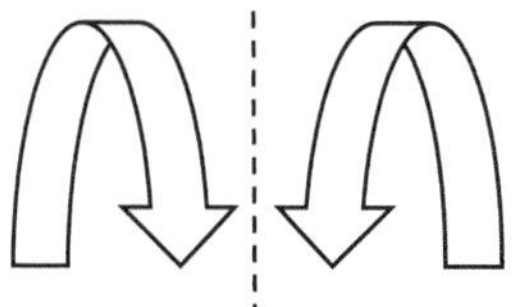

Dilation occurs when you change the size of the original figure by enlarging or shrinking it. The process produces an image that is the exact same shape as the original figure, but is larger or smaller than the original.

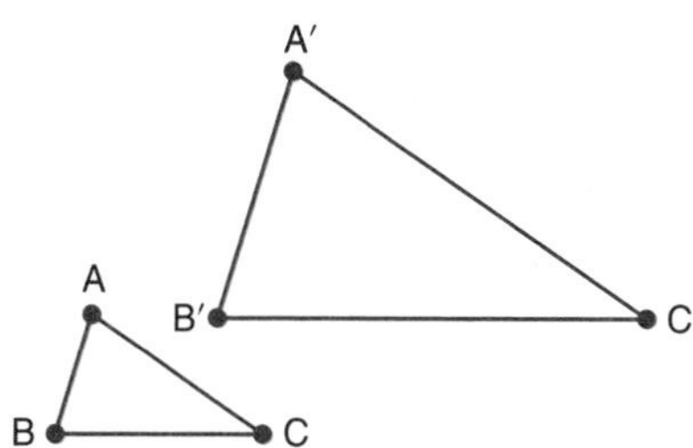

Name ______________________

Exercises IDENTIFY

For each pair of figures, label as translation, rotation, reflection, or dilation.

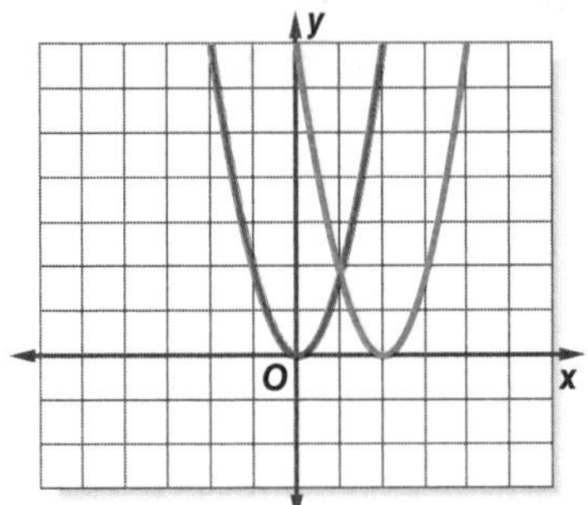

1 ______________________

2 ______________________

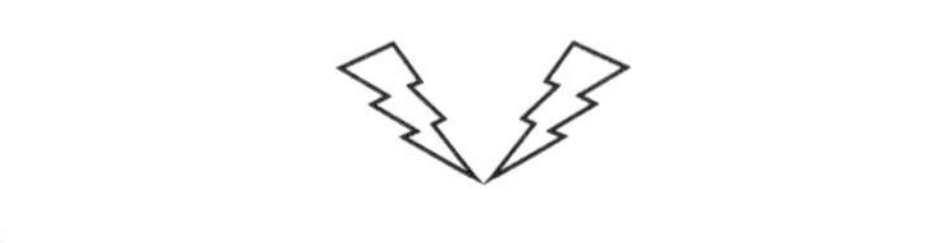

3 ______________________

4 ______________________

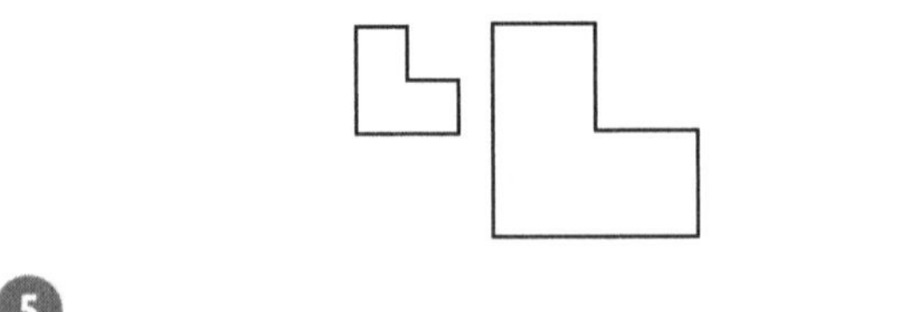

5 ______________________

6 ______________________

7 ______________________

8 ______________________

Identify lines of symmetry.

9 How many lines of symmetry does the figure above have? ____________

10 Draw the lines of symmetry on the figure above. ____________

Name ______________________________

Surface Area of Solid Figures

Not all figures are 2-dimensional. Can you name some common 3-dimensional, or solid, figures?

To describe **solid figures**, you need to know some special terms.

Face: A flat surface of a solid figure. Each face looks like a 2-dimensional figure.

Edge: The line at which two faces meet.

Vertex (of a Solid): A specific point at which *more than* 2 faces meet or where a curve originates.

Base: The face on the bottom of a solid figure.

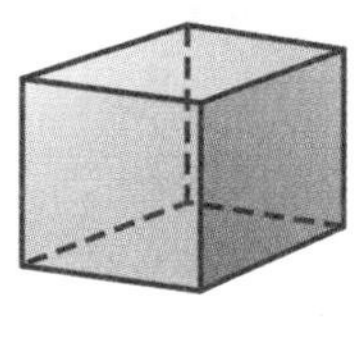
Cube

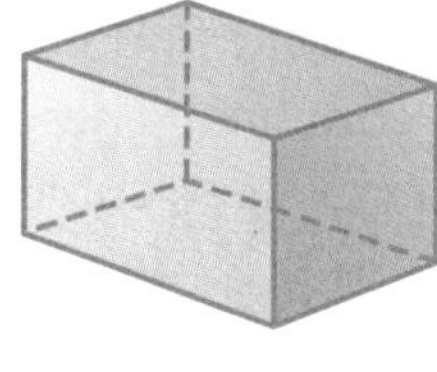
Rectangular Solid

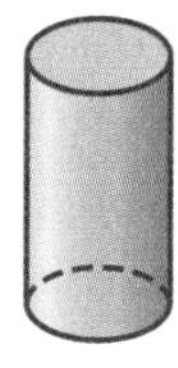
Cylinder

Examples:

To find the surface area of a cube, or a rectangular solid, use the formula: $2lw + 2lh + 2wh$

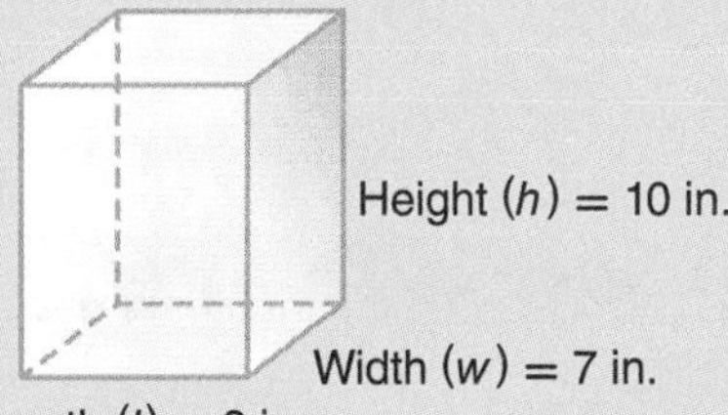

The surface area of the solid above is $(2 \times 8 \times 7) + (2 \times 8 \times 10) + (2 \times 7 \times 10) = 112 + 160 + 140 = 412$ **square inches**

To calculate the surface area of a cylinder, use the formula: $2\pi r^2 + 2\pi rh$.

Radius (r) = 3 in.

Height (h) = 7 in.

The surface area of this cylinder $= 2 \times \pi \times 3^2 + 2 \times \pi \times 3 \times 7 = 18\pi + 42\pi = 60\pi$ **square centimeters**.

Exercises CALCULATE SURFACE AREA

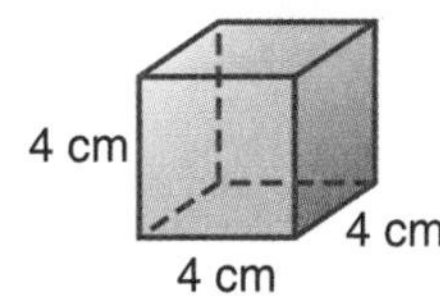

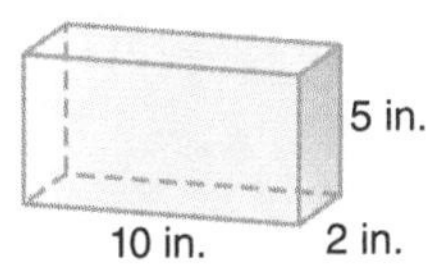

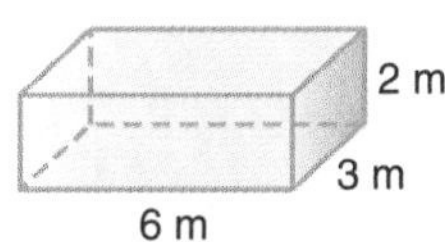

1 ______________________

2 ______________________

3 ______________________

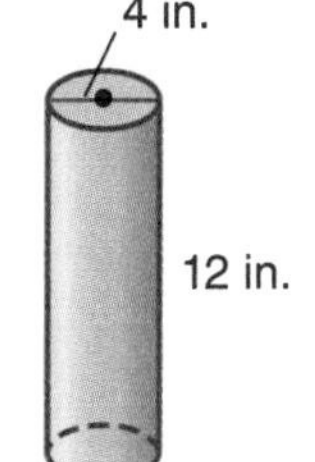

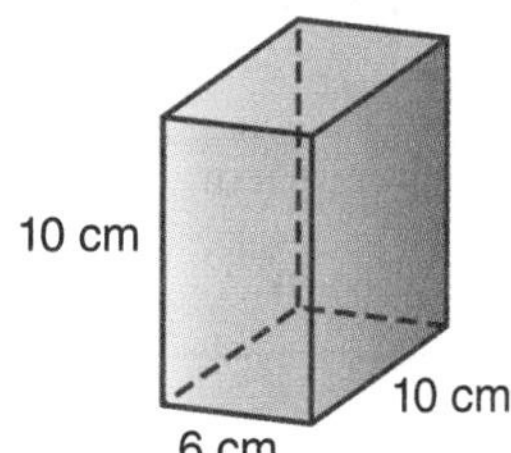

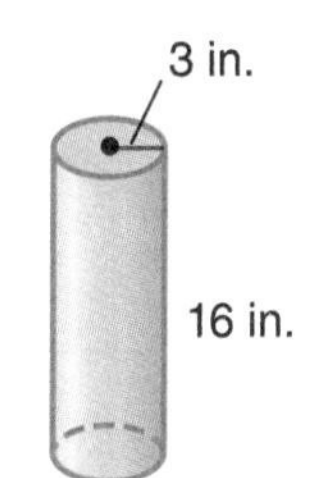

4 ______________________

5 ______________________

6 ______________________

2

Name ______________________________

Volume of Solid Figures

You learned the units used to measure liquid volume in a container. However, what if you want to know a solid figure's **volume**, or how many units it contains? These units are called cubic inches, cubic feet, cubic yards, and cubic miles.

Example:

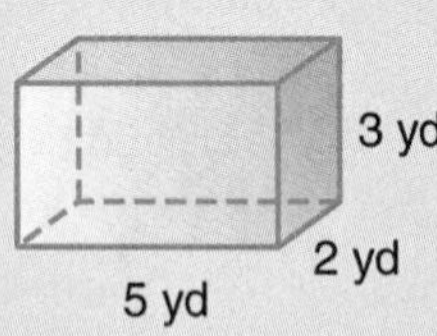

To find the volume of a rectangular solid, multiply length × width × height.

Volume = 5 yd × 2 yd × 3 yd = 30 cu yd

Example:

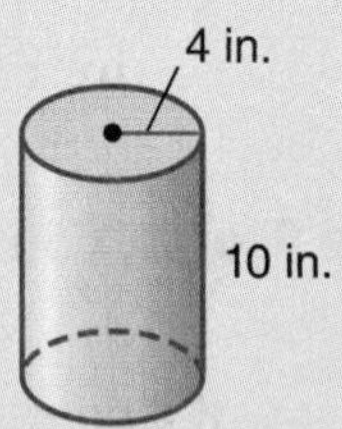

The volume of a cylinder can be calculated by using the formula $V = b \times h$ where the base $= \pi r^2$

Volume $= \pi \times 4^2 \times 10$

$\pi \times 16 \times 10$

160π

Exercises CALCULATE VOLUME

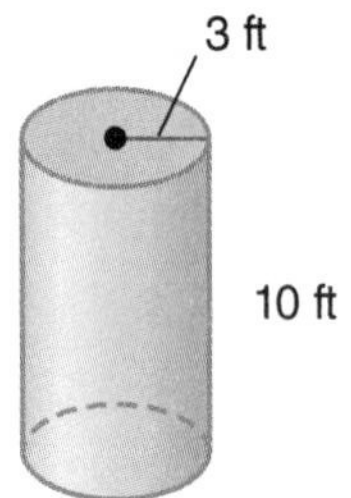

1 ______________________

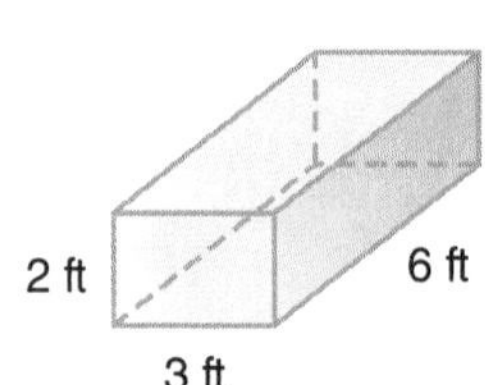

2 

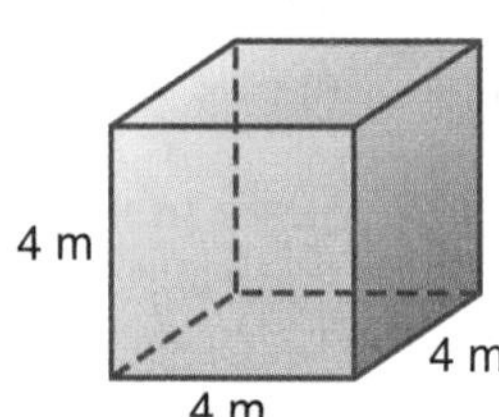

3 

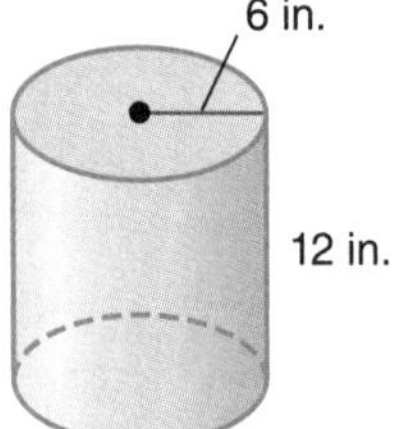

4 ______________________

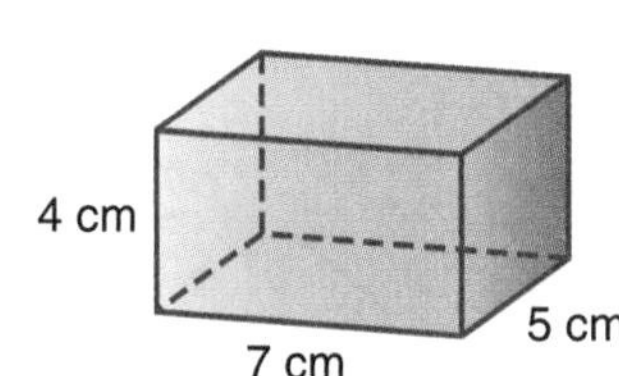

5 

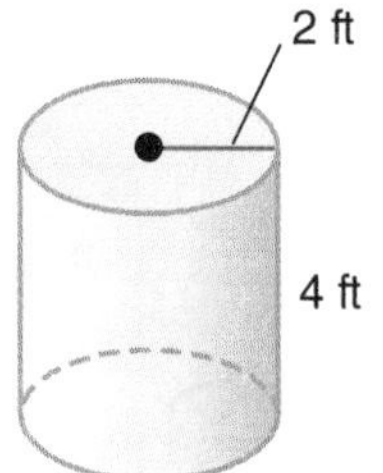

6 ______________________

Name ______________________________

Volume of Solid Figures (cont.)

Examples:

The volume of a cone can be calculated by using the formula

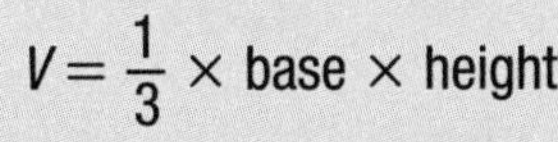

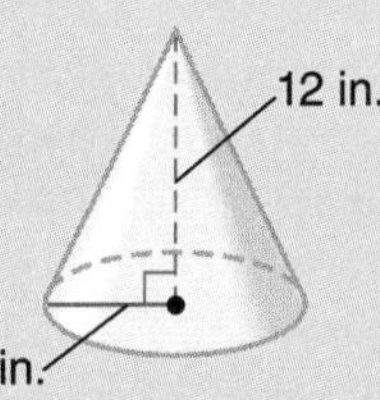

The base can be calculated with πr^2

Volume $= \frac{1}{3} \times \pi \times 6^2 \times 12$

$= \frac{1}{3} \times \pi \times 36 \times 12$

$= 144\pi$ cu in.

The volume of a rectangular pyramid is also calculated using the formula

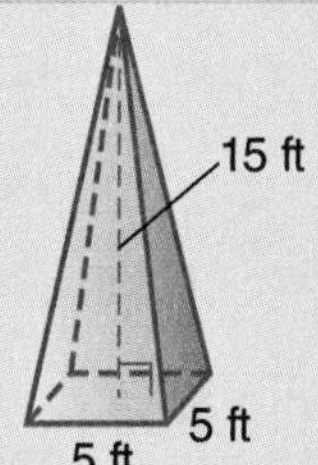

$V = \frac{1}{3} \times b \times h$

The base can be calculated multiplying length $\times$ width.

Volume $= \frac{1}{3} \times 5$ ft $\times 5$ ft $\times 15$ ft

$= \frac{1}{3} \times 375$ cu ft

$= 125$ cu ft

Exercises CALCULATE VOLUME

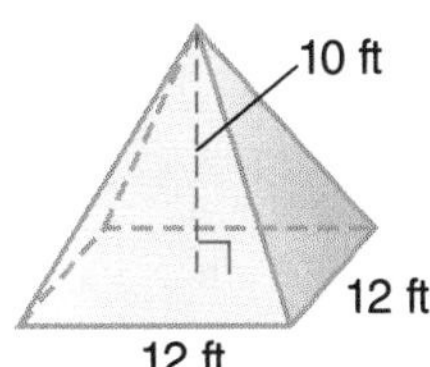

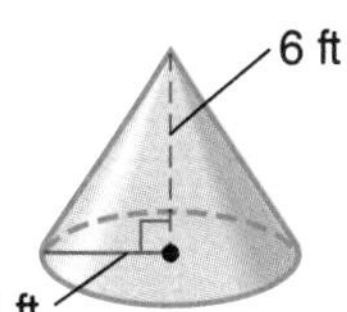

7 ______________________________

8 ______________________________

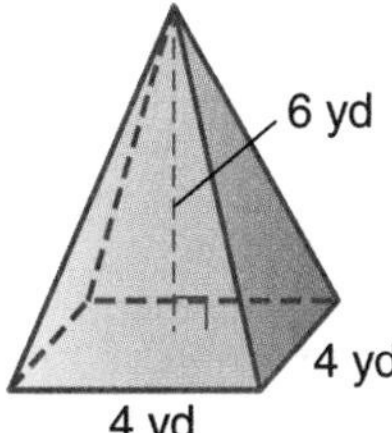

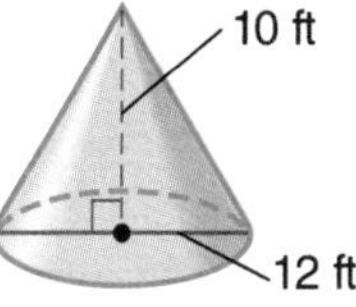

9 ______________________________

10 ______________________________

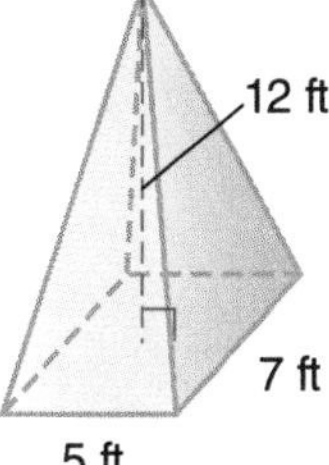

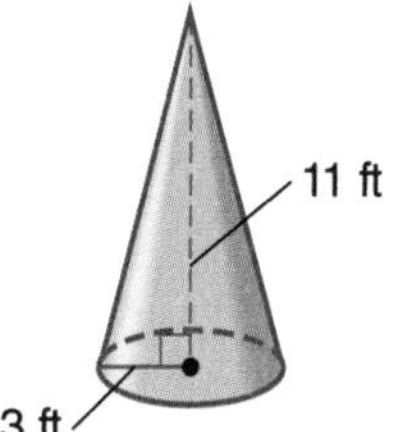

11 ______________________________

12 ______________________________

Test

Name ______________________

Identify each angle as obtuse, acute, or right.

1. 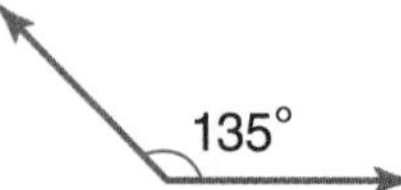

____

2. 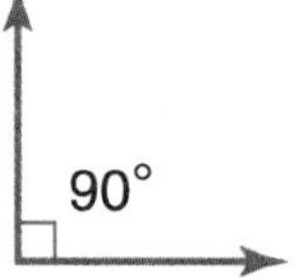

____

3. 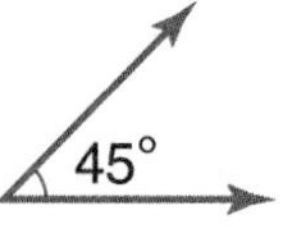

____

Identify each pair of angles as supplementary, complementary, or neither, and explain why.

4. 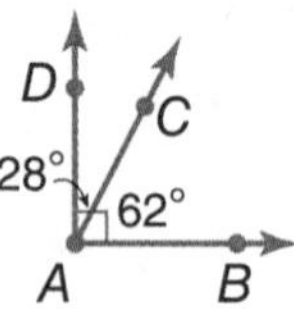

____

____

____

5. 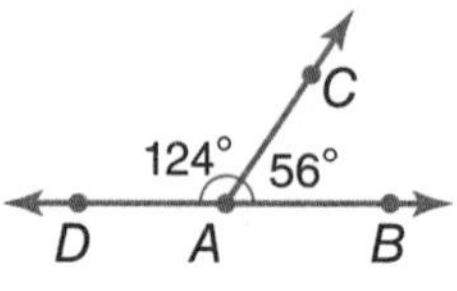

____

____

____

6. 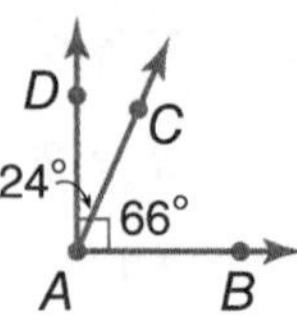

____

____

____

Identify each triangle as scalene, equilateral, or isosceles.

7. 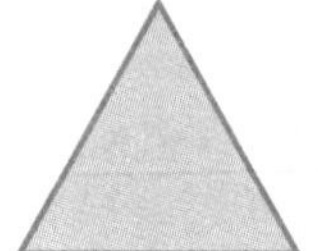

____

8. 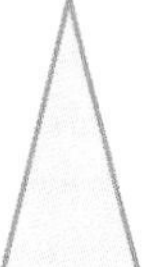

____

9. 

____

Identify each triangle as obtuse, right, or acute.

10. 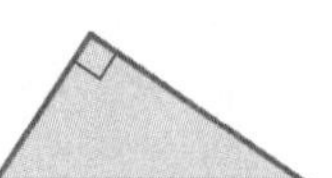

____

11. 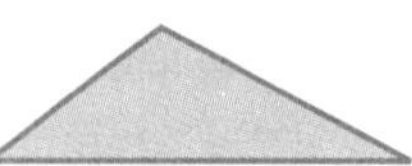

____

12. 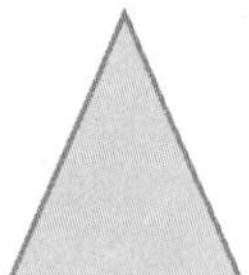

____

13. 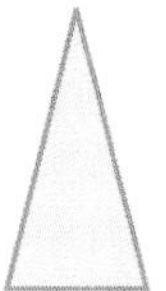

____

Name ____________________

Identify the figures.

14  ____________

15 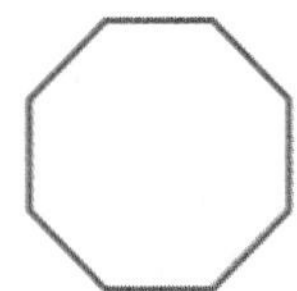 ____________

16 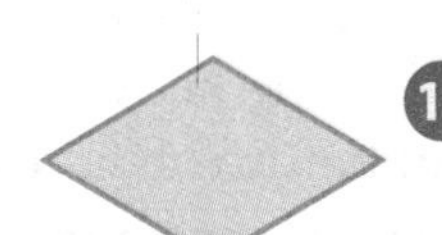 ____________

17  ____________

18 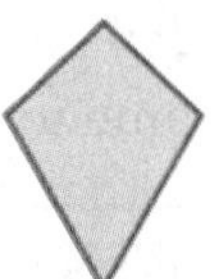 ____________

Fill in the information for each figure.

19 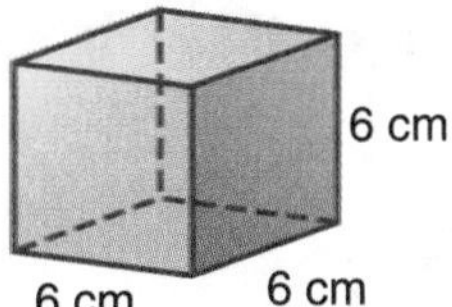

Figure ____________

Volume ____________

Surface Area ________

20 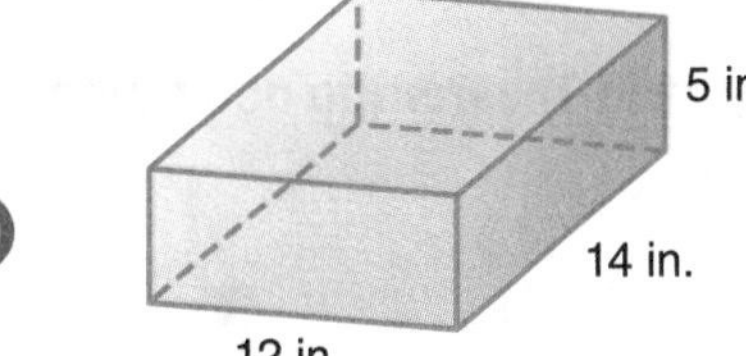

Figure ____________

Volume ____________

Surface Area ________

21 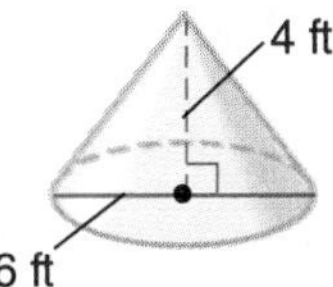

Figure ____________

Volume ____________

22  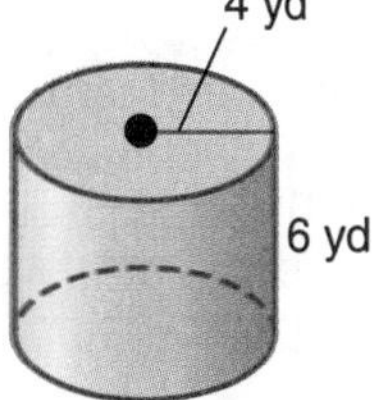

Figure ____________

Volume ____________

Surface Area ________

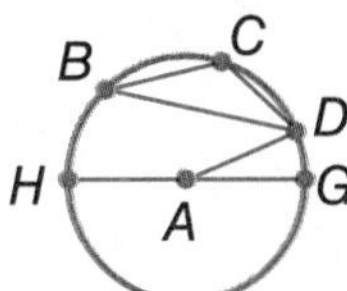

23 Name the center point.

____

24 Which segments are chords?

____

25 Which segment is the diameter?

____

26 Which segments are radii?

____

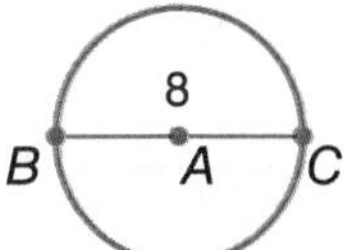

27 What is the circumference of the circle? (Use 3.14 as a value for π).

____

28 What is the area of the circle?

____

Test

Name ______________________________

29 Nathan bought a present for his sister Christine. It came in a box that looked like the figure shown here. Nathan wants to wrap the present before he gives it to his sister. How much wrapping paper does he need?

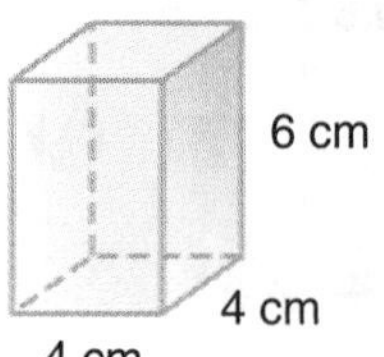

____

Use the Pythagorean Theorem to determine the length of the missing side on these right triangles.

30 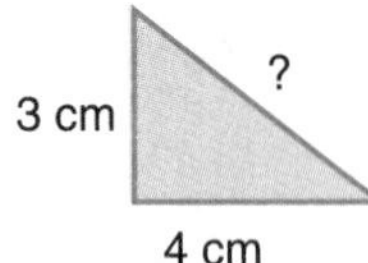

____

31 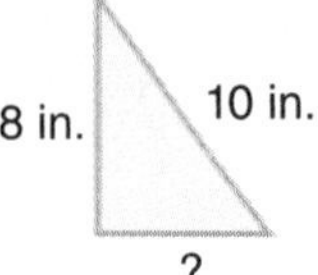

____

32 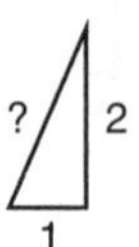

____

33 Which two triangles are similar? ________

Are they congruent? ______________

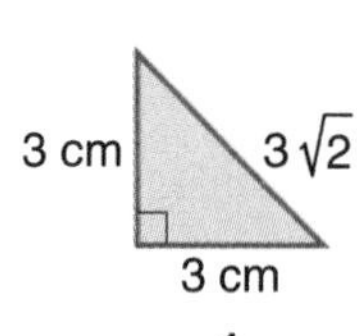

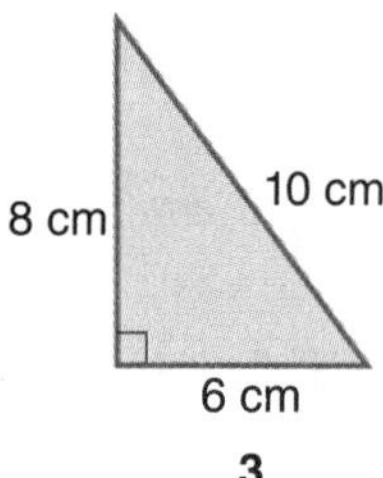

34 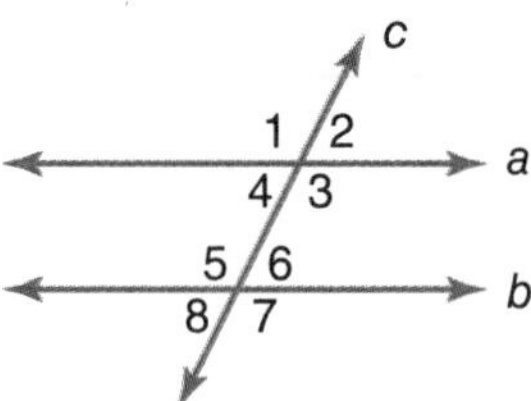

Identify all vertical angle pairs.

____

Are angles 1 and 3 equal in measure?

____

List four supplementary angle pairs.

____

Identify an exterior angle pair. ________

Identify an interior angle pair. ________

35 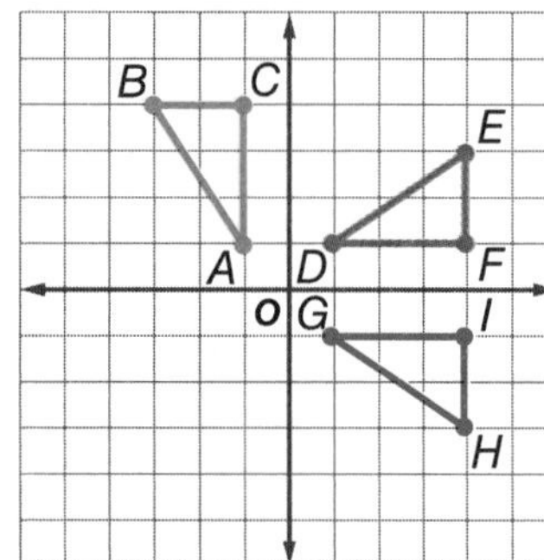

Which triangle is a rotation of triangle *ABC*?

____

Which triangle is a reflection of *DEF*?

____

Name ______________________________

Answers and Explanations

1. Obtuse
2. Right
3. Acute
4. Complementary; angle measurements add to 90°
5. Supplementary add to 180°
6. Complementary add to 90°
7. Equilateral
8. Isosceles
9. Equilateral
10. Right
11. Obtuse
12. Acute
13. Acute
14. Rectangle
15. Octagon
16. Rhombus
17. Trapezoid
18. Kite
19. Cube; Volume: 216 cu cm; SA: 216 sq cm
$V = 6\times6\times6 = 216; SA = 2(6\times6)+2(6\times6)+2(6\times6) = 2(36)+2(36)+2(36) = 72+72+72 = 216$
20. Rectangular solid; Volume: 840 cu cm; SA: 596 sq cm
$V = 12\times14\times5 = 840; SA = 2(12\times14)+2(12\times5)+2(5\times14) = 2(168)+2(60)+2(70) = 336+120+140 = 596$
21. Cone; Volume: 12π cu ft $V = \frac{1}{3}\pi r^2 h = \frac{1}{3}\pi(3^2)(4) = \frac{1}{3}\pi(9)(4) = \frac{1}{3}(36)\pi = 12\pi$
22. Cylinder; Volume: 96π cu yd; SA: 80π sq yd
$V = \pi r^2 h = \pi(4^2)(6) = \pi(16)(6) = 96\pi;\ SA = 2\pi r^2 + 2\pi rh; SA = 2\pi(4^2)+2\pi(4)(6) = 32\pi+48\pi = 80\pi$
23. Point A
24. $\overline{CD}$, $\overline{BD}$, $\overline{BC}$
25. $\overline{HG}$
26. $\overline{AG}$, $\overline{AD}$, $\overline{AC}$
27. 25.12
28. 50.24
29. 128 sq cm $SA = 2(4\times4)+2(4\times6)+2(4\times6) = 2(16)+2(24)+2(24) = 32+48+48 = 128$
30. 5 $3^2+4^2 = c^2;\ 9+16 = c^2;\ 25 = c^2;\ c = \sqrt{25} = 5$
31. 6 $8^2+b^2 = 10^2;\ 64+b^2 = 100;\ b^2 = 100-64;\ b^2 = 36;\ b = \sqrt{36} = 6$
32. $\sqrt{5}$ $1^2+2^2 = c^2;\ 1+4 = c^2;\ 5 = c^2;\ c = \sqrt{5}$
33. ∠2 and ∠3; No, sides are not equal
34. ∠1 and ∠3; ∠2 and ∠4; ∠5 and ∠7; ∠6 and ∠8, yes;
Supplementary: ∠1 and ∠2; ∠2 and ∠3; ∠3 and ∠4; ∠1 and ∠4; ∠5 and ∠6; ∠6 and ∠7; ∠7 and ∠8; ∠8 and ∠5;
Exterior angle pair: ∠1 and ∠7; ∠2 and ∠8;
Interior Angle Pair: ∠3 and ∠5; ∠4 and ∠6
35. △DEF, △GHI

Name ______________________________

Bar Graphs

Graphs are useful ways to display information, or **data**. A **bar graph** uses bars to compare two or more people, places, or things. The bars may be horizontal or vertical. Each bar represents a number. Because the data are shown visually, the bars can be compared to one another. Sometimes different colored bars that represent different kinds of people or things are used.

Examples:

There are 78 students in the eighth grade at Jay County Middle School. Each student voted for his or her favorite kind of pie.

The key tells you which bars stand for girls and which bars stand for boys. The horizontal line, or **axis**, at the bottom of the graph names different kinds of pie.

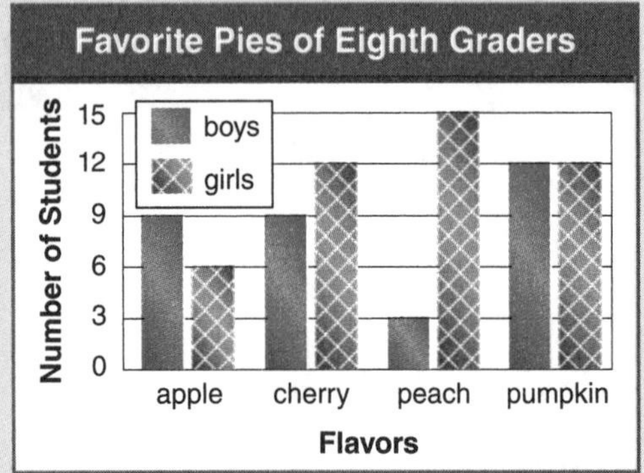

The vertical axis tells you how many boys and how many girls voted for their favorite pie.

How many students in total voted for either apple or peach pie?

Step 1: Find "apple" on the horizontal axis. Look at the top of each bar in the "apple" section, and follow that line back to the vertical axis to find out how many girls voted for apple pie, and how many boys voted for apple pie. 9 boys + 6 girls = 15 students in total voted for apple pie.

Step 2: Find "peach" on the horizontal axis. Repeat the process outlined in Step 1. 3 boys + 15 girls = 18 students.

Step 3: Add: 15 + 18 = 33 students voted for either peach or apple pie.

Exercises INTERPRET

1. On the bar graph, which hair color is the least common?

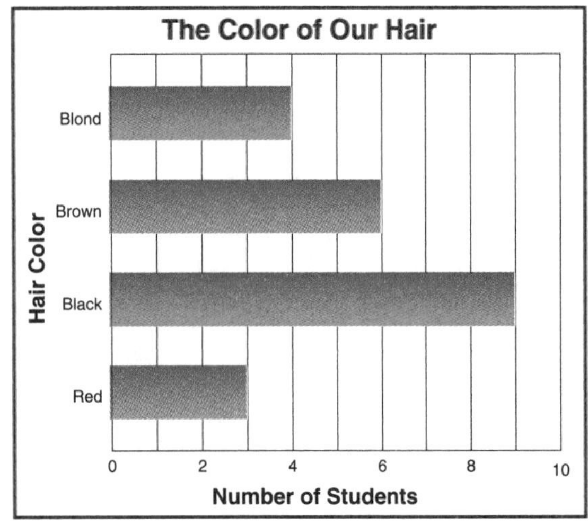

____

2. In which two months did the company lose money?

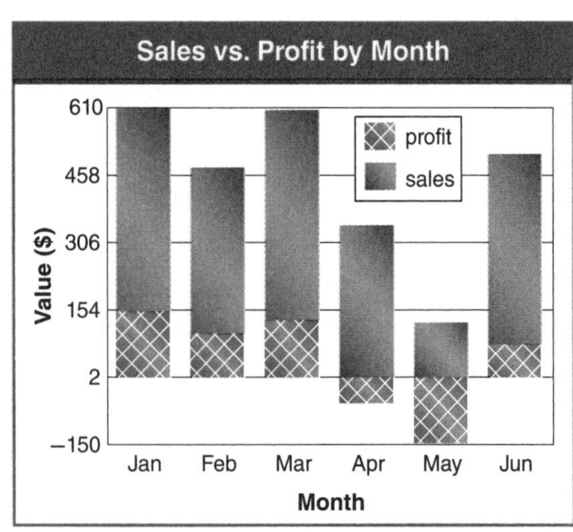

____

Name ______________________________

3 What months had the most and least sales?

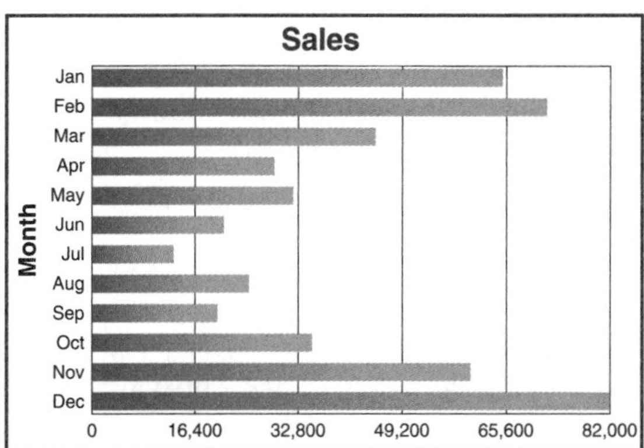

Most ______________________________

Least ______________________________

4 Which two people own the most pairs of shoes?

____

5 Your friend constructed a bar graph to show which types of movies he watches most. Based on this information, what type of movie should you not bring to his house for viewing?

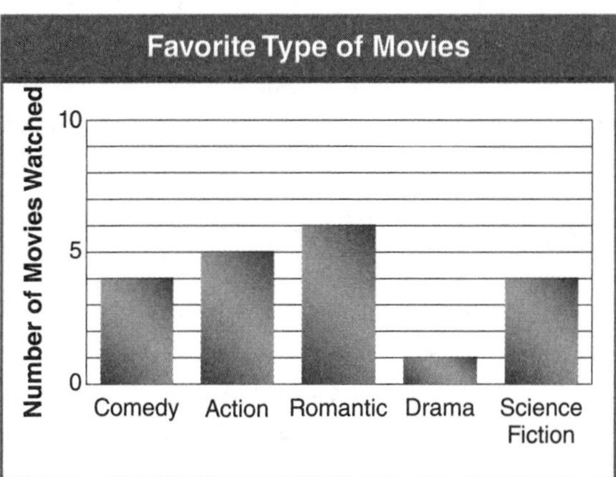

____

6 Which mode of transportation had the most growth in passenger miles and which one had the least?

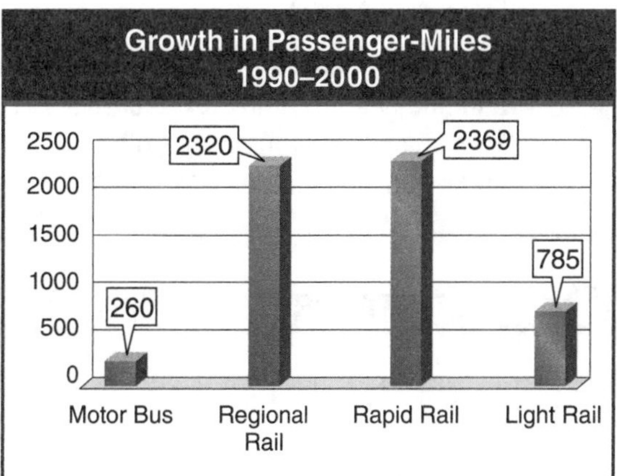

Most ______________________________

Least ______________________________

7 Write a sentence to summarize the trend illustrated in this graph showing park visitors.

____

____

____

____

____

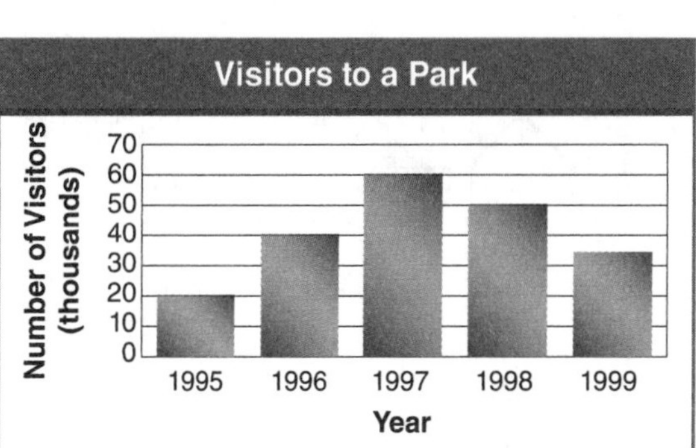

Name ____________________

Line Graphs

A **line graph** is often used to show how information changes as time passes. Each number on the horizontal axis represents a specific time. The distance from one time to another is an **interval**. In a line graph, a steeper line segment shows that more change has occurred during that interval.

Example:

During what time interval did Frank send the most text messages? About how many messages did he send during that interval?

Step 1: Look for the steepest line segment between intervals. That segment is between 4:00 p.m. and 7:00 p.m.

Step 2: Look along the horizontal axis for the time at the beginning of that interval. Then look at where the line is at that time on the vertical axis to find out how many text messages were sent by then. By 4:00 p.m., Frank had sent 20 text messages.

Step 3: Look for the time at the end of that interval and find out how many text messages Frank had sent by then. By 7:00 p.m., Frank had sent 40 messages.

Step 4: Subtract. $40 - 20 = 20$. In the interval between 4:00 p.m. and 7:00 p.m., Frank sent about 20 text messages.

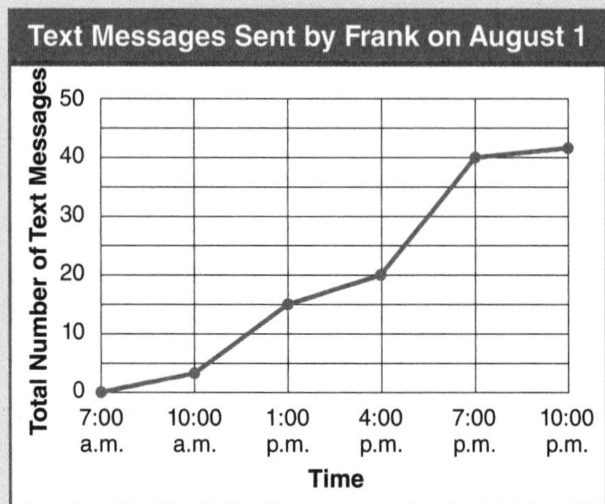

Exercises **INTERPRET**

1. Which month has the highest amount of rainfall?

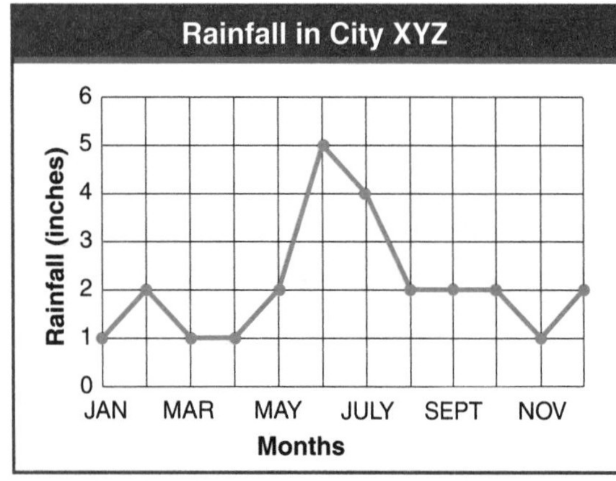

____

____

2. The owner of a produce store studied this line graph showing potato consumption. On what three days should she make sure to have extra potatoes on hand?

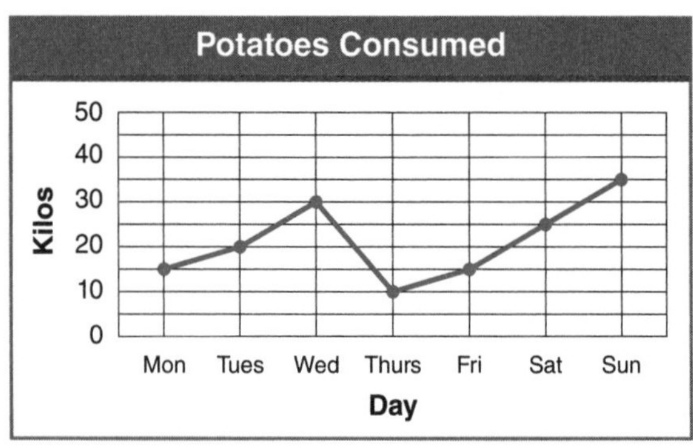

____

____

Name ____________________

3 On which days would you expect usage of electricity to be the highest?

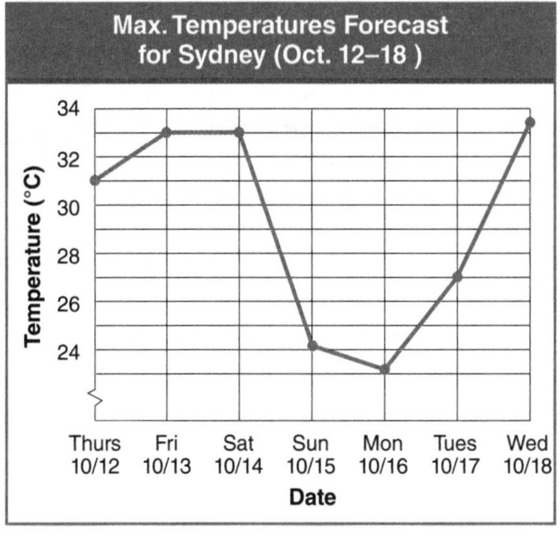

4 Summarize the trend displayed in this graph.

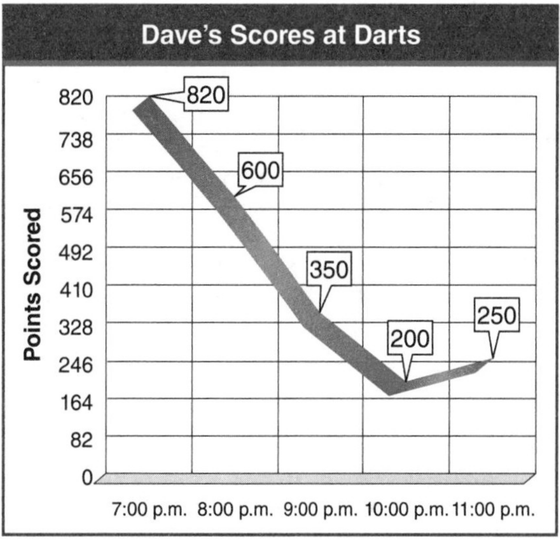

5 Write a sentence summarizing the rapid decrease in value of a car.

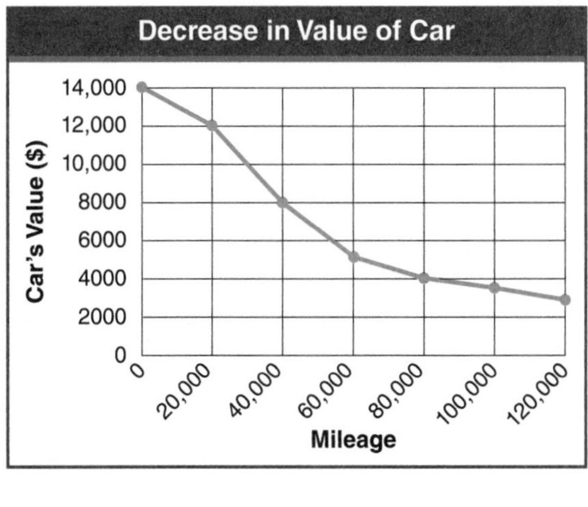

6 On which day did Caroline do the most driving?

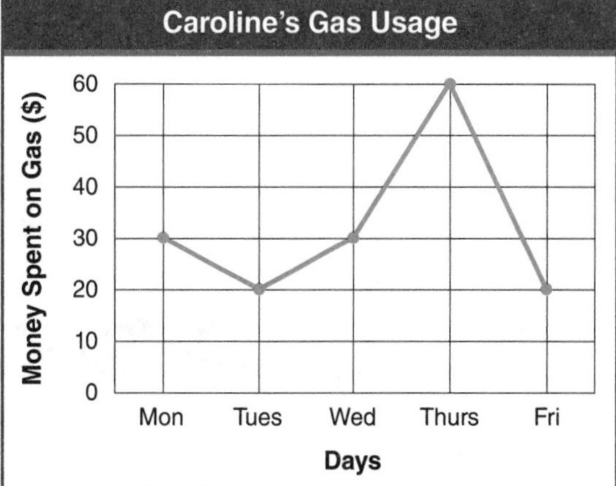

Name ______________________________

Double-Line Graphs

A **double-line graph** often compares how information changes *for two or more* people, places, or things as time passes.

Example:

When had Laura and Timothy both sent *exactly* the same total number of messages? How many total messages were sent by each?

Step 1: Look for a point on the graph where the lines touch one another. Then follow that point down to the horizontal axis to see what time it was. At 10:00 p.m., they had each sent 50 messages.

Exercises INTERPRET

1. Which car is driving toward Taree? Explain.

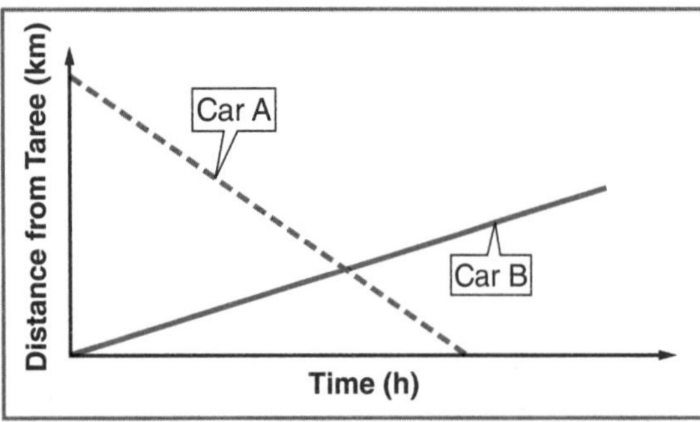

____

2. Which of the two towns has a wider variation in temperatures?

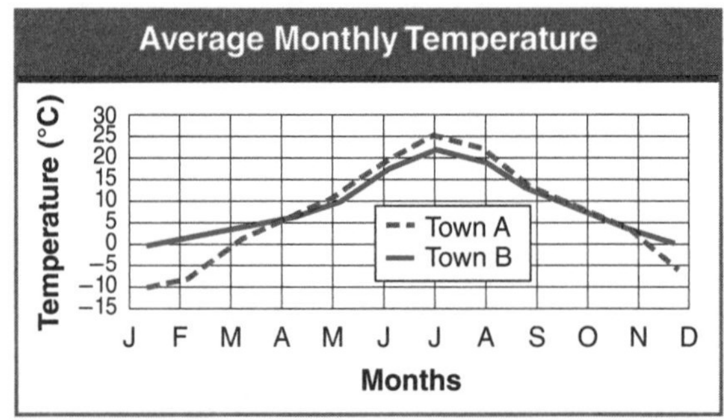

____

3. Based on the double-line graph below, what can you say happened in the year 2003? Write a sentence summarizing the data.

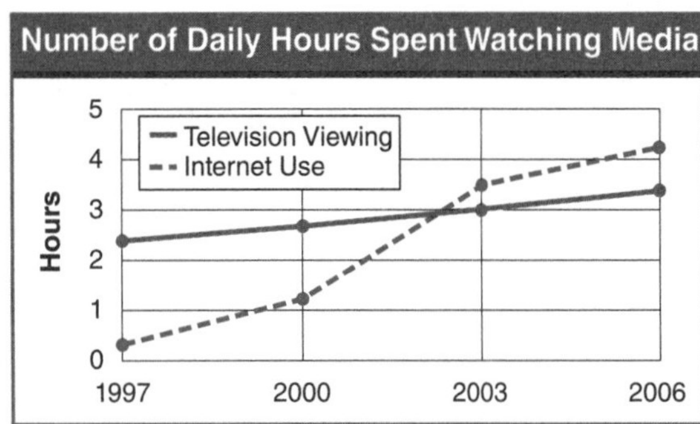

____

____

4. Write a sentence explaining what has happened to urban and rural populations in the U.S. since 1900.

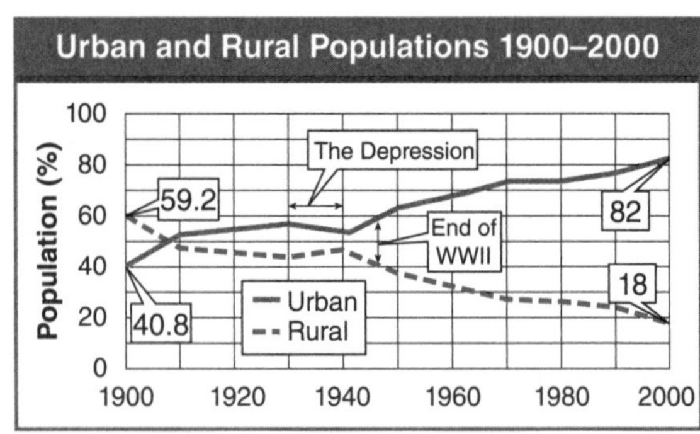

____

____

Name ______________________________

Circle Graphs

A **circle graph** compares parts, or segments, of a whole to the whole. Some people also call a circle graph a pie chart, because it looks like a pie that has been sliced. When you read a circle graph, you are comparing parts to each other and to the whole. However, sometimes you can calculate a part exactly.

Examples:

Which kind of coin did Olivia save most?

Step 1: Find the largest **segment** on the graph.

Step 2: Read the label for that segment. Olivia saved more quarters than any other kind of coin.

Olivia saved a total of 64 coins. How many of them were pennies?

Step 1: Look at the whole circle again. You may not be able to tell exactly how big each part is. However, you can estimate. If you compare pennies and dimes to the whole circle, those two **segments** account for half the circle.

Step 2: Multiply $\frac{1}{2} \times 64 = 32$. Altogether there are 32 pennies and dimes.

Step 3: Now compare the pennies and the dimes to each other. The segments look the same. So $\frac{1}{2}$ of those 32 coins are pennies and $\frac{1}{2}$ are dimes.

Step 4: Multiply $\frac{1}{2} \times 32 = 16$. There are 16 pennies.

Coins in Olivia's Bank

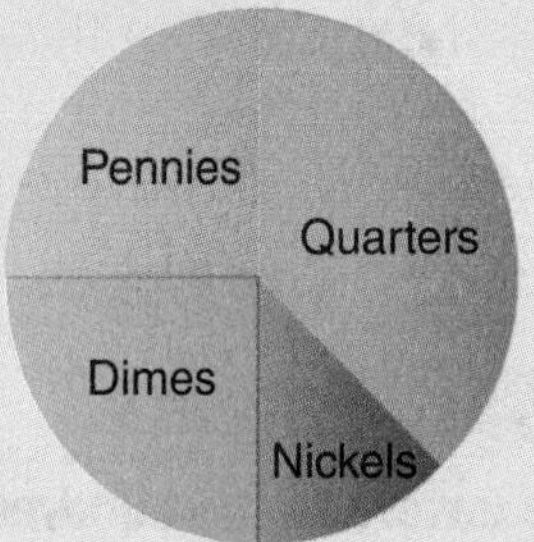

Exercises INTERPRET

1. What are the three major areas of consumer expenditures?

Consumer Expenditures
Avg. Total Expenditures: $29,846

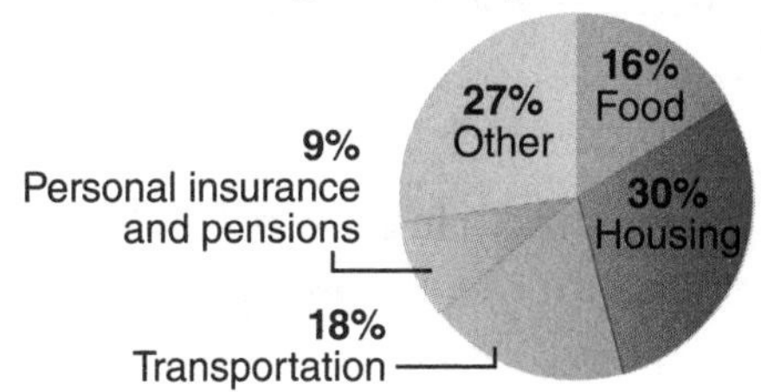

____

____

2. Name the two regions that represent more than 50% of the company sales.

Sales by Region

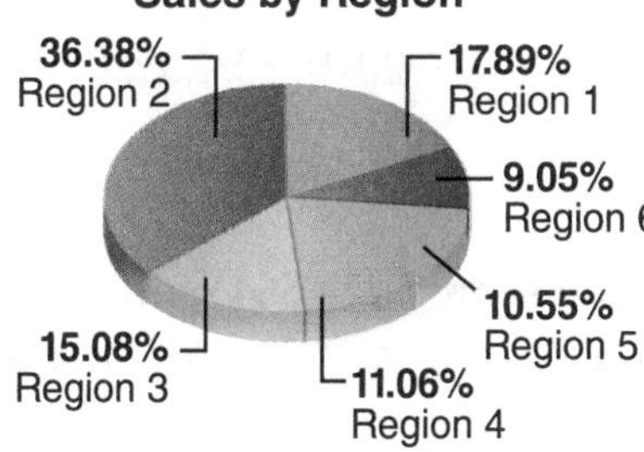

____

____

Name ____________________

Measures of Central Tendency

Statistics is a branch of mathematics that studies data expressed as numbers. In the data, the numbers answer questions such as: How many? How long? How far? How big?

Suppose you have this group of numbers: 21, 10, 18, 10, 14, 7, 10, 14

Begin by arranging them in order: 7, 10, 10, 10, 14, 14, 18, 21

The **range** is the greatest number minus the smallest number. $21 - 7 = 14$

The **mean** (sometimes called the average) is the total of the whole collection divided by the number of addends. $104 \div 8 = 13$

The **median** is the number in the middle. If your collection has an even number of addends, the median is the average of the two middle ones. $(10 + 14) \div 2 = 24 \div 2 = 12$

The **mode** is the number that appears most frequently in the collection. In this example, the mode is 10.

Example:

Find the mean of 5, 3, 6, 10, 5, 2, 4.

Step 1: Add the numbers.
$5 + 3 + 6 + 10 + 5 + 2 + 4 = 35$

Step 2: Divide by the number of addends.
$35 \div 7 = 5$

Remember...

The range, mean, median, and mode numbers *may* all be different! *Or* some of them *may* be identical.

Exercises CALCULATE

Round all answers to the hundredths place.

1. 1, 2, 3, 4, 9, 8, 7, 6, 5 Mean ____ Median ____ Range ____ Mode ____
2. 10, 15, 20, 60, 110, 10, 10, 45 Mean ____ Median ____ Range ____ Mode ____
3. 23, 23, 24, 25, 48, 56, 32, 1, 2 Mean ____ Median ____ Range ____ Mode ____
4. −10, −20, −20, 0, 10, 20, 20 Mean ____ Median ____ Range ____ Mode ____

Solve.

5. Adam scored 114,564 points on the first level of his computer game. He scored 113,098 on the second level, and 125,888 on the third level. How many points did he average per level?
6. Robert wants to divide his penny collection into bags that average 15 pennies each. If he has 1710 pennies in his collection, how many bags will he use?
7. Elena picked 252 tomatoes from her 12 tomato plants. On average, how many tomatoes did each plant yield?
8. Elba Dean can ride her bicycle an average of 81 miles a day. If she wants to visit her cousin 324 miles away, how many days will it take for her to ride there?

Name ____________________

Stem-and-Leaf Plots

A **stem-and-leaf plot** organizes data by the place value of digits. Think of it as a plant with stems. Each stem may have a different number of leaves.

Example:

Math Test Scores in Mrs. Castro's Class

Stems	Leaves
6	6 7 8
7	4 5 5
8	2 4 6 8 8
9	0 0 2 8

To read this, attach each leaf to its stem. In Mrs. Castro's class, the test scores were **66**, **67**, **68**, **74**, **75**, **75**, **82**, **84**, **86**, **88**, **88**, **90**, **90**, **92**, and **98**.

To find the range in a stem-and-leaf plot, look at the first leaf on the first stem and the last leaf on the last stem. Add them and divide by two.

Range = $(66 + 98) \div 2 = 164 \div 2 = 82$

Exercises INTERPRET

1. Make a list all of the points scored in the basketball games.

Points Scored in Basketball Games

Stem	Leaves
3	9
4	0 1 5 7 7 7 9
5	2 6 6 6

____

____

2. Make a list of the data shown below.

Stem	Leaf
12	0 5 8 8
13	0 1 2 4 6 7 9
14	1 2 3 5 5 9
15	
16	1 5

____

____

3. Using the stem-and-leaf plot, determine the median age of people at the family reunion, the range, and the mode of the ages.

Ages of People at the Family Reunion

Stem	Leaves
0	1 8 9
3	2 4 7
4	5
5	1 5
8	1

Median ____________________

Range ____________________

Mode ____________________

4. In a biology class, eight students collected shrubs for a study. The number of shrubs collected by the students were 4, 8, 12, 16, 21, 21, and 23. Make a stem-and-leaf plot of these numbers.

Shrubs Collected by Students

Stem	Leaf

Name ______________________________

Box-and-Whisker Plots

A **box-and-whisker plot** looks at data to tell where most of the numbers lie. This type of plot shows the medians in the data.

Example:

You have recorded the heights, in inches, of the 13 children you baby-sit for, and arranged these numbers in order: 21, 23, 26, 30, 34, 34, 36, 36, 37, 38, 40, 48, 52.

The **lower extreme** is the lowest number in your data, 21. The **upper extreme** is the highest number in your data, 52. The median of all the numbers in the data is the middle number, 36.

The **lower quartile** is the median of the numbers below the median. $(26 + 30) \div 2 = 28$

The **upper quartile** is the median of the numbers above the median. $(38 + 40) \div 2 = 39$

You have four sections on your line of data: each relative to its quartile mark, and each quartile mark relative to the median. Each quartile contains $\frac{1}{4}$ of the data.

What's the range of the lowest quartile?

Step 1: Find the lower extreme and the lower quartile. 21 and 28

Step 2: Subtract the lower extreme from the lower quartile. $28 - 21 = 7$

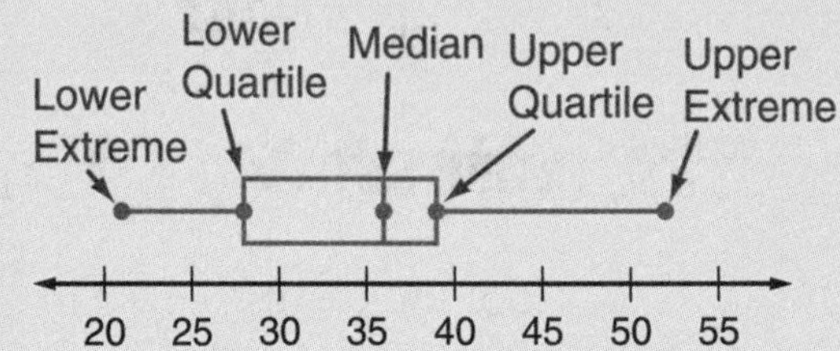

Exercises INTERPRET

1 Give the lower quartile for the box-and-whisker plot.

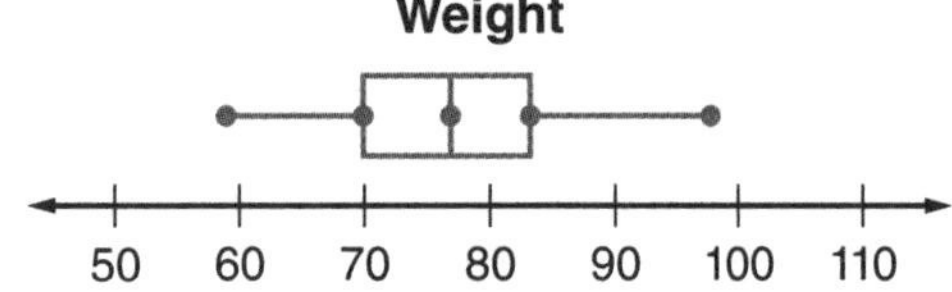

____

2 What is the range for this box-and-whisker plot?

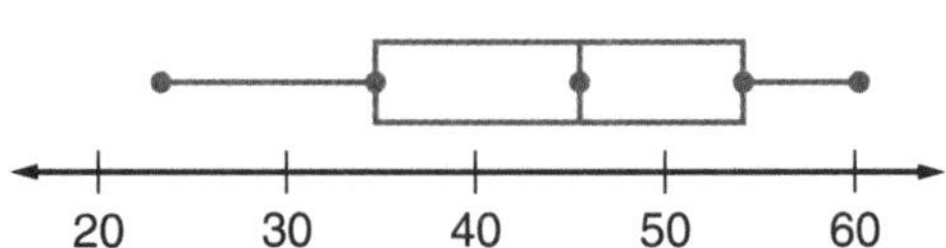

____

3 Create a box-and-whisker plot from this information.

Summary	
Lower Extreme	5
Lower Quartile	8.5
Median	12
Upper Quartile	14
Upper Extreme	20

4 What is the range and median of this box-and-whisker plot?

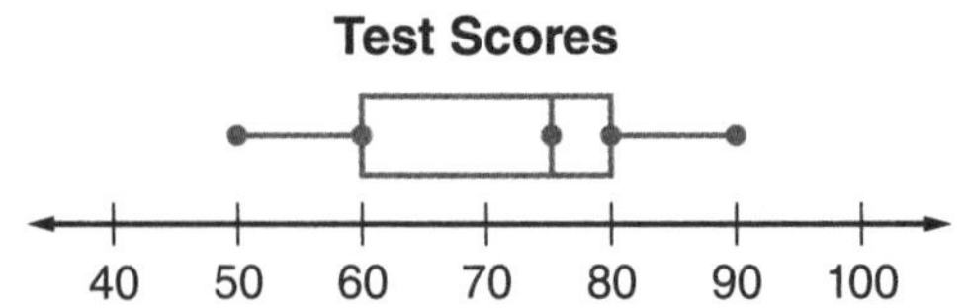

Range ______________________________

Median ______________________________

Name ______________________________

Tree Diagrams

A **tree diagram** can be used to show possible combinations of people, places, or things. It looks like a set of trees with branches.

Example:

At a community cookout, you can buy a ticket that allows you to choose one main item, and one side dish. The tree diagram shows the possible combinations.

To find out how many possible combinations there are, count the number of branches. In this example there are nine branches. How many possible combinations would there be if you could also order chips as a side dish?

Add potato chips as a branch on *each* main item. Since there are 3 items, add $9 + 3 = 12$

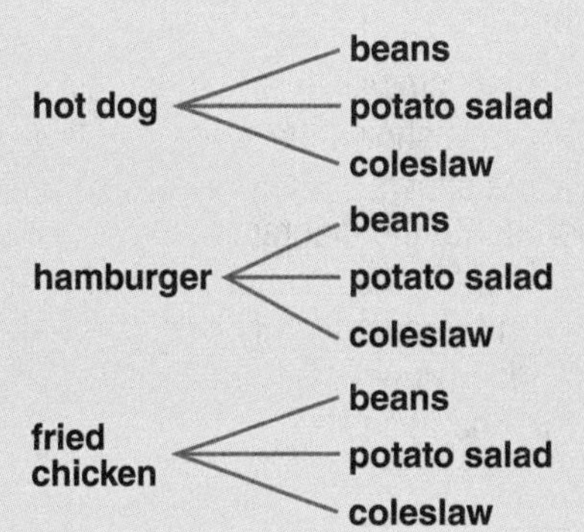

Exercises DIAGRAM

1. Phil first rolls a 6-sided number cube then flips a coin. Draw a tree diagram that shows all the possible outcomes of Phil's actions. How many different outcomes are there?

   ____

   How many outcomes exist where Phil rolls an even number and he flips a coin "heads"?

   ____

2. Felicia is laying out her wardrobe for an upcoming vacation. She will be gone 4 days. She lays out 4 shirts (blue, black, red, yellow), 3 pairs of pants (black, tan, white), and 3 pairs of shoes (black, brown, red). Draw a tree diagram to show all of the different combinations of outfits that Felicia could wear on the trip. How many combinations are there?

   ____

   How many choices does Felicia have that include red shoes?

   ____

Name ______________________________

Venn Diagrams

A **Venn Diagram** is used to show *groups* of data and can also show if and when some of the data is placed in more than one group.

Example:

The left circle shows the days Edna played *only* Baseball Blaster. The right circle shows the days she played *only* Football Fun. The overlap area shows the days she played *both* games. Some data does not fit into the diagram at all. Using the data shown in this diagram, identify the day Edna played none of the games identified in the data and tell why you choose that day. In this case, the day shown outside the diagram is the day Edna played none of the games listed.

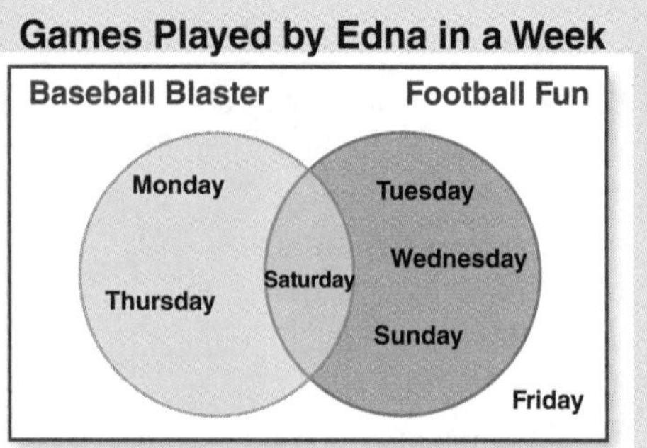

Exercises DIAGRAM

1. Ramon surveyed a group of 50 people at the town meeting about the expansion of the town zoo and the construction of a bike path. He found that of the 50 people he surveyed, 32 people supported expanding the zoo and 30 people supported constructing a bike path. Twelve people supported both projects. Fill in the Venn Diagram to represent the results of the survey.

Support Zoo Expansion   Support Bike Path

How many people supported the town zoo only? ______

How many supported the bike path only? ____________

2. The manager of the local clothing store wants to know which jeans to stock for the upcoming back-to-school sale. He reviews the numbers from last year's sale and finds that the store sold 120 pairs of jeans. 80 were boot-cut, and 60 were stone-washed. Assuming the store only stocked those two styles of jeans, how many of the jeans sold were both stone-washed and boot-cut?

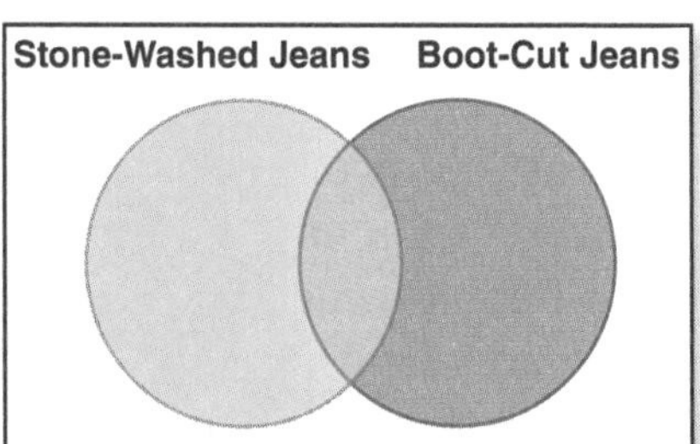

____

How many of the jeans were just stone-washed and not boot-cut? ______________

How many were just boot-cut and not stone-washed? ______________

Complete the Venn Diagram to show the data.

Name ______________________________

Calculating Probabilities

Probability is the likelihood of something happening in the future. Knowing how to calculate probability will help you predict future events, although not with 100 percent accuracy!

The simple formula to figure probability (P) is the number of favorable outcomes (f) divided by the total number of possible outcomes (o). You could express this formula as an equation.

$P = \frac{f}{o}$

Remember...

Probability only shows what is most likely to happen, not what will *definitely* happen. It is certainly possible that a person could throw a 6-sided number cube and that three fives, or 30 fives, or indeed 300 fives in a row would show—although the probability is great that this would not happen!

Example:

If you roll a 6-sided number cube, there are six possible outcomes. Each side has a different number of spots. The cube could show 1, 2, 3, 4, 5, or 6 spots.

What is the probability of the side with four spots being on top after the cube is thrown? The probability of rolling a 4 is $\frac{1}{6}$.

What is the probability of a 5 or a 6 not being on top after a cube is thrown?

Step 1: Decide how many favorable outcomes there are. In this case $6 - 2 = 4$

Step 2: Set up your equation. $P = \frac{4}{6}$

Step 3: You could simplify that fraction. $\frac{4}{6} = \frac{2}{3}$

If you were to roll the cube three times, you would probably have a favorable outcome two of those times.

Exercises INTERPRET

1. If you place 14 marbles in a bag with 7 red, 4 orange, and 3 black, what is the probability of blindly pulling a red marble from the bag?

   ____

2. If there are 20 males and 15 females in your class, and the teacher wants to appoint one person to be in charge of attendance, what is the probability that this person will be a female?

   ____

3. A survey was taken at school and all 525 students were asked if they belonged to a club. 212 people responded that they did belong to a club. What is the probability that if you randomly chose a person walking down the hall, that this person would belong to a club?

   ____

4. Someone mistakenly put three boxes of hardboiled eggs in with the regular farm eggs that totaled 156 boxes. What is the probability that someone buying a box of eggs will get a box of hardboiled eggs?

   ____

Name ______________________________

Use the spinner graphic to answer questions 1–4. What is the probability of:

1. Spinning an odd number? ____________________

2. Spinning a 2? ____________________

3. Spinning either a 2 or 4? ____________________

4. Spinning a 1? ____________________

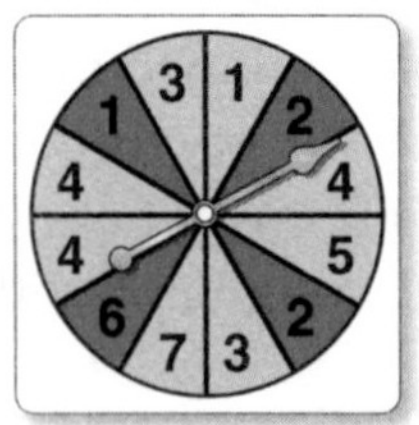

Use the Stem-and-Leaf Plot to answer

5. What is the range of the data?

____

6. What is the median of the data?

____

7. What is the mean of the data?

____

8. What is the mode of the data?

____

Stem-and-Leaf Plot

4	5 6
5	6 8
6	1 7
7	2 7 8
8	9
9	4

Use the Tree Diagram to answer questions 9–12.

9. How many different combinations of outfits can be created from the choices?

____

10. How many possibilities are there that include green-striped shirts?

____

11. How many possibilities are there that include a yellow tie and gray pants?

____

12. How many possibilities do NOT include a blue tie?

____

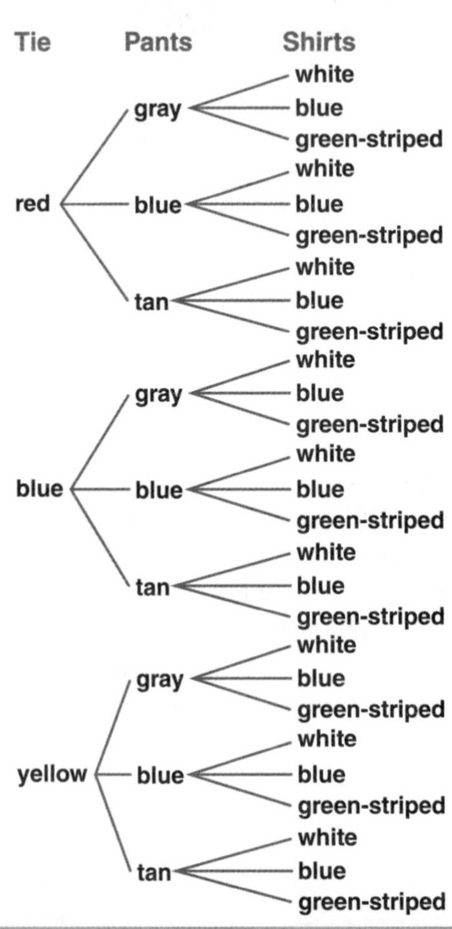

Name ____________________

Use the box-and-whisker plot to answer questions 13–15.

Weight of Pet Cats (kg)

5.0 5.25 5.5 5.75 6.0 6.25 6.5 6.75 7.0

13. What is the median of this data plot?

____

14. What is the range of the data?

____

15. What is the upper quartile?

____

Students in James's health class were polled on their favorite health food snack. The results are displayed on the graph.

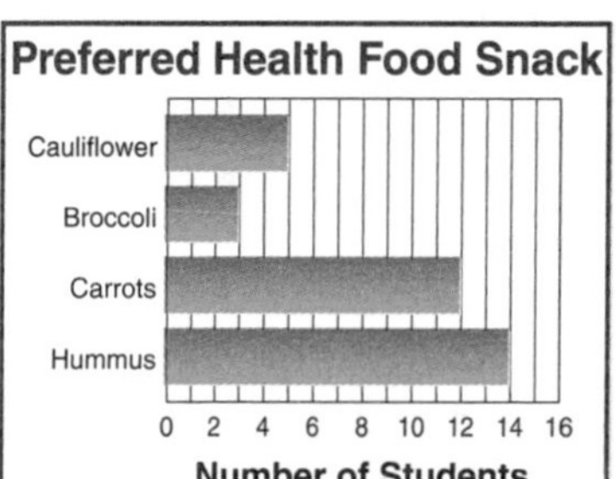

16. What is the least favorite health food snack?

____

17. What is the favorite health food snack?

____

18. How many more people preferred carrots to cauliflower?

____

Janice was making a schedule to determine how many volunteers she needed for the nature center guided tours. She charted the number of visitors to the nature center during the prior summer.

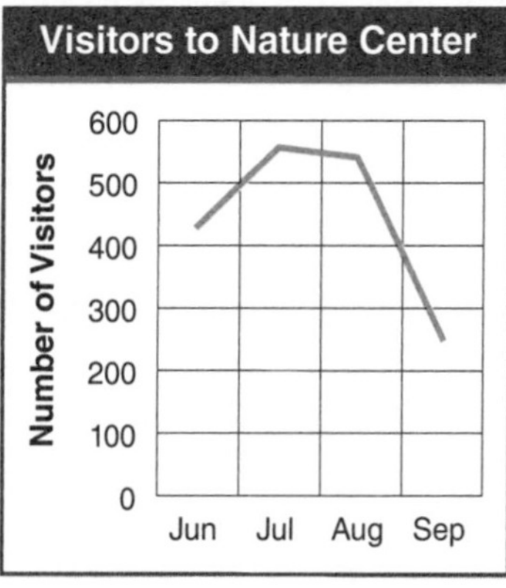

19. What month had the most visitors?

____

20. What month had the fewest visitors?

____

21. During what months should Janice increase her staffing to meet the demand for guided tours?

____

Name ______________________________

Peggy charted bike rentals for the previous month.

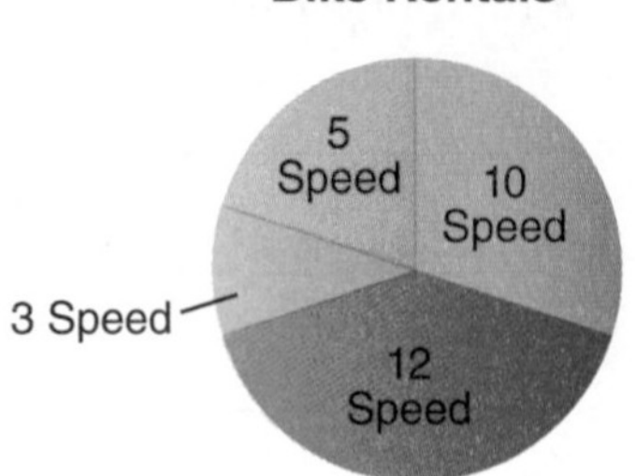

22 What was the most popular kind of bike rented?

____

23 Which kind of bike speed was the least popular?

____

Coach Taylor made a chart of the performance of his two best hitters.

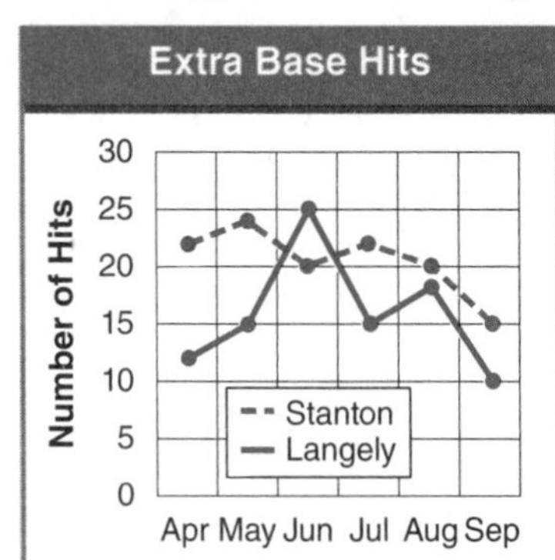

24 In which month did Langely hit more extra base hits than Stanton?

____

25 How many more extra base hits did Stanton have than Langely in the month of September?

____

26 Who had the lowest number of hits in any month? Which month?

____

27 In which month did Langley and Stanton come closest to having an equal number of extra base hits?

____

28 Use the Venn Diagram to display the following data: 25 students take Algebra I, 22 students take U.S. History, and 8 students take both courses.

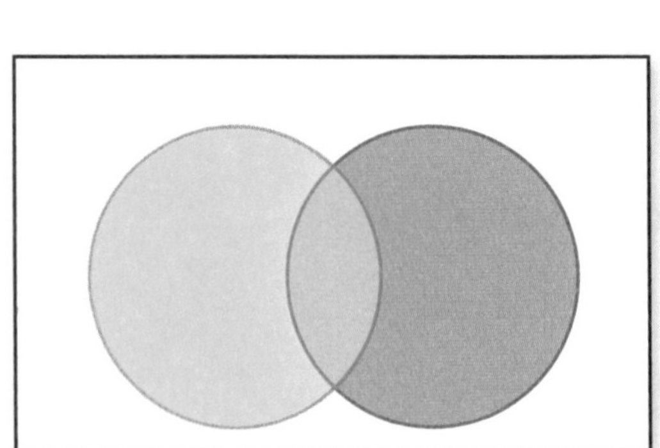

Name ______________________________

Answers and Explanations

1. $\frac{1}{2}$ There are 6 odd sections out of 12 total, so $\frac{6}{12}=\frac{1}{2}$.

2. $\frac{1}{6}$ There are 2 sections marked "2" out of 12 total, so $\frac{2}{12}=\frac{1}{6}$.

3. $\frac{5}{12}$ There are 2 sections marked "2" and 3 sections marked "4" out of 12 total, so $\frac{5}{12}$.

4. $\frac{1}{6}$ There are 2 sections marked "1" out of 12 total, so $\frac{2}{12}=\frac{1}{6}$.

5. 49 $94-45=49$

6. 67 There are 11 values, so the median is the sixth value, which is 67.

7. 67.5 $\frac{45+46+56+58+61+67+72+77+78+89+94}{11}=\frac{743}{11}=67.5$

8. There is no mode.

9. 27 Count the ends of the trees. Each of the three trees has 9, so $3\times 9=27$.

10. 9 Each of the 9 final branches includes a green-striped shirt.

11. 3 The bottom tree is for yellow ties. The top branch of that tree is for gray pants and there are 3 options there from that branch.

12. 18 Two of the three trees do NOT have a blue tie and each tree has 9 ends, so $2\times 9=18$.

13. 6 The line that goes through the box is the median.

14. 1.5 $6.5-5=1.5$

15. 6.25 The right-side border of the box begins the upper quartile.

16. Broccoli The shortest bar is for broccoli.

17. Hummus The longest bar is for hummus.

18. 7 12 chose carrots and 5 chose cauliflower; $12-5=7$

19. July The highest part of the line is in July.

20. September The lowest part of the line is in September.

21. July–August July and August have the most visitors.

22. 12 speed The largest section is for 12-speed.

23. 3 speed The smallest section is for 3-speed.

24. June The red line is higher in June.

25. 5 In September, Stanton hit 15 and Langely hit 10; $15+10=5$

26. Langley has the lowest point on either line in September.

27. August The closest the lines come together is in August.

28.

Posttest

Name ______________________________

Complete the following test items.

1. Robin runs 24 kilometers a week. If she continues to run at this rate, how many kilometers will she run in a year? ______________

2. The fashion department at an outlet store had a sale on t-shirts. There were 1124 t-shirts in stock at the beginning of the sale and another 426 more were ordered. At the end of the sale the store still had 335 t-shirts in stock. How many t-shirts were sold during the sale? ______________

3. Ronnie has 12 lengths of garden hose. Each is $6\frac{3}{4}$ meters long. How many meters of garden hose does Ronnie have to divide among 6 people working in the community garden? ______________

   How much hose will each person receive? ______________

4. Don has 112 quarts of tomato sauce to divide among the 12 contestants in a pasta cooking contest. How many cups is that per contestant? ______________

5. $6\frac{5}{8} + 3\frac{1}{4} + \frac{1}{6} + 1\frac{1}{3} =$ ______________

6. $-10 + 15 - (-6) + 5(-4) + \frac{16}{-8} =$ ______________

7. Solve for x: $x - 8 = 16$ ______________

8. Solve for x: $3x + 6 = 30$ ______________

9. Solve: $12 + (11 - 7)^2 - (16 \div 2) + 4(8 \times 2) - 3(8 - 2) =$ ______________

10. Restate in exponent form, then solve: $4 \times 4 \times 4 \times 3 \times 3 + 5 \times 5 =$

    ____

11. 4.65 meters = ________ inches (Use 2.54 cm = 1 inch)

12. 16 yards = ________ centimeters

13. What is the area of the rectangle?

    ____

    What is the perimeter of the rectangle?

    ____

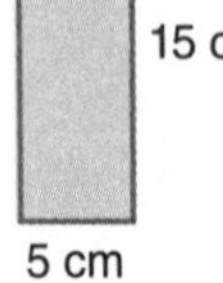

14. What is the area of the circle? (Use 3.14 for π.)

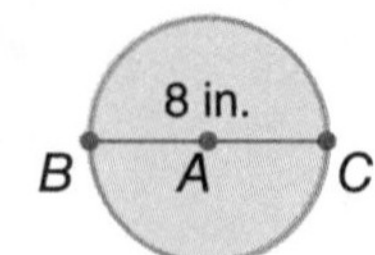

    ____

    What is the circumference of the circle?

    ____

Name ______________________

Posttest

15 Identify each angle as obtuse, acute, or right.

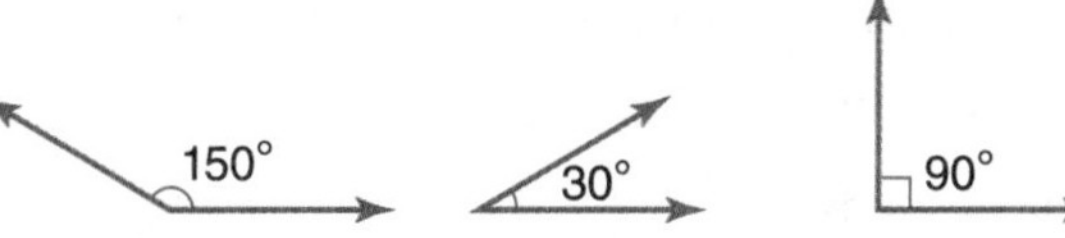

______ ______ ______

16 Identify each triangle as scalene, isosceles, or equilateral.

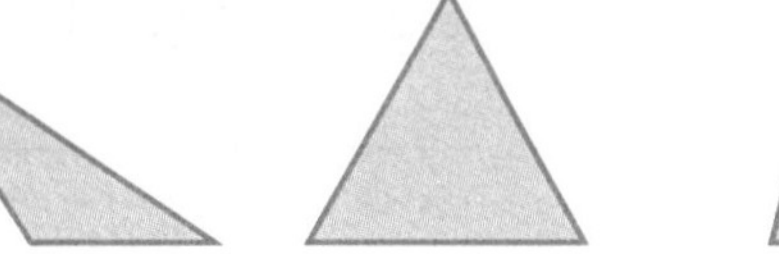
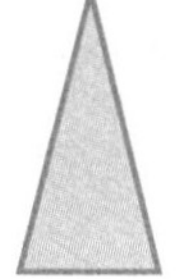

______ ______ ______

Calculate and reduce the fractions.

17 $\frac{5}{12} \times 168 =$ ______

18 $\left(\frac{1}{3} \times \frac{9}{14}\right) \times \frac{14}{3} =$ ______

19 $\frac{56}{65} \div 14 =$ ______

20 Give the coordinates for points on the grid.

A ______ B ______

C ______ D ______

What is the slope of a line drawn between points D and A?

______

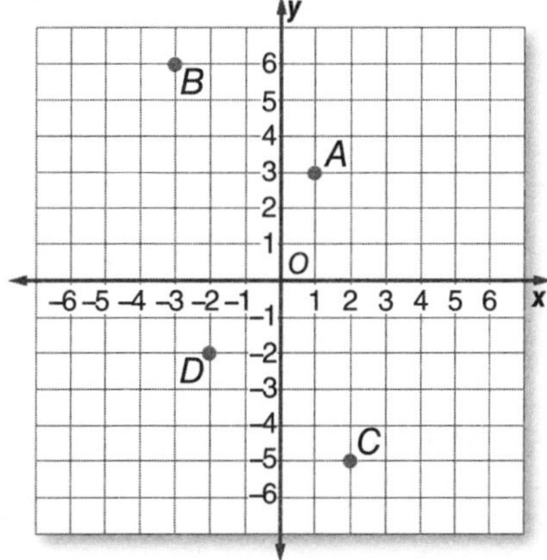

21 What is the measure of angle DBC?

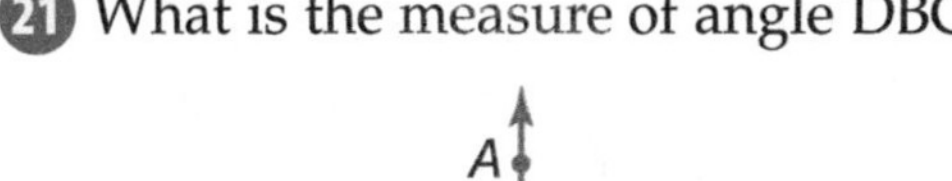
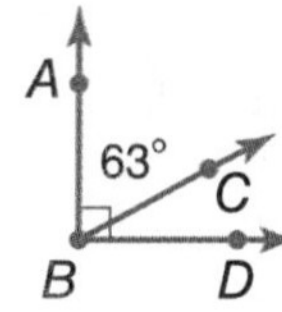

______

22 $0.345\overline{)0.595}$

23 $3\overline{)0.5596}$

24 What is 30% of 0.802?

______

25 What is $\frac{3}{8}$ of 96%?

______

26 Restate 5.625 as an improper fraction and a mixed number.

Improper Fraction ______ Mixed Number ______

27 Put the following numbers in order from least to greatest.
2.356, 1.3561, 3.56302, 2.5631, 2.35692, 1.35688, 2.5622, 1.599

______

28 Solve for x. $\frac{45}{64} = \frac{x}{192}$ ______

29 Restate $2\frac{7}{25}$ as a decimal. ______

Posttest

Name ____________________

30 An item costs you \$13.50 to produce. What price would you charge if you wanted to mark up the item by 20%?

____

31 Darma deposits \$500 in a bank account that earns 2.5% simple interest. How much money will she have in the account after 1 year? ____________________

After 2 years? ____________________

32 Identify each quadrilateral.

  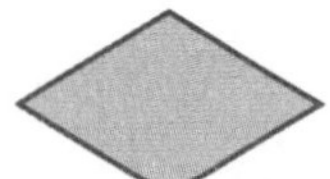 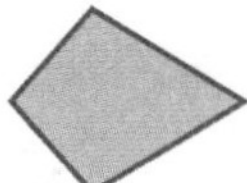 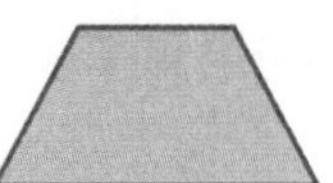

__________ __________ __________ __________ __________

33 Jim earns money by mowing lawns in his neighborhood. If he can mow 3 lawns in an hour, how many lawns can he mow in 30 hours?

____

34 The amount of water that the town of Bellville uses during the summer months averages 47,005 gallons per day. If the town reduces its water usage by 12%, how much water will be saved per day?

____

35 $\frac{6}{7} - \frac{2}{7} + \frac{5}{7} + \frac{3}{7} - \frac{1}{7} =$ ____________________

36 $\frac{15}{16} \times 3\frac{1}{5} =$ ____________________

37 $10^7 \times 10^2 =$ ____________________

38 $4^6 \div 4^3 =$ ____________________

39 Solve for x: $2x - 4.8 > 5.2$ ____________________

40 What is the square root of 169?

____

41 What is the mode of the data distribution?

____

What is the median?

____

Stem	Leaf
3	2 3
4	2 3 6 8
5	4 7 7 7
6	1 2 4 4 6
7	1 4

42 What is the range of the data in the box-and-whisker plot?

____

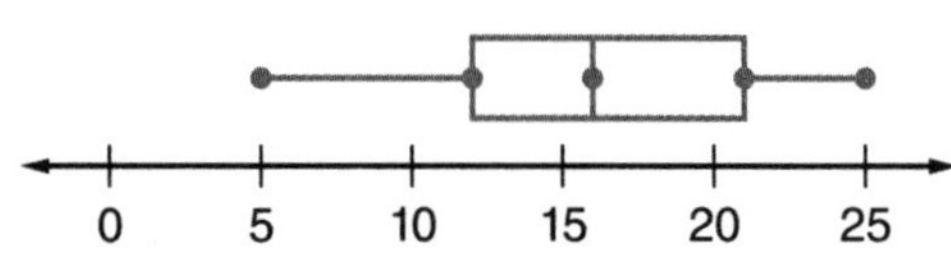

Name ______________________________

Posttest

43 What fruit is the least preferred by the students? ____________
What is the second most preferred fruit? ______________

44 Clarence collected about 5 more stamps than what person? ____________
Who collected the second fewest stamps? ______________

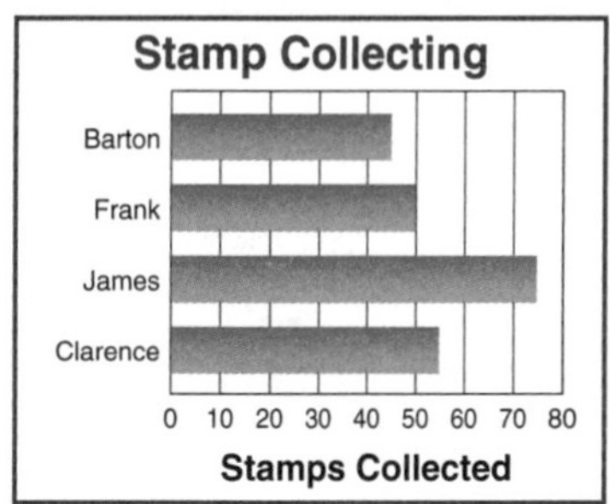

45 How many possible combinations are there?

____

Bread	Cold Cuts	Cheese
rye	chicken	Swiss
		American
		cheddar
	turkey	Swiss
		American
		cheddar
	bologna	Swiss
		American
		cheddar
whole wheat	chicken	Swiss
		American
		cheddar
	turkey	Swiss
		American
		cheddar
	bologna	Swiss
		American
		cheddar

46

t
A B a
D C
E F b
H G

Name two pairs of alternate interior angles.

__________ and __________

__________ and __________

Name two pairs of alternate exterior angles.

__________ and __________

__________ and __________

Name a pair of vertical angles.

__________ and __________

Name two pairs of supplementary angles.

__________ and __________

__________ and __________

47 Use the Pythagorean Theorem to find the value of x. ________________

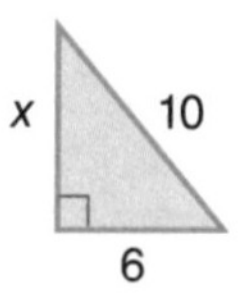

48 Name 2 line segments. ____________

Name 4 rays. ________________

Name a line. ________________

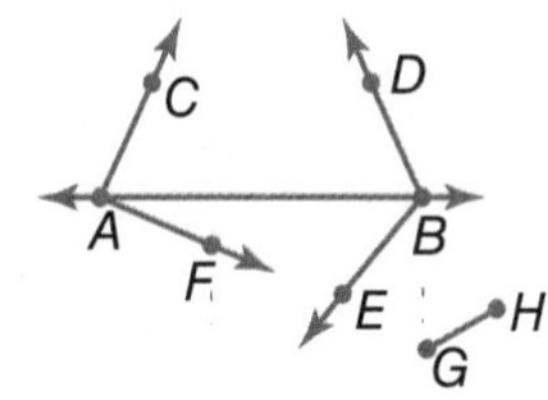

Posttest

Name ______________________________

Calculate the volume and surface area of the figures shown.

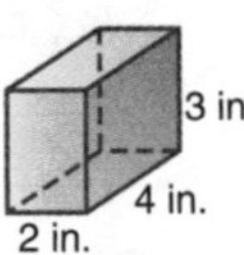

Volume ______________

Surface Area ______________

50

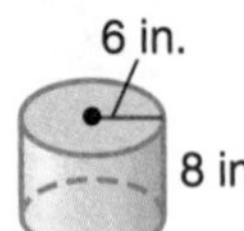

Volume ______________

Surface Area ______________

51

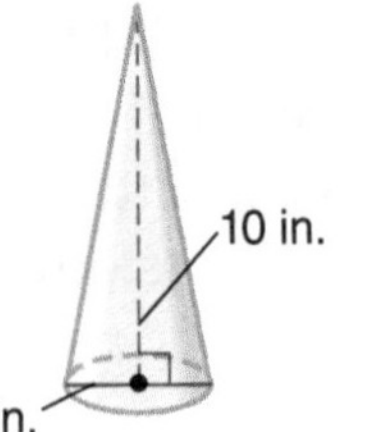

Volume ______________

52 Estimate the value of $\sqrt{140}$ ______________. Of $\sqrt{48}$ ______________

53 Convert $0.\overline{573}$ to a fraction. ______________

54 Solve $3(2x + 4) = 6(x + 2)$. ______________

55 Solve $26x + 4 = 6 + 26x - 3$. ______________

56 Complete and graph the function table for $y = x^2$.

Is it a linear or nonlinear function?

____

x	y
–2	
–1	
0	
1	
2	

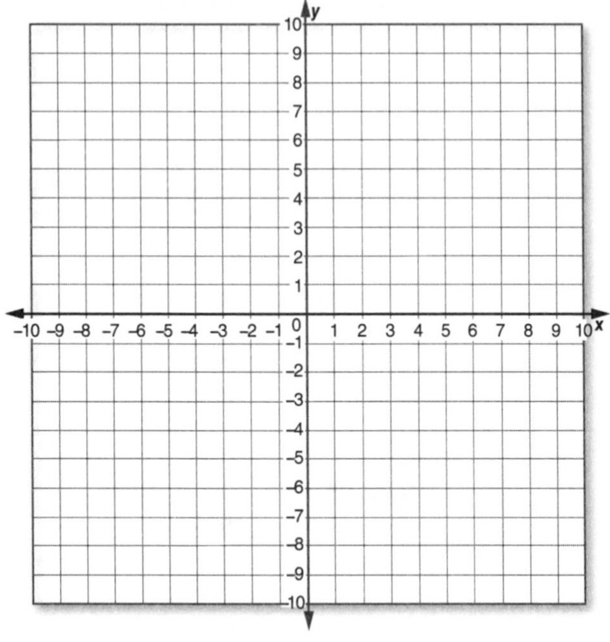

Name ___________________________

Posttest

57 Look at the graph below.

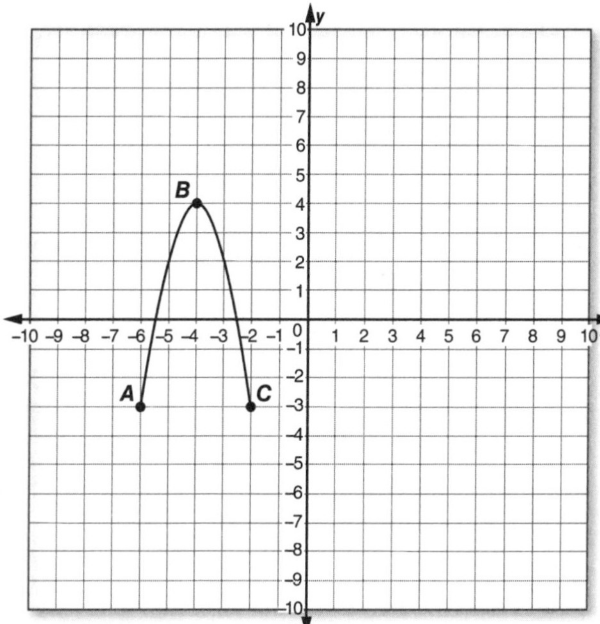

The function is increasing between points

____

The function is decreasing between points

____

58 How many times greater is 12×10^3 than 4×10^2?

59 Are these polygons similar? __________ If so, what is the scale factor? __________

15
7 7
3

90
42 42
18

60 What type of transformation is shown below? ___________________________

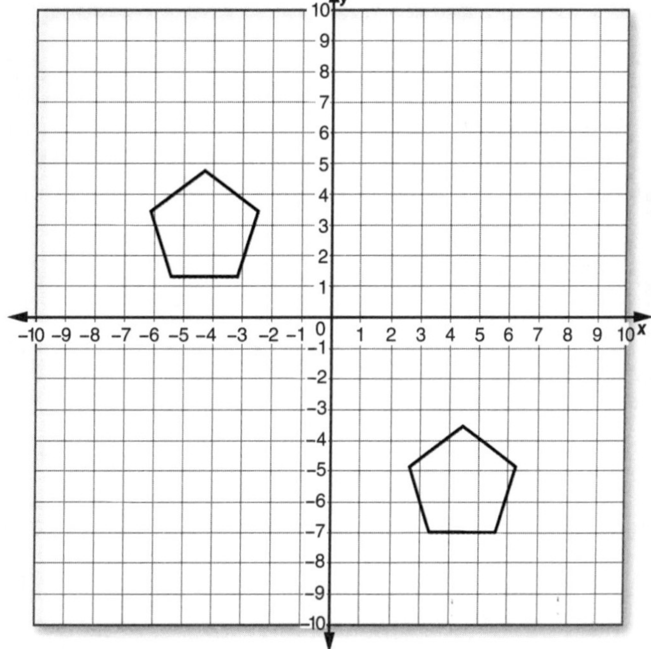

Name ______________________________

Answers and Explanations for Posttest

1. 1248 km — $\frac{24\text{ km}}{1\text{ week}} = \frac{y\text{ km}}{52\text{ weeks (1 year)}}; y = 24 \times 52 = 1,248$

2. 1215 t-shirts — $1124 + 426 - 335 = 1,215$

3. 81 meters; $13\frac{1}{2}$ meters — $6\frac{3}{4} \times 12 = \frac{27}{4} \times \frac{12}{1} = \frac{27}{1} \times \frac{3}{1} = 81; 81 \div 6 = 13\frac{1}{2}$

4. $37\frac{1}{3}$ cups — $112 \times 2 = 224$ pt; $224 \times 2 = 448$ cups; $448 \div 12 = 37\frac{1}{3}$

5. $11\frac{3}{8}$ — $6 + 3 + 1 = 10; \frac{15}{24} + \frac{6}{24} + \frac{4}{24} + \frac{8}{24} = \frac{33}{24} = 1\frac{9}{24} = 1\frac{3}{8}; 10 + 1\frac{3}{8} = 11\frac{3}{8}$

6. -11 — $-10 + 15 + 6 - 20 + \frac{16}{-8} = -10 + 15 + 6 - 20 - 2 = -11$

7. $x = 24$

$$\begin{aligned} x - 8 &= 16 \\ +8 \quad & +8 \\ x &= 24 \end{aligned}$$

8. $x = 8$

$$\begin{aligned} 3x + 6 &= 30 \\ -6 \quad & -6 \\ \frac{3x}{3} &= \frac{24}{3} \\ x &= 8 \end{aligned}$$

9. 66 — $12 + 4^2 - 8 + 4(16) - 3(6) = 12 + 16 - 8 + 4(16) - 3(6) = 12 + 16 - 8 + 64 - 18 = 66$

10. $4^3 \times 3^2 + 5^2 = 601$ — $4^3 \times 3^2 + 5^2 = 64 \times 9 + 25 = 576 + 25 = 601$

11. 183.1 inches — $4.65\text{ m} \times 100 = 465$ cm; $465 \div 2.54 = 183.1$ in.

12. 1463 cm — $16 \times 0.914 = 14.624$ m; $14.624 \times 100 = 1462.4$ cm

13. 75 sq cm; 40 cm — $5 \times 15 = 75; 5 + 5 + 15 + 15 = 40.$

14. 50.24 sq in.; 25.12 in. — $A = \pi r^2 = \pi \times (4^2) = 3.14 \times 16 = 50.24; C = \pi d = 3.14 \times 8 = 25.12$

15. Obtuse, acute, right

16. Scalene, equilateral, isosceles

17. 70 — $\frac{5}{\cancel{12}_1} \times \frac{\cancel{168}^{14}}{1} = 70$

18. 1 — $\frac{1}{\cancel{3}_1} \times \frac{\cancel{9}^3}{14} = \frac{3}{14}; \frac{3}{14} \times \frac{14}{3} = 1$

19. $\frac{4}{65}$ — $\frac{\cancel{56}^4}{65} \times \frac{1}{\cancel{14}_1} = \frac{4}{65}$

20. A (1, 3); B (−3, 6); C (2, −5); D (−2, −2); $\frac{5}{3}$ — $s = \frac{y_2 - y_1}{x_2 - x_1} = \frac{3 - (-2)}{1 - (-2)} = \frac{5}{3}$

21. 27 degrees — $90° - 63° = 27°$

22. 1.7

$$0.35.\overline{)0.59.5} = 1.7$$

$$\begin{array}{r} 35 \\ \hline 245 \\ 245 \\ \hline 0 \end{array}$$

23. 0.18653

$$3\overline{)0.55960} = 0.18653\ldots$$

$$\begin{array}{r} 3 \\ \hline 25 \\ 24 \\ \hline 19 \\ 18 \\ \hline 16 \\ 15 \\ \hline 10 \\ 9 \\ \hline 10\ldots \end{array}$$

24. 0.2406 $0.3 \times 0.802 = 0.2406$

25. 36% $\frac{3}{8} \times 96 = \frac{3}{1} \times 12 = 36$

26. $\frac{45}{8}; 5\frac{5}{8}$ $5.625 = \frac{5625}{1000} = \frac{225}{40} = \frac{45}{8} = 5\frac{5}{8}$

27. 1.3561, 1.35688, 1.599, 2.356, 2.35692, 2.5622, 2.5631, 3.56302

28. 135 $45 \times 192 = 64x; 8{,}640 = 64x; x = 135$

29. 2.28

$$2 + \quad 25\overline{)7.00} = 0.28$$

$$\begin{array}{r} 50 \\ \hline 200 \\ 200 \\ \hline 0 \end{array}$$

30. \$16.20 $13.50 \times 0.2 = 2.70; 13.50 + 2.70 = \$16.20$

31. \$512.50; \$525.00 $\$500 \times 0.025 = \$12.50; \$500 + \$12.50 = \$512.50; \$12.5 \times 2 = \$25; \$500 + \$25 = \$525$

32. Square, rectangle, rhombus, kite, trapezoid

33. 90 lawns $\frac{3 \text{ lawns}}{1 \text{ hour}} = \frac{x \text{ lawns}}{30 \text{ hours}}; (3)(30) = (1)(x); x = 90$

34. 5,640.6 gallons $47{,}005 \times 0.12 = 5{,}640.6$

35. $\frac{11}{7}$ or $1\frac{4}{7}$ $\frac{6-2+5+3-1}{7} = \frac{11}{7} = 1\frac{4}{7}$

36. 3 $\frac{15}{16} \times \frac{16}{5} = \frac{3}{1} \times \frac{1}{1} = 3$

37. 10^9 $10^{7+2} = 10^9$

38. 4^3 $4^{6-3} = 4^3$

39. $x > 5$ $2x - 4.8 + 4.8 > 5.2 + 4.8; 2x > 10; \frac{2x}{2} > \frac{10}{2}; x > 5$

40. 13 $13 \times 13 = 169$

Name ______________________________

41. 57; 57 — The number 57 appears three times, more than any other number; There are 17 values, so the median is value number 9, which is 57.

42. 20 — $25-5=20$

43. Pineapple; Banana

44. Frank; Frank

45. 18

46. Alternate interior angles: ∠D and ∠F; ∠E and ∠C;
Alternate exterior angles: ∠A and ∠G; ∠B and ∠H;
Vertical angles: ∠A and ∠C; ∠B and ∠D; ∠E and ∠G; ∠F and ∠H;
Supplementary angles: ∠A and ∠B; ∠B and ∠C; ∠A and ∠D; ∠E and ∠F; ∠F and ∠G; ∠G and ∠H; ∠H and ∠E; ∠H and ∠A; ∠G and ∠B; ∠E and ∠B; ∠F and ∠A; and others

47. 8 — $a^2+b^2=c^2$; $a^2+6^2=10^2$; $a^2+36=100$; $a^2=64$; $a=\sqrt{64}=8$

48. Line segments: $\overline{AB}, \overline{AF}, \overline{AC}, \overline{DB}, \overline{BE}, \overline{HG}$;
Rays: $\overrightarrow{AF}, \overrightarrow{AC}, \overrightarrow{BE}, \overrightarrow{BD}, \overrightarrow{AB}, \overrightarrow{BA}$, Line $\overleftrightarrow{AB}$

49. Volume = 24 cu in.; SA = 52 sq in. — $V=lwh=4\times3\times2=24$; $SA=2(4\times3)+2(4\times2)+2(3\times2)=2(12)+2(8)+2(6)=24+16+12=52$

50. Volume = 288π cu units; SA = 168π sq units — $V=\pi r^2h=\pi\times6^2\times8=\pi\times36\times8=288\pi$; $SA=2(\pi r^2)+(\pi dh)$ $=2(\pi6^2)+\pi(12)(8)=2(36\pi)+96\pi=72\pi+96\pi$ $=156\pi$

51. Volume = $\frac{40}{3}\pi$ cubic units — $V=\frac{1}{3}Bh=\frac{1}{3}(\pi r^2)(h)=\frac{1}{3}(\pi2^2)(10)=\frac{1}{3}(4\pi)(10)=\frac{1}{3}(40)\pi=\frac{40}{3}\pi$

52. 11.8; 6.9 — $\sqrt{144}=12$, so $\sqrt{140}\cong11.8$; $\sqrt{49}=7$, so $\sqrt{48}\approx6.9$

53. $\frac{573}{999}=\frac{191}{333}$ — $x=0.573\ldots$; $1000x=573.573\ldots$; $1000x-x=573.573\ldots-x$; $999x=573$; $x=\frac{573}{999}=\frac{191}{333}$

54. Infinite solutions — $6x+12=6x+12$,. which is true no matter what x is.

55. No solutions — $26x+4-26x=6+26x-3-26x$; $4=6-3$; so we are left with $4=3$, which is not true.

56. Nonlinear

x	y
−2	4
−1	1
0	0
1	1
2	4

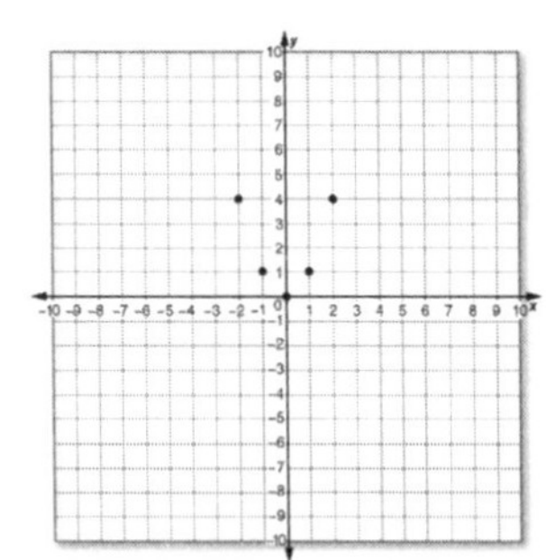

57. A and B; B and C

58. 30 — $\frac{12\times10^3}{4\times10^2}=3\times10^1=3\times10=30$

59. Yes; the larger is 6 times bigger than the smaller. — $\frac{42}{7}=6$; $\frac{90}{15}=6$; $\frac{18}{3}=6$

60. translation

Glossary

Acute Angle: An angle with a measure of less than 90°. *(p. 129)*

Acute Triangle: A triangle with only acute angles, angles less than 90°. *(p. 133)*

Addend: Any number that is added to another number. *(p. 14)*

Algebraic Expression: A group of letters, numbers, and symbols used in a series of operations. *(p. 77)*

Angle: Two rays that share an endpoint. *(p. 129)*

Area: The measure of a 2- or 3-dimensional figure's interior, given in square units. *(p. 104)*

Associative Property of Addition: States that addends may be grouped in any order without changing the sum. *(p. 14)*

Associative Property of Multiplication: States that numbers may be grouped in any way without changing the product. *(p. 14)*

Bar Graph: A graph that uses numbers to compare two or more people, places, or things. Each bar represents a number and may be represented horizontally or vertically. *(p. 150)*

Base: The face on the bottom of a solid figure. *(p. 143)*

Base of an Exponent: The number being used as the factor when writing in exponential form. In the statement 10^3, the base is 10. *(p. 67)*

Box-and-Whisker Plot: Organizes data to show where the most data points lie and also shows the median of the data. *(p. 158)*

Carry: To place an extra digit—when adding or multiplying—in the next place-value column on the left. *(p. 10)*

Celsius: Used in the metric system to measure temperature and expressed as °C, also expressed as Centigrade. *(p. 121)*

Chord: A line segment with both endpoints on a circle's circumference. *(p. 139)*

Circle: A 2-dimensional figure with every point on its circumference an equal distance from its center point. *(p. 139)*

Circle Graph: Shows parts of a whole as a percentage to the whole and is also known as a pie chart. *(p. 155)*

Circumference: The length of distance around a circle's perimeter. *(p. 139)*

Coefficient: The number that replaces the symbol × and multiplies the variable in a multiplication expression. The statement 9*m* shows 9 as the coefficient and *m* as the variable. *(p. 77)*

Common Denominator: A number which can be divided evenly by all the denominators in a group of fractions. *(p. 22)*

Common Multiple: A number that is a multiple of all the numbers in a given set. *(p. 22)*

Commutative Property of Addition: States that numbers may be added in any order without changing the sum. *(p. 14)*

Commutative Property of Multiplication: States that multiplication may be done in any order without changing the product. *(p. 14)*

Complementary Angles: Two angles that form a right angle. Their sum is 90°. *(p. 130)*

Congruent: A term used to describe something that is equal. *(p. pp. 133–134)*

Cross-multiplying: A method for finding a missing numerator or denominator. *(p. 51)*

Customary Units of Length: Measurements expressed in inches *(in.)*, feet *(ft)*, yards *(yd)*, and miles *(mi)*. *(p. 110)*

Customary Units of Weight: Measurements expressed in ounces *(oz)*, pounds *(lb)*, and *tons*. *(p. 112)*

Data: Information that is gathered and sometimes displayed in graphs and charts. *(p. 150)*

Degrees: The units used to describe temperature. *(p.121)*

Denominator: The number below the line in a fraction. *(p. 18)*

Diameter: A chord that passes through a circle's center point. *(p. 139)*

Dilation: Changing the size of the original figure by enlarging or shrinking it. *(p. 141)*

Discount: A reduction in the cost of an item from the usual price. *(p. 56)*

Distributive Property of Multiplication: States that each number may be multiplied separately and added together. *(p. 14)*

Dividend: The number to be divided in a division problem. *(p. 14)*

Divisor: The number by which another number—the dividend—will be divided. *(p. 14)*

Double-Line Graph: Compares how information changes as time passes between two or more people, places, or things. *(p. 154)*

Edge: The line on a solid figure where two faces meet. *(p. 143)*

Equality Property of Addition: States that when adding a number on one side of an equation, you must add the same number on the other side of an equation. Both sides will then still be equal. *(p. 14)*

Equality Property of Division: States that when dividing a number on one side of an equation, you must divide by the same number on the other side of the equation. Both sides will then still be equal. *(p. 14)*

Equality Property of Multiplication: States that when multiplying a number on one side of an equation, you must multiply by the same number on the other side of the equation. Both sides will then still be equal. *(p. 14)*

Equality Property of Subtraction: States that when subtracting a number on one side of an equation, you must subtract the same number on the other side of the equation. Both sides will then still be equal. *(p. 14)*

Equation: A mathematical statement used to show that two amounts are equal. *(p. 51)*

Equilateral Triangle: A triangle with all three sides being the same length. *(p. 133)*

Exponent: The number that tells how many times the base number is multiplied by itself. The exponent ^{3} in 10^3 shows $10 \times 10 \times 10$. *(p. 67)*

Exterior Angle: An angle located outside parallel lines when a line intersects the parallel lines. *(p. 130)*

Face: The flat surface of a solid figure. On a solid figure each face looks two-dimensional. *(p. 143)*

Factors: The numbers multiplied in a multiplication exercise. *(p. 40)*

Fahrenheit: The customary system used to measure temperature and expressed as °F. *(p. 121)*

Fluid ounces: A measurement used for liquids. *(p. 119)*

Function Table: Used to show a relation between an ordered pair. *(p. 92)*

Identity Elements: Numbers in a problem that do not affect the answer. Only addition and multiplication have identity elements. *(p. 14)*

Improper Fraction: A fraction greater than 1 because its numerator is greater than its denominator. *(p. 18)*

Interest: The percent of the principal charged by the bank for money borrowed, or paid to a person with money in a savings account. *(p. 60)*

Interior Angle: An angle located inside parallel lines when a line intersects the parallel lines. *(p. 130)*

Intersecting Lines: Lines that meet or cross each other at a specific point. *(p. 127)*

Interval: The distance between each measurement of time on a line graph. *(p. 60)*

Irrational Number: The square root of a number that is not a perfect square. *(p. 71)*

Isosceles Triangle: A triangle with two sides the same length, but the third side being a different length. *(p. 133)*

Kite: A quadrilateral with two angles that are equal, two touching sides that are equal in length, and the other two touching sides are equal in length. *(p. 137)*

Line: A straight path that goes in both directions and does not end. A line is measured in length. *(p. 127)*

Linear Function: A function for which the graph of the function is a straight line. *(p. 101)*

Line Graph: Often used to show a change in information as time passes. The distance from one time to another is an interval. *(p. 152)*

Line Segment: A specific part of a line that ends at two identified points. *(p. 128)*

Liquid Volume: Units of liquid a container can hold and expressed in cups *(c)*, pints *(pt)*, quarts *(qt)*, and gallons *(gal)*. *(p. 111)*

Lower Extreme: The lowest number in a group of data used in a box-and-whisker plot. *(p. 158)*

Lower Quartile: The median of numbers from the lower extreme to the median on a box-and-whisker plot. *(p. 158)*

Mark-up: The percent by which something is increased before it is sold. *(p. 56)*

Mean: The total number of the whole collection divided by the number of addends. *(p. 156)*

Glossary

Median: The middle number in a set of numbers when the numbers are arranged from least to greatest. *(p. 156)*

Metric Units of Length: Measurements expressed in millimeters *(mm)*, centimeters *(cm)*, meters *(m)*, and kilometers *(km)*. *(p. 115)*

Metric Units of Liquid Volume: Measurements expressed in liter *(L), milliliters (mL), centiliters (cL), and kiloliters (kL)*. *(p. 116)*

Metric Units of Mass: Measurements expressed in grams *(g)*, milligrams *(mg)*, centigrams *(cg)*, and kilograms *(kg)*. *(p. 117)*

Mixed Number: A number with a whole number part and a fraction part. *(p. 18)*

Mode: The number that appears most often in a set of numbers. *(p. 156)*

Negative Number: A number less than 0 and identified with the minus sign. *(p. 15)*

Nonlinear Function: A function for which the graph of the function is not a straight line. *(p. 101)*

Numerator: The number above the line in a fraction. *(p. 18)*

Obtuse Angle: An angle with a measure of more than 90°. *(p. 129)*

Obtuse Triangle: A triangle with one obtuse angle. *(p. 133)*

Order of Operations: Rules that tell the steps to follow when doing a computation. *(p. 13)*

Origin of a Circle: The circle's center point. *(p. 139)*

Percent Change: The amount of change from a starting point. *(p. 56)*

Perfect Square: Numbers that result from squaring an integer. *(p. 70)*

Perimeter: The distance around a figure. Measured in customary or metric units. *(p. 113)*

Pi: The ratio of a circle's diameter to its circumference—a ratio that is exactly the same for every circle. A circle's circumference equals pi times its diameter. A circle's area equals pi times the square of its radius. Pi is often rounded to 3.14. *(p. 140)*

Point: An exact location in space that has no dimensions and cannot be measured. A point is usually represented by a dot. *(p. 127)*

Polygon: Any closed two-dimensional figure that is made up of line segments. Triangles and quadrilaterals are two types of polygons. *(p. 138)*

Power of 10: In a place-value chart, each place value is 10 times the place value of the number to its right. *(p. 41)*

Principal: The amount borrowed or deposited into a bank. *(p. 60)*

Probability: The likelihood of an event happening in the future. *(p. 161)*

Product: The result, or answer, of a multiplication problem. *(p. 13)*

Property of Additive Inverse: States that when adding a negative number to its inverse the sum will be 0. For example: $-8 + 8 = 0$. *(p. 15)*

Proportion: An equation that shows two ratios are equal. *(p. 51)*

Pythagorean Theorem: In a right triangle, the square of the length of the hypotenuse is equal to the sum of the squares of the lengths of the other two sides. *(p. 135)*

Quadrilateral: A two-dimensional figure with four sides and four angles. *(p. 137)*

Quotient: The result of dividing one number by another. *(p. 17)*

Radical Sign: The symbol used to indicate a square root. *(p. 70)*

Radius: A line segment that starts at a circle's center point and extends to its perimeter. *(p. 139)*

Range: The greatest number minus the smallest number in a set of numbers. *(p. 156)*

Rate: A comparison of two different units or numbers. *(p. 53)*

Ratio: A comparison of two numbers using division. *(p. 50)*

Rational Number: Any real number that can be made by dividing two integers. *(p. 42)*

Ray: A part of a line that extends from a specific point in only one direction. *(p. 128)*

Reciprocals: Two fractions that look like upside-down reflections of one another. *(p. 27)*

Rectangle: A quadrilateral with four right angles. A rectangle's opposite sides are parallel and the same length. *(p. 137)*

Reflection: Creating a mirror image of the original figure. *(p. 141)*

Regroup: In place value, to use part of the value from one place in another place to make adding or subtracting possible. *(p. 11)*

Remainder: The number left over in whole-number division when you can no longer divide any further. *(p. 18)*

Rhombus: A figure with parallel sides of equal length and equal opposite angles. *(p. 137)*

Right Angle: An angle that measures exactly 90°. *(p. 129)*

Right Triangle: A triangle with one right angle, an angle with a measure of exactly 90°. *(p. 133)*

Rotation: Occurs when a figure is moved around a point or line. The shape remains the same but the orientation changes. *(p. 141)*

Scalene Triangle: A triangle with all three sides being of different lengths. *(p. 133)*

Scientific Notation: A way of writing numbers as the product of a power of 10 and a decimal that is greater than 1 but less than 10. *(p. 72)*

Similar Triangles: Triangles with the same shape but with different sizes. *(p. 134)*

Slope: The amount by which a line rises or falls as you read a coordinate grid from left to right. *(p. 97)*

Solid Figure: A three-dimensional figure such as a cube or pyramid. *(p. 143)*

Square: A quadrilateral with four right angles and four sides that are the same length. *(p. 137)*

Square Root: A number that when multiplied by itself equals a given number. *(p. 70)*

Statistics: A branch of math that answers questions about how many, how long, how often, how far, or how big. *(p. 156)*

Stem-and-Leaf Plot: Used to organize data and compare it. A stem-and-leaf plot organizes data from least to greatest using the digits or the greatest place value to group data. *(p. 157)*

Supplementary Angles: Any two angles that add up to a sum of 180°. *(p. 130)*

Symmetry: Results when a figure is folded down the center and the parts are identical. *(p. 141)*

Translation: Occurs when an identical figure is drawn and then moved in any direction. *(p. 141)*

Tree Diagram: Used to show possible combinations of data including people, places, or things in a diagram that looks like a tree with branches. *(p. 159)*

Trapezoid: A figure with two opposite sides that are parallel, but the sides are different lengths. *(p. 137)*

Triangle: A two-dimensional figure with three sides. *(p. 133)*

Upper Extreme: The highest number in a group of data used in a box-and-whisker plot. *(p. 158)*

Upper Quartile: The median of the numbers from the median to the upper extreme on a box-and-whisker plot. *(p. 158)*

Variable: An unknown number usually expressed as a letter and used in Algebra. In the statement $n - 18$, n is the variable. *(p. 77)*

Venn Diagram: A diagram used to show data and how different sets of data can overlap. *(p. 160)*

Vertex: The specific point of a ray, also called an endpoint. *(p. 128)*

Vertex of a Solid: A specific point at which more than two faces meet, or a point where a curve begins. *(p. 143)*

Vertical Angles: The angles opposite each other when two lines intersect. *(p. 130)*

Volume: The number of units a solid figure contains, expressed in cubic inches, feet, yards, or miles. *(p. 144)*

Whole Number: A number that does not include a fraction or decimal. *(p. 18)*

Zero Property of Multiplication: States that any number times zero equals zero. *(p. 14)*

Answers and Explanations

Chapter 1: Fundamentals

Lesson 1.1

1. 13 $(7)\times(2)-(9)+2^3=7\times2-9+8=14-9+8$
$=5+8=13$

2. 0 $(1)\times(2)-2^3+6=1\times2-8+6=2-8+6=-6+6=0$

3. 64 $(3)^3+(5)^2+5-2+3^2=27+25+5-2+9=64$

4. 45 $(10)\times(3)+42-3^3=10\times3+42-27=30+42-27$
$=45$

5. 6 $2^3-2^3+9-(3)=0+9-3=6$

6. 11 $4^2-(8-5)+(4+2)-2^3=4^2-3+6-2^3$
$=16-3+6-8=11$

7. 3 $(5)+(3)-(3)-2=5+3-3-2=5-2=3$

8. 21 $(7)\times(3)\times1^2=7\times3\times1=21$

Chapter 2: Negative Numbers

Lesson 2.1

1. FE G C A BD
−9 −8 −7 −6 −5 −4 −3 −2 −1 0 1 2

F (−8.5); E (−8); G (−4.5);
C (−2.5); A (−1); B (1); D (1.5)

2. 8, 4.6, 3.3, 3, −3, −3.3, −4.3, −6, −6.6, −6.7, −8.1

3. $<$

4. $<$

5. $>$

6. $<$

7. $>$

8. $<$

9. $=$

10. $<$

11. $<$

Lesson 2.2

1. 139 $171-32=139$

2. −84 $145-61=84; -84$

3. −1 $112-111=1; -1$

4. 399 $715-316=399$

5. 426 $1101-561-114=540-114=426$

6. −181 $365+111=476; 476-295=181; -181$

7. −847 $210+210+427=847; -847$

8. 28 $71-53+10=18+10=28$

9. 79 $301-222=79$

10. 65 $118-181+128;\ 118+128=246; 246-181=65$

11. 89 $214-125=89$

12. −20 $(85+24)-(19+110)=109-129; 129-109$
$=20; -20$

13. −82 $79+30=109; 109-27=82; -82$

14. −169 $213+119=332; 332-163=169; -169$

15. 28 $42+22-67+31=95-67=28$

16. 12 $12+29-29=12+0=12$

Lesson 2.3

1. 15 $5\times3=15$

2. −150 $15\times10=150; -150$

3. −10 $100\div10=10; -10$

4. 75 $25\times3=75$

5. −225 $15\times15=225; -225$

6. −300 $12\times5\times5=12\times25=300; -300$

7. −28 $2\times14=28; -28$

8. −231 $11\times21=231; -231$

9. 225 $15\times5\times3=15\times15=225$

10. −618 $3\times103\times2=309\times2=618; -618$

11. 14 $20\div20=1; 1\times14=14$

12. 2420 $22\times11\times10=242\times10=2420$

13. 112 $8\times14=112$

14. −3 $132\div44=3; -3$

15. 15 $(150\div30)\times3=5\times3=15$

16. 12 $55\div55=1; 1\times12=12$

17. −2 $90\div3\div15=30\div15=2; -2$

18. 169 $52\times13\div4=676\div4=169$

Chapter 3: Fractions and Mixed Numbers

Lesson 3.1

1. $21\frac{1}{3}$ $\frac{64}{3}=21\text{ R}1=21\frac{1}{3}$

2. $25\frac{1}{4}$ $\frac{101}{4}=25\text{ R}1=25\frac{1}{4}$

3. $7\frac{1}{2}$ $\frac{15}{2}=7\text{ R}1=7\frac{1}{2}$

4. $17\frac{1}{3}$ $\frac{52}{3}=17\text{ R}1=17\frac{1}{3}$

5. $5\frac{1}{2}$ $\frac{66}{12}=5\text{ R}6=5\frac{6}{12}=5\frac{1}{2}$

6. $12\frac{5}{11}$ $\frac{137}{11}=12\text{ R}5=12\frac{5}{11}$

7. 11 $\frac{176}{16}=11\text{ R}0=11$

8. $7\frac{5}{8}$ $\frac{61}{8}=7\text{ R}5=7\frac{5}{8}$

9. $52\frac{2}{3}$ cups $\frac{158}{3}=52\text{ R}2=52\frac{2}{3}$

10. $35\frac{1}{2}$ yards $\frac{142}{4}=35\text{ R}2=35\frac{2}{4}=35\frac{1}{2}$

Answers and Explanations

Lesson 3.2

1. $\frac{23}{4}$ $\quad \frac{(5\times4)+3}{4}=\frac{20+3}{4}=\frac{23}{4}$
2. $\frac{54}{7}$ $\quad \frac{(7\times7)+5}{7}=\frac{49+5}{7}=\frac{54}{7}$
3. $\frac{282}{11}$ $\quad \frac{(25\times11)+7}{11}=\frac{275+7}{11}=\frac{282}{11}$
4. $\frac{124}{5}$ $\quad \frac{(24\times5)+4}{5}=\frac{120+4}{5}=\frac{124}{5}$
5. $\frac{213}{13}$ $\quad \frac{(16\times13)+5}{13}=\frac{208+5}{13}=\frac{213}{13}$
6. $\frac{205}{14}$ $\quad \frac{(14\times14)+9}{14}=\frac{196+9}{14}=\frac{205}{14}$
7. $\frac{481}{9}$ $\quad \frac{(53\times9)+4}{9}=\frac{477+4}{9}=\frac{481}{9}$
8. $\frac{71}{4}$ $\quad \frac{(17\times4)+3}{4}=\frac{68+3}{4}=\frac{71}{4}$
9. 32 times $\quad \frac{(10\times3)+2}{3}=\frac{30+2}{3}=\frac{32}{3}$; $\frac{32}{3}\div\frac{1}{3}=\frac{32}{3}\times\frac{3}{1}=32$
10. 3 pies $\quad \frac{25}{3}=8\frac{1}{3}; 8\frac{1}{3}-6=2\frac{1}{3}$, so 3 more

Lesson 3.3

1. $\frac{6}{4}$ or $1\frac{1}{2}$ $\quad \frac{3+3}{4}=\frac{6}{4}=\frac{3}{2}=1\frac{1}{2}$
2. 1 $\quad \frac{1+4}{5}=\frac{5}{5}=1$
3. $\frac{10}{8}$ or $1\frac{1}{4}$ $\quad \frac{5+5}{8}=\frac{10}{8}=1\frac{2}{8}=1\frac{1}{4}$
4. $\frac{11}{9}$ or $1\frac{2}{9}$ $\quad \frac{7+4}{9}=\frac{11}{9}=1\frac{2}{9}$
5. $\frac{7}{11}$ $\quad \frac{4+3}{11}=\frac{7}{11}$
6. $\frac{20}{17}$ or $1\frac{3}{17}$ $\quad \frac{15+5}{17}=\frac{20}{17}=1\frac{3}{17}$
7. $\frac{21}{9}$ or $2\frac{1}{3}$ $\quad \frac{7+14}{9}=\frac{21}{9}=2\frac{3}{9}=2\frac{1}{3}$
8. $\frac{7}{3}$ or $2\frac{1}{3}$ $\quad \frac{2+5}{3}=\frac{7}{3}=2\frac{1}{3}$
9. $1\frac{1}{7}$ quarts $\quad \frac{1}{7}+\frac{2}{7}+\frac{5}{7}=\frac{1+2+5}{7}=\frac{8}{7}=1\frac{1}{7}$
10. No, they only surveyed $\frac{8}{9}$ of the class $\quad \frac{2}{9}+\frac{5}{9}+\frac{1}{9}=\frac{2+5+1}{9}=\frac{8}{9}$
11. $\frac{1}{2}$ $\quad \frac{3-1}{4}=\frac{2}{4}=\frac{1}{2}$
12. $\frac{1}{3}$ $\quad \frac{3-2}{3}=\frac{1}{3}$
13. $\frac{1}{3}$ $\quad \frac{8-5}{9}=\frac{3}{9}=\frac{1}{3}$
14. $\frac{3}{4}$ $\quad \frac{7-1}{8}=\frac{6}{8}=\frac{3}{4}$
15. $\frac{2}{7}$ $\quad \frac{5-3}{7}=\frac{2}{7}$
16. 0 $\quad \frac{1-1}{2}=\frac{0}{2}=0$
17. $\frac{1}{3}$ $\quad \frac{2-1}{3}=\frac{1}{3}$
18. 1 $\quad \frac{5-2}{3}=\frac{3}{3}=1$
19. $\frac{1}{2}$ quart $\quad \frac{7}{8}-\frac{3}{8}=\frac{7-3}{8}=\frac{4}{8}=\frac{1}{2}$
20. Yes, she has $\frac{1}{2}$ pound left $\quad \frac{19}{16}-\frac{11}{16}=\frac{19-11}{16}=\frac{8}{16}=\frac{1}{2}; \frac{1}{2}>\frac{7}{16}$

Lesson 3.4

1. $1\frac{3}{20}$ $\quad \frac{15}{20}+\frac{8}{0}=\frac{23}{20}=1\frac{3}{20}$
2. $\frac{22}{21}$ or $1\frac{1}{21}$ $\quad \frac{15}{21}+\frac{7}{21}=\frac{22}{21}=1\frac{1}{21}$
3. $\frac{73}{60}$ or $1\frac{13}{60}$ $\quad \frac{33}{60}+\frac{40}{60}=\frac{73}{60}=1\frac{13}{60}$
4. $\frac{9}{52}$ $\quad \frac{13}{52}-\frac{4}{52}=\frac{9}{52}$
5. $\frac{5}{36}$ $\quad \frac{9}{36}-\frac{4}{36}=\frac{5}{36}$
6. $\frac{3}{7}$ $\quad \frac{2}{21}+\frac{7}{21}=\frac{9}{21}=\frac{3}{7}$
7. $\frac{91}{33}$ or $2\frac{25}{33}$ $\quad \frac{102}{33}-\frac{11}{33}=\frac{91}{33}=2\frac{25}{33}$
8. $\frac{73}{42}$ or $1\frac{31}{42}$ $\quad \frac{66}{42}+\frac{7}{42}=\frac{73}{42}=1\frac{31}{42}$
9. $\frac{1}{15}$ $\quad \frac{11}{15}-\frac{10}{15}=\frac{1}{15}$
10. $\frac{19}{56}$ $\quad \frac{35}{56}-\frac{16}{56}=\frac{19}{56}$
11. $\frac{131}{77}$ or $1\frac{54}{77}$ $\quad \frac{98}{77}+\frac{33}{77}=\frac{131}{77}=1\frac{54}{77}$
12. $\frac{19}{60}$ $\quad \frac{55}{60}-\frac{36}{60}=\frac{19}{60}$

Lesson 3.5

1. $16\frac{1}{4}$ $\quad 12+3=15; \frac{2}{4}+\frac{3}{4}=\frac{5}{4}=1\frac{1}{4}; 15+1\frac{1}{4}=16\frac{1}{4}$
2. $17\frac{54}{77}$ $\quad 13+4=17; \frac{33}{77}+\frac{21}{77}=\frac{54}{77}; 17\frac{54}{77}$

Answers and Explanations

3. $8\frac{37}{56}$ $5+3=8;\ \frac{16}{56}+\frac{21}{56}=\frac{37}{56};\ 8\frac{37}{56}$

4. $10\frac{5}{12}$ $3+7=10;\ \frac{4}{24}+\frac{6}{24}=\frac{10}{24}=\frac{5}{12};\ 10\frac{5}{12}$

5. $7\frac{20}{33}$ $4+3=7;\ \frac{9}{33}+\frac{11}{33}=\frac{20}{33};\ 7\frac{20}{33}$

6. $16\frac{9}{10}$ $11+5=16;\ \frac{5}{10}+\frac{4}{10}=\frac{9}{10};16\frac{9}{10}$

7. $10\frac{4}{63}$ $4+5=9;\ \frac{49}{63}+\frac{18}{63}=\frac{67}{63}=1\frac{4}{63};9+1\frac{4}{63}$ $=10\frac{4}{63}$

8. $29\frac{13}{55}$ $13+15=28;\ \frac{33}{55}+\frac{35}{55}=\frac{68}{55}=1\frac{13}{55};$ $28+1\frac{13}{55}=29\frac{13}{55}$

9. $50\frac{17}{78}$ $22+27=49;\ \frac{65}{78}+\frac{30}{78}=\frac{95}{78}=1\frac{17}{78};$ $49+1\frac{17}{78}=50\frac{17}{78}$

10. $8\frac{27}{55}$ $1+7=8;\ \frac{5}{55}+\frac{22}{55}=\frac{27}{55};8\frac{27}{55}$

11. $58\frac{13}{18}$ $44+14=58;\ \frac{9}{18}+\frac{4}{18}=\frac{13}{18};\ 58\frac{13}{18}$

12. $20\frac{1}{21}$ $9+10=19;\ \frac{15}{21}+\frac{7}{21}=\frac{22}{21}=1\frac{1}{21};\ 19+1\frac{1}{21}=20\frac{1}{21}$

13. $6\frac{101}{117}$ $11-4=7;\ \frac{65}{117}-\frac{81}{117}=-\frac{16}{117};\ 7-\frac{16}{117}=6\frac{101}{117}$

14. $3\frac{1}{30}$ $13-10=3;\ \frac{5}{30}-\frac{4}{30}=\frac{1}{30};\ 3\frac{1}{30}$

15. $1\frac{1}{2}$ $15-14=1;\ \frac{4}{6}-\frac{1}{6}=\frac{3}{6}=\frac{1}{2};\ 1\frac{1}{2}$

16. $9\frac{11}{36}$ $20-11=9;\ \frac{27}{36}-\frac{16}{36}=\frac{11}{36};\ 9\frac{11}{36}$

17. $10\frac{5}{42}$ $13-3=10;\ \frac{35}{42}-\frac{30}{42}=\frac{5}{42};\ 10\frac{5}{42}$

18. $4\frac{19}{55}$ $23-19=4;\ \frac{44}{55}-\frac{25}{55}=\frac{19}{55};\ 4\frac{19}{55}$

19. $9\frac{19}{22}$ $13-3=10;\ \frac{8}{22}-\frac{11}{22}=-\frac{3}{22};\ 10-\frac{3}{22}=9\frac{19}{22}$

20. $\frac{8}{9}$ $11-10=1;\ \frac{6}{9}-\frac{7}{9}=-\frac{1}{9};\ 1-\frac{1}{9}=\frac{8}{9}$

21. $36\frac{2}{51}$ $77-41=36;\ \frac{17}{51}-\frac{15}{51}=\frac{2}{51};\ 36\frac{2}{51}$

22. $6\frac{1}{2}$ $9-3=6;\ \frac{10}{14}-\frac{3}{14}=\frac{7}{14}=\frac{1}{2};\ 6\frac{1}{2}$

23. $19\frac{19}{40}$ $31-12=19;\ \frac{35}{40}-\frac{16}{40}=\frac{19}{40};\ 19\frac{19}{40}$

24. $12\frac{19}{21}$ $45-32=13;\ \frac{7}{21}-\frac{9}{21}=-\frac{2}{21};\ 13-\frac{2}{21}=12\frac{19}{21}$

Lesson 3.6

1. $\frac{2}{5}$ $\frac{8}{20}\div\frac{4}{4}=\frac{2}{5}$

2. $\frac{1}{12}$ $\frac{49}{588}\div\frac{49}{49}=\frac{1}{12}$

3. $\frac{5}{18}$ $\frac{525}{1890}\div\frac{15}{15}=\frac{35}{126}\div\frac{7}{7}=\frac{5}{18}$

4. $\frac{3}{55}$ $\frac{168}{3080}\div\frac{8}{8}=\frac{21}{385}\div\frac{7}{7}=\frac{3}{55}$

5. $\frac{4}{25}$ $\frac{24}{150}\div\frac{6}{6}=\frac{4}{25}$

6. $\frac{3}{91}$ $\frac{18}{546}\div\frac{6}{6}=\frac{3}{91}$

7. $\frac{5}{14}$ $\frac{120}{336}\div\frac{12}{12}=\frac{10}{28}\div\frac{2}{2}=\frac{5}{14}$

8. $\frac{22}{65}$ $\frac{220}{650}\div\frac{10}{10}=\frac{22}{65}$

9. $\frac{1}{6}$ $\frac{3}{18}\div\frac{3}{3}=\frac{1}{6}$

10. $\frac{21}{55}$ $\frac{42}{110}\div\frac{2}{2}=\frac{21}{55}$

11. $\frac{39}{68}$ $\frac{3276}{5712}\div\frac{12}{12}=\frac{273}{476}\div\frac{7}{7}=\frac{39}{68}$

12. $\frac{343}{1000}$ $\frac{686}{2000}\div\frac{2}{2}=\frac{343}{1000}$

13. $\frac{2}{3}$ $\frac{210}{315}\div\frac{5}{5}=\frac{42}{63}\div\frac{21}{21}=\frac{2}{3}$

14. $\frac{1}{8}$ $\frac{66}{528}\div\frac{66}{66}=\frac{1}{8}$

15. $\frac{12}{55}$ $\frac{360}{1650}\div\frac{30}{30}=\frac{12}{55}$

16. $\frac{91}{256}$ $\frac{182}{512}\div\frac{2}{2}=\frac{91}{256}$

Chapter 4: Multiplying Fractions

Lesson 4.1

1. $3\frac{1}{4}$ $\frac{13}{4}=3\frac{1}{4}$

2. $4\frac{2}{7}$ $\frac{30}{7}=4\frac{2}{7}$

3. $8\frac{1}{4}$ Reduce first: $11\times\frac{3}{4}=\frac{33}{4}=8\frac{1}{4}$

4. 18 Reduce first: $6\times\frac{3}{1}=18$

5. $6\frac{3}{10}$ Reduce first: $\frac{9}{1}\times\frac{7}{10}=\frac{63}{10}=6\frac{3}{10}$

6. $3\frac{11}{17}$ $\frac{62}{17}=3\frac{11}{17}$

7. $1\frac{3}{4}$ Reduce first: $1\times\frac{7}{4}=\frac{7}{4}=1\frac{3}{4}$

Answers and Explanations

8. $12\frac{8}{11}$ $\frac{140}{11}=12\frac{8}{11}$

9. $2\frac{2}{9}$ Reduce first: $4\times\frac{5}{9}=\frac{20}{9}=2\frac{2}{9}$

10. $4\frac{2}{3}$ $\frac{14}{3}=4\frac{2}{3}$

11. $9\frac{3}{5}$ $\frac{48}{5}=9\frac{3}{5}$

12. $5\frac{1}{2}$ Reduce first: $1\times\frac{11}{2}=\frac{11}{2}=5\frac{1}{2}$

13. $37\frac{5}{7}$ $\frac{264}{7}=37\frac{5}{7}$

14. $11\frac{1}{2}$ Reduce first: $1\times\frac{23}{2}=\frac{23}{2}=11\frac{1}{2}$

15. 18 Reduce first: $3\times\frac{6}{1}=18$

16. $8\frac{8}{9}$ Reduce first: $5\times\frac{16}{9}=\frac{80}{9}=8\frac{8}{9}$

17. $17\frac{1}{2}$ gallons Reduce first: $28\times\frac{5}{8}=7\times\frac{5}{2}=\frac{35}{2}=17\frac{1}{2}$

18. $10\frac{2}{7}$ hours $8\times\frac{9}{7}=\frac{72}{7}=10\frac{2}{7}$

Lesson 4.2

1. $\frac{2}{3}$ $\frac{\cancel{3}^{1}}{\cancel{2}_{1}}\times\frac{\cancel{4}^{2}}{\cancel{9}_{3}}=\frac{2}{3}$

2. $\frac{2}{9}$ $\frac{\cancel{5}^{1}}{\cancel{9}_{3}}\times\frac{\cancel{12}^{4}}{\cancel{30}_{6}}=\frac{4}{18}=\frac{2}{9}$

3. $\frac{6}{35}$ $\frac{\cancel{15}^{5}}{\cancel{21}_{7}}\times\frac{6}{25}=\frac{\cancel{5}^{1}}{7}\times\frac{6}{\cancel{25}_{5}}=\frac{6}{35}$

4. $\frac{1}{4}$ $\frac{1}{2}\times\frac{1}{2}=\frac{1}{4}$

5. $\frac{1}{2}$ $\frac{\cancel{2}^{1}}{\cancel{3}_{1}}\times\frac{\cancel{3}^{1}}{\cancel{4}_{2}}=\frac{1}{2}$

6. $\frac{4}{7}$ $\frac{\cancel{5}^{1}}{\cancel{4}_{1}}\times\frac{\cancel{16}^{4}}{\cancel{35}_{7}}=\frac{4}{7}$

7. $\frac{1}{10}$ $\frac{\cancel{5}^{1}}{\cancel{18}_{2}}\times\frac{\cancel{9}^{1}}{\cancel{25}_{5}}=\frac{1}{10}$

8. $\frac{1}{8}$ $\frac{\cancel{4}^{1}}{\cancel{14}_{1}}\times\frac{\cancel{28}^{2}}{\cancel{64}_{16}}=\frac{2}{16}=\frac{1}{8}$

9. $\frac{1}{2}$ $\frac{\cancel{13}^{1}}{\cancel{22}_{2}}\times\frac{\cancel{11}^{1}}{\cancel{13}_{1}}=\frac{1}{2}$

10. $\frac{2}{3}$ $\frac{\cancel{12}^{1}}{\cancel{13}_{1}}\times\frac{\cancel{52}^{4}}{\cancel{72}_{6}}=\frac{4}{6}=\frac{2}{3}$

11. $\frac{4}{225}$ $\frac{2}{15}\times\frac{2}{15}=\frac{4}{225}$

12. $\frac{1}{5}$ $\frac{\cancel{21}^{3}}{\cancel{24}_{3}}\times\frac{\cancel{8}^{1}}{\cancel{35}_{5}}=\frac{3}{15}=\frac{1}{5}$

13. $1\frac{1}{2}$ $\frac{\cancel{48}^{3}}{\cancel{21}_{1}}\times\frac{\cancel{42}^{2}}{\cancel{64}_{4}}=\frac{6}{4}=\frac{3}{2}=1\frac{1}{2}$

14. $\frac{1}{2}$ $\frac{\cancel{7}^{1}}{\cancel{9}_{1}}\times\frac{\cancel{9}^{1}}{\cancel{14}_{2}}=\frac{1}{2}$

15. $\frac{3}{10}$ $\frac{\cancel{15}^{3}}{\cancel{18}_{2}}\times\frac{\cancel{9}^{1}}{\cancel{25}_{5}}=\frac{3}{10}$

16. $\frac{4}{9}$ $\frac{\cancel{10}^{2}}{\cancel{13}_{1}}\times\frac{\cancel{26}^{2}}{\cancel{45}_{9}}=\frac{4}{9}$

17. $\frac{5}{64}$ miles $\frac{1}{4}\times\frac{5}{16}=\frac{5}{64}$ mile

18. $1\frac{2}{9}$ gallons $\frac{\cancel{22}^{11}}{\cancel{6}_{3}}\times\frac{1}{3}=\frac{11}{9}=1\frac{2}{9}$ gal

Lesson 4.3

1. $\frac{3}{4}$ $\frac{\cancel{27}^{3}}{4}\times\frac{1}{\cancel{9}_{1}}=\frac{3}{4}$

2. $\frac{5}{12}$ $\frac{1}{\cancel{10}_{2}}\times\frac{\cancel{25}^{5}}{6}=\frac{5}{12}$

3. $3\frac{1}{2}$ $\frac{\cancel{49}^{7}}{\cancel{4}_{2}}\times\frac{\cancel{2}^{1}}{\cancel{7}_{1}}=\frac{7}{2}=3\frac{1}{2}$

4. 4 $\frac{\cancel{22}^{2}}{\cancel{7}_{1}}\times\frac{\cancel{14}^{2}}{\cancel{11}_{1}}=\frac{4}{1}=4$

5. $1\frac{1}{2}$ $\frac{\cancel{2}^{1}}{\cancel{5}_{1}}\times\frac{\cancel{15}^{3}}{\cancel{4}_{2}}=\frac{3}{2}=1\frac{1}{2}$

6. 3 $\frac{\cancel{33}^{3}}{\cancel{7}_{1}}\times\frac{\cancel{7}^{1}}{\cancel{11}_{1}}=\frac{3}{1}=3$

7. $1\frac{1}{5}$ $\frac{\cancel{22}^{2}}{5}\times\frac{3}{\cancel{11}_{1}}=\frac{6}{5}=1\frac{1}{5}$

8. 1 $\frac{\cancel{13}^{1}}{\cancel{4}_{1}}\times\frac{\cancel{4}^{1}}{\cancel{13}_{1}}=1$

9. 4 $\frac{\cancel{18}^{2}}{5_{1}}\times\frac{\cancel{10}^{2}}{\cancel{9}_{1}}=\frac{4}{1}=4$

10. 1 $\frac{\cancel{3}^{1}}{\cancel{13}_{1}}\times\frac{\cancel{13}^{1}}{\cancel{3}_{1}}=\frac{1}{1}=1$

11. $\frac{2}{3}$ $\frac{\cancel{11}^{1}}{3}\times\frac{2}{\cancel{11}_{1}}=\frac{2}{3}$

12. $1\frac{1}{5}$ $\frac{\cancel{26}^{2}}{5}\times\frac{3}{\cancel{13}_{1}}=\frac{6}{5}=1\frac{1}{5}$

13. $1\frac{3}{4}$ $\frac{\cancel{21}^{7}}{4}\times\frac{1}{\cancel{3}_{1}}=\frac{7}{4}=1\frac{3}{4}$

14. $\frac{4}{5}$ $\quad \frac{\cancel{14}^{2}}{5}\times\frac{2}{\cancel{7}_{1}}=\frac{4}{5}$

15. $\frac{27}{40}$ $\quad \frac{9}{4}\times\frac{3}{10}=\frac{27}{40}$

16. 2 $\quad \frac{\cancel{10}^{2}}{\cancel{3}_{1}}\times\frac{\cancel{3}^{1}}{\cancel{5}_{1}}=\frac{2}{1}=2$

17. $15\frac{3}{10}$ yards $\quad \frac{\cancel{102}^{51}}{5}\times\frac{3}{\cancel{4}_{2}}=\frac{153}{10}=15\frac{3}{10}$ yards

18. $2\frac{1}{4}$ hours $\quad \frac{\cancel{27}^{9}}{\cancel{8}_{4}}\times\frac{\cancel{2}^{1}}{\cancel{3}_{1}}=\frac{9}{4}=2\frac{1}{4}$ yards

Lesson 4.4

1. $20\frac{5}{8}$ $\quad \frac{11}{2}\times\frac{15}{4}=\frac{165}{8}=20\frac{5}{8}$

2. $6\frac{8}{15}$ $\quad \frac{7}{3}\times\frac{14}{5}=\frac{98}{15}=6\frac{8}{15}$

3. $25\frac{27}{35}$ $\quad \frac{41}{5}\times\frac{22}{7}=\frac{902}{35}=25\frac{27}{35}$

4. $21\frac{7}{12}$ $\quad \frac{7}{4}\times\frac{37}{3}=\frac{259}{12}=21\frac{7}{12}$

5. $11\frac{2}{3}$ $\quad \frac{5}{\cancel{2}_{1}}\times\frac{\cancel{14}^{7}}{3}=\frac{35}{3}=11\frac{2}{3}$

6. $9\frac{23}{28}$ $\quad \frac{25}{\cancel{8}_{4}}\times\frac{\cancel{22}^{11}}{7}=\frac{275}{28}=9\frac{23}{28}$

7. $74\frac{2}{3}$ $\quad \frac{56}{\cancel{5}_{1}}\times\frac{\cancel{20}^{4}}{3}=\frac{224}{3}=74\frac{2}{3}$

8. $49\frac{2}{5}$ $\quad \frac{19}{\cancel{2}_{1}}\times\frac{\cancel{26}^{13}}{5}=\frac{247}{5}=49\frac{2}{5}$

9. 12 $\quad \frac{\cancel{5}^{1}}{\cancel{3}_{1}}\times\frac{\cancel{36}^{12}}{\cancel{5}_{1}}=\frac{12}{1}=12$

10. $30\frac{5}{8}$ $\quad \frac{35}{4}\times\frac{7}{2}=\frac{245}{8}=30\frac{5}{8}$

11. $19\frac{1}{32}$ $\quad \frac{29}{8}\times\frac{21}{4}=\frac{609}{32}=19\frac{1}{32}$

12. 21 $\quad \frac{\cancel{14}^{7}}{\cancel{3}_{1}}\times\frac{\cancel{9}^{3}}{\cancel{2}_{1}}=\frac{21}{1}=21$

13. $6\frac{18}{25}$ $\quad \frac{\cancel{16}^{8}}{5}\times\frac{21}{\cancel{10}_{5}}=\frac{168}{25}=6\frac{18}{25}$

14. $22\frac{32}{55}$ $\quad \frac{54}{5}\times\frac{23}{11}=\frac{1242}{55}=22\frac{32}{55}$

15. $36\frac{4}{45}$ $\quad \frac{203}{9}\times\frac{8}{5}=\frac{1624}{45}=36\frac{4}{45}$

16. $40\frac{1}{28}$ $\quad \frac{59}{4}\times\frac{19}{7}=\frac{1121}{28}=40\frac{1}{28}$

Chapter 5: Dividing Fractions

Lesson 5.1

1. $\frac{3}{8}$ $\quad \frac{3}{2\times4}=\frac{3}{8}$

2. $\frac{3}{32}$ $\quad \frac{6}{16}=\frac{3}{8};\frac{3}{8}\div4=\frac{3}{8\times4}=\frac{3}{32}$

3. $\frac{2}{27}$ $\quad \frac{\cancel{6}^{2}}{27\times\cancel{3}_{1}}=\frac{2}{27}$

4. $\frac{1}{48}$ $\quad \frac{1}{12\times4}=\frac{1}{48}$

5. $\frac{3}{19}$ $\quad \frac{18}{57}=\frac{6}{19};\frac{6}{19}\div2=\frac{\cancel{6}^{3}}{19\times\cancel{2}_{1}}=\frac{3}{19}$

6. $\frac{2}{15}$ $\quad \frac{\cancel{14}^{2}}{15\times\cancel{7}_{1}}=\frac{2}{15}$

7. $\frac{4}{81}$ $\quad \frac{4}{9\times9}=\frac{4}{81}$

8. $\frac{1}{18}$ $\quad \frac{\cancel{12}^{1}}{18\times\cancel{12}_{1}}=\frac{1}{18}$

9. $\frac{2}{11}$ $\quad \frac{\cancel{16}^{4}}{22\times\cancel{4}_{1}}=\frac{4}{22}=\frac{2}{11}$

10. $\frac{5}{19}$ $\quad \frac{\cancel{15}^{5}}{19\times\cancel{3}_{1}}=\frac{5}{19}$

11. $\frac{2}{31}$ $\quad \frac{\cancel{12}^{2}}{31\times\cancel{6}_{1}}=\frac{2}{31}$

12. $\frac{11}{252}$ $\quad \frac{\cancel{55}^{11}}{63\times\cancel{20}_{4}}=\frac{11}{252}$

13. $\frac{1}{159}$ $\quad \frac{\cancel{33}^{3}}{477\times\cancel{11}_{1}}=\frac{3}{477}=\frac{1}{159}$

14. $\frac{1}{42}$ $\quad \frac{\cancel{3}^{1}}{14\times\cancel{9}_{3}}=\frac{1}{42}$

15. $\frac{3}{31}$ $\quad \frac{\cancel{15}^{3}}{31\times\cancel{5}_{1}}=\frac{3}{31}$

16. $\frac{4}{63}$ $\quad \frac{\cancel{16}^{4}}{63\times\cancel{4}_{1}}=\frac{4}{63}$

17. $\frac{3}{32}$ pounds each $\quad \frac{3}{4}\div8=\frac{3}{4\times8}=\frac{3}{32}$

18. $\frac{6}{25}$ yards $\quad \frac{18}{25}\div3=\frac{\cancel{18}^{6}}{25\times\cancel{3}_{1}}=\frac{6}{25}$

Lesson 5.2

1. 50 $\quad 5\times\frac{10}{1}=50$

2. 15 $\quad \cancel{9}^{3}\times\frac{5}{\cancel{3}_{1}}=15$

Answers and Explanations

3. 16 $\quad \cancel{14}^{2} \times \frac{8}{\cancel{7}_{1}} = 16$

4. 27 $\quad \cancel{12}^{3} \times \frac{9}{\cancel{4}_{1}} = 27$

5. 16 $\quad \cancel{12}^{4} \times \frac{4}{\cancel{3}_{1}} = 16$

6. 54 $\quad \cancel{42}^{6} \times \frac{9}{\cancel{7}_{1}} = 54$

7. 72 $\quad \cancel{45}^{9} \times \frac{8}{\cancel{5}_{1}} = 72$

8. 84 $\quad \cancel{24}^{12} \times \frac{7}{\cancel{2}_{1}} = 84$

9. 40 $\quad \cancel{16}^{8} \times \frac{5}{\cancel{2}_{1}} = 40$

10. $13\frac{1}{3}$ $\quad 5 \times \frac{8}{3} = \frac{40}{3} = 13\frac{1}{3}$

11. 28 $\quad \cancel{16}^{4} \times \frac{7}{\cancel{4}_{1}} = 28$

12. 143 $\quad \cancel{39}^{13} \times \frac{11}{\cancel{3}_{1}} = 143$

13. 55 $\quad \cancel{15}^{5} \times \frac{11}{\cancel{3}_{1}} = 55$

14. 8 $\quad \cancel{14}^{2} \times \frac{4}{\cancel{7}_{1}} = 8$

15. 99 $\quad \cancel{27}^{9} \times \frac{11}{\cancel{3}_{1}} = 99$

16. 88 $\quad \cancel{33}^{11} \times \frac{8}{\cancel{3}_{1}} = 88$

17. 225 packages $\quad 60 \div \frac{4}{15} = \cancel{60}^{15} \times \frac{15}{\cancel{4}_{1}} = 225$

18. 25 stops $\quad 20 \div \frac{4}{5} = \cancel{20}^{5} \times \frac{5}{\cancel{4}_{1}} = 25$

Lesson 5.3

1. $\frac{16}{7}$ $\quad \frac{\cancel{6}^{2}}{7} \times \frac{8}{\cancel{3}_{1}} = \frac{16}{7} = 2\frac{2}{7}$

2. $\frac{16}{7}$ $\quad \frac{\cancel{4}^{2}}{\cancel{14}_{7}} \times \frac{\cancel{16}^{8}}{\cancel{2}} = \frac{16}{7} = 2\frac{2}{7}$

3. $\frac{14}{27}$ $\quad \frac{2}{9} \times \frac{7}{3} = \frac{14}{27}$

4. 2 $\quad \frac{1}{\cancel{4}_{1}} \times \frac{\cancel{8}^{2}}{1} = \frac{2}{1} = 2$

5. $\frac{9}{13}$ $\quad \frac{\cancel{5}^{1}}{13} \times \frac{9}{\cancel{5}_{1}} = \frac{9}{13}$

6. $\frac{49}{9}$ $\quad \frac{7}{9} \times \frac{7}{1} = \frac{49}{9} = 5\frac{4}{9}$

7. $\frac{3}{13}$ $\quad \frac{1}{13} \times \frac{3}{1} = \frac{3}{13}$

8. $\frac{5}{2}$ $\quad \frac{5}{\cancel{17}_{1}} \times \frac{\cancel{17}^{1}}{2} = \frac{5}{2} = 2\frac{1}{2}$

9. $\frac{16}{5}$ $\quad \frac{4}{5} \times \frac{4}{1} = \frac{16}{5} = 3\frac{1}{5}$

10. $\frac{3}{8}$ $\quad \frac{\cancel{15}^{3}}{\cancel{24}_{8}} \times \frac{\cancel{3}^{1}}{\cancel{5}_{1}} = \frac{3}{8}$

11. $\frac{42}{121}$ $\quad \frac{6}{11} \times \frac{7}{11} = \frac{42}{121}$

12. $\frac{1}{2}$ $\quad \frac{\cancel{13}^{1}}{\cancel{17}_{1}} \times \frac{\cancel{17}^{1}}{\cancel{26}_{2}} = \frac{1}{2}$

13. $\frac{9}{22}$ $\quad \frac{3}{\cancel{11}_{1}} \times \frac{\cancel{33}^{3}}{22} = \frac{9}{22}$

14. 3 $\quad \frac{\cancel{4}^{1}}{\cancel{7}_{1}} \times \frac{\cancel{21}^{3}}{\cancel{4}_{1}} = \frac{3}{1} = 3$

15. $\frac{3}{2}$ $\quad \frac{\cancel{9}^{3}}{\cancel{14}_{2}} \times \frac{\cancel{7}^{1}}{\cancel{3}_{1}} = \frac{3}{2} = 1\frac{1}{2}$

16. $\frac{9}{25}$ $\quad \frac{3}{5} \times \frac{3}{5} = \frac{9}{25}$

17. 14 muffins $\quad \frac{7}{8} \div \frac{1}{16} = \frac{7}{\cancel{8}_{1}} \times \frac{\cancel{16}^{2}}{1} = 14$

18. $7\frac{1}{2}$ miles $\quad \frac{15}{16} \div \frac{1}{8} = \frac{15}{\cancel{16}_{2}} \times \frac{\cancel{8}^{1}}{1} = \frac{15}{2} = 7\frac{1}{2}$

Lesson 5.4

1. $1\frac{5}{14}$ $\quad \frac{19}{6} \div \frac{7}{3} = \frac{19}{\cancel{6}_{2}} \times \frac{\cancel{3}^{1}}{7} = \frac{19}{14} = 1\frac{5}{14}$

2. $1\frac{59}{189}$ $\quad \frac{31}{7} \div \frac{27}{8} = \frac{31}{7} \times \frac{8}{27} = \frac{248}{189} = 1\frac{59}{189}$

3. $2\frac{1}{28}$ $\quad \frac{38}{7} \div \frac{8}{3} = \frac{\cancel{38}^{19}}{7} \times \frac{3}{\cancel{8}_{4}} = \frac{57}{28} = 2\frac{1}{28}$

4. $1\frac{122}{207}$ $\quad \frac{47}{9} \div \frac{23}{7} = \frac{47}{9} \times \frac{7}{23} = \frac{329}{207} = 1\frac{122}{207}$

5. $2\frac{1}{18}$ $\quad \frac{37}{5} \div \frac{18}{5} = \frac{37}{\cancel{5}_{1}} \times \frac{\cancel{5}^{1}}{18} = \frac{37}{18} = 2\frac{1}{18}$

6. $1\frac{3}{4}$ $\quad \frac{17}{4} \div \frac{17}{7} = \frac{\cancel{17}^{1}}{4} \times \frac{7}{\cancel{17}_{1}} = \frac{7}{4} = 1\frac{3}{4}$

7. $1\frac{2}{29}$ $\quad \frac{31}{9} \div \frac{29}{9} = \frac{31}{\cancel{9}_{1}} \times \frac{\cancel{9}^{1}}{29} = \frac{31}{29} = 1\frac{2}{29}$

8. $\frac{74}{121}$ $\quad \frac{37}{11} \div \frac{11}{2} = \frac{37}{11} \times \frac{2}{11} = \frac{74}{121}$

9. $1\frac{73}{104}$ $\quad \frac{59}{13} \div \frac{8}{3} = \frac{59}{13} \times \frac{3}{8} = \frac{177}{104} = 1\frac{73}{104}$

10. $2\frac{30}{169}$ $\quad \frac{46}{13} \div \frac{13}{8} = \frac{46}{13} \times \frac{8}{13} = \frac{368}{169} = 2\frac{30}{169}$

11. $\frac{117}{140}$ $\quad \frac{13}{7} \div \frac{20}{9} = \frac{13}{7} \times \frac{9}{20} = \frac{117}{140}$

12. $1\frac{14}{15}$ $\quad \frac{29}{8} \div \frac{15}{8} = \frac{29}{\cancel{8}_1} \times \frac{\cancel{8}^1}{15} = \frac{29}{15} = 1\frac{14}{15}$

13. $\frac{54}{91}$ $\quad \frac{18}{7} \div \frac{13}{3} = \frac{18}{7} \times \frac{3}{13} = \frac{54}{91}$

14. $2\frac{3}{5}$ $\quad \frac{13}{2} \div \frac{5}{2} = \frac{13}{\cancel{2}_1} \times \frac{\cancel{2}^1}{5} = \frac{13}{5} = 2\frac{3}{5}$

15. $4\frac{2}{9}$ $\quad \frac{38}{5} \div \frac{9}{5} = \frac{38}{\cancel{5}_1} \times \frac{\cancel{5}^1}{9} = \frac{38}{9} = 4\frac{2}{9}$

16. $\frac{7}{18}$ $\quad \frac{11}{9} \div \frac{22}{7} = \frac{\cancel{11}^1}{9} \times \frac{7}{\cancel{22}_2} = \frac{7}{18}$

17. $2\frac{1}{7}$ miles per hour $\quad 3\frac{3}{4} \div 1\frac{3}{4} = \frac{15}{4} \div \frac{7}{4} = \frac{15}{\cancel{4}_1} \times \frac{\cancel{4}^1}{7} = \frac{15}{7} = 2\frac{1}{7}$

18. $5\frac{17}{20}$ pounds $\quad 14\frac{5}{8} \div 2\frac{1}{2} = \frac{117}{8} \div \frac{5}{2} = \frac{117}{\cancel{8}_4} \times \frac{\cancel{2}^1}{5} = \frac{117}{20} = 5\frac{17}{20}$

Chapter 6: Understanding Decimals

Lesson 6.1

1. 49
2. 98
3. 157
4. 3027
5. 189
6. 2245
7. 280
8. 429
9. 124.6
10. 175.5
11. 349.5
12. 313.4
13. 375.8
14. 44.0
15. 567.0
16. 61.2
17. 1536.34
18. 32.46
19. 119.00
20. 523.76
21. 1099.99
22. 1.12
23. 33.44
24. 555.56
25. 729.240
26. 409.134
27. 8056.708
28. 549.595
29. 99.800
30. 177.556
31. 2012.205
32. 901.901

Lesson 6.2

1. 1.313

$$\begin{array}{r} 0.3125 \\ 1+16\overline{)\,5.00} \\ \underline{48} \\ 20 \\ \underline{16} \\ 40 \\ \underline{32} \\ 80 \\ \underline{80} \\ 0 \end{array}$$

2. 2.571

$$\begin{array}{r} 0.5714\ldots \\ 2+7\overline{)\,4.000} \\ \underline{35} \\ 50 \\ \underline{49} \\ 10 \\ \underline{7} \\ 30 \\ \underline{28} \\ 2\ldots \end{array}$$

3. 0.240

$$\begin{array}{r} 0.24 \\ 200\overline{)48.00} \\ \underline{400} \\ 800 \\ \underline{800} \\ 0 \end{array}$$

4. 3.750

$$\begin{array}{r} 0.75 \\ 3+500\overline{)375.00} \\ \underline{3500} \\ 2500 \\ \underline{2500} \\ 0 \end{array}$$

5. 0.030

$$\begin{array}{r} 0.03 \\ 200\overline{)6.00} \\ \underline{600} \\ 0 \end{array}$$

6. 7.394

$$\begin{array}{r} 0.39393\ldots \\ 7+33\overline{)13.0000} \\ \underline{99} \\ 310 \\ \underline{297} \\ 130 \\ \underline{99} \\ 310 \\ \underline{297} \\ 130\ldots \end{array}$$

Answers and Explanations

7. 0.333

$$\begin{array}{r} 0.33\ldots \\ 156\overline{)52.000} \\ \underline{468} \\ 520 \\ \underline{468} \\ 520\ldots \end{array}$$

8. 4.733

$$\begin{array}{r} 0.7333\ldots \\ 4+15\overline{)\ 11.0000} \\ \underline{105} \\ 50 \\ \underline{45} \\ 50 \\ \underline{45} \\ 50\ldots \end{array}$$

9. 1.001

$$\begin{array}{r} 0.0005 \\ 1+2000\overline{)1.0000} \\ \underline{10000} \\ 0 \end{array}$$

10. 2.440

$$\begin{array}{r} 0.44 \\ 2+75\overline{)33.0} \\ \underline{300} \\ 300 \\ \underline{300} \\ 0 \end{array}$$

Lesson 6.3

1. $\frac{13}{10}$ $1\frac{3}{10}=\frac{13}{10}$
2. $\frac{3}{5}$ $\frac{6}{10}=\frac{3}{5}$
3. $\frac{147}{250}$ $\frac{588}{1000}=\frac{147}{250}$
4. $\frac{31}{8}$ $3+\frac{875}{1000}=3+\frac{35}{40}=3+\frac{7}{8}=\frac{31}{8}$
5. $\frac{27}{4}$ $6+\frac{75}{100}=6+\frac{3}{4}=\frac{27}{4}$
6. $\frac{9}{8}$ $1+\frac{125}{1000}=1+\frac{5}{40}=1+\frac{1}{8}=\frac{9}{8}$
7. $\frac{163}{50}$ $3+\frac{26}{100}=3+\frac{13}{50}=\frac{163}{50}$
8. $\frac{13}{40}$ $\frac{325}{1000}=\frac{13}{40}$
9. $\frac{5}{8}$ $\frac{625}{1000}=\frac{25}{40}=\frac{5}{8}$
10. $\frac{3}{4}$ $\frac{75}{100}=\frac{3}{4}$

Lesson 6.4

1. 0.1332, 1.031, 1.3, 1.322, 1.5, 1.505, 1.55, 13.1
2. 0.075, 0.34, 0.705, 0.75, 0.751, 1.675, 1.68, 7.51
3. 0.00175, 0.01695, 0.017, 0.107, 0.17, 1.07, 1.7
4. 0.405, 0.415, 0.420, 0.45, 0.451, 0.625, 1.4
5. 0.333, 0.33, 0.25, 0.155, 0.15, 0.125
6. 1.001, 0.334, 0.3334, 0.332, 0.3033, 0.3, 0.0335
7. 0.751, 0.7501, 0.75, 0.707, 0.667, 0.6667, 0.6
8. 0.68, 0.6665, 0.63, 0.6, 0.59996, 0.55, 0.06665

Chapter 7: Adding and Subtracting Decimals

Lesson 7.1

1. 167.9817

$$\begin{array}{r} 145.4150 \\ 22.1000 \\ +\ 0.4667 \\ \hline 167.9817 \end{array}$$

2. 838.131

$$\begin{array}{r} 436.911 \\ +401.220 \\ \hline 838.131 \end{array}$$

3. 139.011543

$$\begin{array}{r} 57.477000 \\ 81.534000 \\ +\ 0.000543 \\ \hline 139.011543 \end{array}$$

4. 20.2349

$$\begin{array}{r} 12.2320 \\ 3.0010 \\ +5.0019 \\ \hline 20.2349 \end{array}$$

5. 76.156

$$\begin{array}{r} 73.045 \\ 0.011 \\ +3.100 \\ \hline 76.156 \end{array}$$

6. 24.31

$$\begin{array}{r} 11.0809 \\ +13.2291 \\ \hline 24.3100 \end{array}$$

7. 16.948

$$\begin{array}{r} 0.882 \\ 15.600 \\ +0.466 \\ \hline 16.948 \end{array}$$

8. 46.4309

$$\begin{array}{r} 44.3200 \\ +2.1109 \\ \hline 46.4309 \end{array}$$

9. 34.2252 meters

$$\begin{array}{r} 11.3240 \\ 12.6742 \\ +10.2270 \\ \hline 34.2252 \end{array}$$

10. 3.8463 inches

$$\begin{array}{r} 1.9030 \\ 1.6778 \\ +1.2655 \\ \hline 3.8463 \end{array}$$

Lesson 7.2

1. 11.9375

6 1 7 11 1

$$\begin{array}{r} 17.3820 \\ -5.4445 \\ \hline 11.9375 \end{array}$$

2. 12.4382

7 9 9 10 1

$$\begin{array}{r} 28.0010 \\ -15.5628 \\ \hline 12.4382 \end{array}$$

3. 100.3899

$$\begin{array}{r} {\scriptstyle 7\,16\,9\,1} \\ 102.8700 \\ -2.4801 \\ \hline 100.3899 \end{array}$$

4. 4.7797

$$\begin{array}{r} {\scriptstyle 7\ \ 12\ 10\ 9\ 1} \\ 38.3102 \\ -33.5305 \\ \hline 4.7797 \end{array}$$

5. 5.5563

$$\begin{array}{r} {\scriptstyle 12\ \ 12\ 12\ 1} \\ 13.3333 \\ -7.7770 \\ \hline 5.5563 \end{array}$$

6. 13.7372

$$\begin{array}{r} {\scriptstyle 8\ \ 10\ 10\ 1} \\ 19.1113 \\ -5.3741 \\ \hline 13.7372 \end{array}$$

7. 462.6875

$$\begin{array}{r} {\scriptstyle 4\ \ 9\ 9\ 11\ 1} \\ 575.0020 \\ -112.3145 \\ \hline 462.6875 \end{array}$$

8. 2.16069

$$\begin{array}{r} {\scriptstyle 8\ \ 1\ 6\ 9\ 10\ 1} \\ 9.07010 \\ -6.90941 \\ \hline 2.16069 \end{array}$$

9. 0.384 meters

$$\begin{array}{r} {\scriptstyle 7\ 17\ 1} \\ 5.8833 \\ -5.4993 \\ \hline 0.3840 \end{array}$$

10. 8.0284 inches

$$\begin{array}{r} {\scriptstyle 6\ 13\ 1} \\ 9.7740 \\ -1.7456 \\ \hline 8.0284 \end{array}$$

Chapter 8: Multiplying and Dividing Decimals

Lesson 8.1

1. 478.17 — $189 \times 253 = 47,817$ and there are 2 decimal places, so 478.17
2. 17.45458 — $718 \times 2431 = 1745,458$ and there are 5 decimal places, so 17.45458
3. 62.625 — $15 \times 4175 = 62,625$ and there are 3 decimal places, so 62.625
4. 11.9391 — $17 \times 7023 = 119,391$ and there are 4 decimal places, so 11.9391
5. 598.29 — $77 \times 7770 = 598,290$ and there are 3 decimal places, so 598.290
6. 36.3 — $15 \times 242 = 3630$ and there are 2 decimal places, so 36.30
7. 145.6 — $16 \times 91 = 1456$ and there is 1 decimal place, so 145.6
8. 348.315 — $55 \times 6333 = 348,315$ and there are 3 decimal places, so 348.315
9. 33.3 gallons — $12 \times 2775 = 33,300$ and there are 3 decimal places, so 33.300
10. Yes, the total weight of the packages is 880.3328 pounds — $64 \times 137552 = 8,803,328$ and there are 4 decimal places so 880.3328

Lesson 8.2

1. 74.28

$$\begin{array}{r} 74.279\ldots \\ 4.51.\overline{)335.00.00} \\ 3157 \\ \hline 1930 \\ 1804 \\ \hline 1260 \\ 902 \\ \hline 3580 \\ 3157 \\ \hline 4230 \\ 4059 \\ \hline 171\ldots \end{array}$$

2. 58.59

$$\begin{array}{r} 58.591\ldots \\ 7.1.\overline{)416.0.000} \\ 355 \\ \hline 610 \\ 568 \\ \hline 420 \\ 355 \\ \hline 650 \\ 639 \\ \hline 110 \\ 71 \\ \hline 39\ldots \end{array}$$

3. 27.76

$$\begin{array}{r} 27.756\ldots \\ 7.71.\overline{)214.00.000} \\ 1542 \\ \hline 5980 \\ 5397 \\ \hline 5830 \\ 5397 \\ \hline 4330 \\ 3855 \\ \hline 4750 \\ 4626 \\ \hline 124\ldots \end{array}$$

4. 1.65

$$\begin{array}{r} 1.65 \\ 88\overline{)145.20} \\ 88 \\ \hline 572 \\ 528 \\ \hline 440 \\ 440 \\ \hline 0 \end{array}$$

5. 0.65

$$\begin{array}{r} 0.65 \\ 88\overline{)24.05} \\ 222 \\ \hline 185 \\ 185 \\ \hline 0 \end{array}$$

6. 20.00

$$\begin{array}{r} 20.0 \\ 2.24.\overline{)44.80.} \\ 448 \\ \hline 0 \end{array}$$

Answers and Explanations

7. 2.22

$$\begin{array}{r} 2.22 \\ 25\overline{)55.50} \\ \underline{50} \\ 55 \\ \underline{50} \\ 50 \\ \underline{50} \\ 0 \end{array}$$

8. 35.00

$$\begin{array}{r} 35. \\ 7.8.\overline{)273.0.} \\ \underline{234} \\ 390 \\ \underline{390} \\ 0 \end{array}$$

Unit 1 Review

1. integer, rational
2. rational
3. whole, integer, rational
4. rational
5. rational
6. rational
7. rational
8. rational

9. $-\frac{23}{1}$ To change a whole number to a fraction, write the number as the numerator and 1 as the denominator.

10. $\frac{39}{250}$ $\frac{156}{1000} = \frac{39}{250}$

11. $\frac{484}{25}$ $19 + \frac{36}{100} = 19\frac{9}{25} = \frac{19 \times 25 + 9}{25} = \frac{484}{25}$

12. $\frac{26}{3}$ $\frac{8 \times 3 + 2}{3} = \frac{26}{3}$

13. $-\frac{8}{1}$ To change a whole number to a fraction, write the number as the numerator and 1 as the denominator.

14. $\frac{25}{9}$ $\frac{2 \times 9 + 7}{9} = \frac{25}{9}$

15. $\frac{389}{200}$ $1 + \frac{945}{1000} = 1\frac{189}{200} = \frac{1 \times 200 + 189}{200} = \frac{389}{200}$

16. $\frac{39}{5}$ $7 + \frac{8}{10} = 7\frac{4}{5} = \frac{7 \times 5 + 4}{5} = \frac{39}{5}$

17. $\frac{27}{2}$ $\frac{13 \times 2 + 1}{2} = \frac{27}{2}$

18. $\frac{3819}{50}$ $76 + \frac{38}{100} = 76\frac{19}{50} = \frac{76 \times 50 + 19}{50} = \frac{3819}{50}$

19. $-\frac{302}{1}$ To change a whole number to a fraction, write the number as the numerator and 1 as the denominator.

20. $9\frac{1}{3}$ or $\frac{28}{3}$ $x = 0.333\ldots; 10(x) = 3.333\ldots;$ $10x - x = 3.333\ldots - 0.333\ldots; 9x = 3;$ $x = \frac{1}{3}; 9 + \frac{1}{3} = 9\frac{1}{3} = \frac{28}{3}$

Chapter 9: Ratios and Proportions

Lesson 9.1

1. $\frac{5}{4}$ 5 oz. plaster to 4 oz. water $= \frac{5}{4}$

2. $\frac{3}{2}$ 3 pillowcases to 2 sheets $= \frac{3}{2}$

3. $\frac{2}{1}$ 2 forks to 1 knife $= \frac{2}{1}$

4. $\frac{4}{3}; \frac{3}{4}$ 4 pepperoni to 3 olives $= \frac{4}{3}$; 3 olives to 4 pepperoni $= \frac{3}{4}$

5. $\frac{4}{3}$ 8 seventh graders to 6 eighth graders $= \frac{8}{6} = \frac{4}{3}$

6. $\frac{1}{1}$ 1 cup sugar to 1 cup peanut butter $= \frac{1}{1}$

7. 18 boys to girls $= \frac{5}{6}; 15 \div 5 = 3; 6 \times 3 = 18$

8. 21 boys to girls $= \frac{4}{3}; 12 \div 4 = 3; 3 \times 3 = 9; 12 + 9 = 21$

Lesson 9.2

1. True $\frac{36}{81} \div \frac{9}{9} = \frac{4}{9}$

2. False $\frac{35}{42} \div \frac{7}{7} = \frac{5}{6}$

3. True $\frac{12}{9} \div \frac{3}{3} = \frac{4}{3}$

4. False $\frac{16}{18} \div \frac{2}{2} = \frac{8}{9}$

5. True $\frac{125}{300} \div \frac{25}{25} = \frac{5}{12}$

6. False $\frac{36}{32} \div \frac{4}{4} = \frac{9}{8}$

7. True $\frac{84}{132} \div \frac{12}{12} = \frac{7}{11}$

8. True $\frac{25}{40} \div \frac{5}{5} = \frac{5}{8}$

9. $n = 60$ $10 \times 36 = 6 \times n; 360 = 6n; 60 = n$

10. $x = 6$ $4 \times 24 = x \times 16; 96 = 16x; 6 = x$

11. $y = 39$ $13 \times 78 = 26 \times y; 1014 = 26y; 39 = y$

12. $m = 5$ $11 \times 60 = m \times 132; 660 = 132m; 5 = m$

13. $n = 27$ $18 \times 42 = 28 \times n; 756 = 28n; 27 = n$

14. $x = 5$ $x \times 57 = 19 \times 15; 57x = 285; x = 5$

15. $x = 29$ $x \times 104 = 52 \times 58; 104x = 3016; x = 29$

16. $n = 12$ $18 \times 10 = 15 \times n; 180 = 15n; 12 = n$

17. 16.2 points $\frac{486 \text{ points}}{6 \text{ games}} = \frac{x \text{ points}}{1 \text{ game}}$; $(486)(1) = (6)(x)$; $486 = 6x; 81 = x$; $81 \div 5$ players $= 16.2$

18. the 12-pack $\frac{12 \text{ sodas}}{\$5.50} = \frac{1 \text{ soda}}{x}$; $(12)(x) = (5.50)(1)$; $12x = 5.5; x = 0.458 = \$0.46$; $\frac{6 \text{ sodas}}{\$3.50} = \frac{1 \text{ soda}}{x}$; $(6)(x) = (3.55)(1)$; $6x = 3.55; x = 0.591 = \$0.59$

19. \$245.96 $\frac{0.86 \text{ Euros}}{1 \text{ dollar}} = \frac{x \text{ Euros}}{286 \text{ dollars}}$; $(0.86)(286) = (1)(x); 245.96 = x$

20. 8 bags $\frac{\$0.85}{1 \text{ bag}} = \frac{\$7.50}{x \text{ bags}}$; $(0.85)(x) = (1)(7.5)$; $0.85x = 7.5; x = 8.82$

Lesson 9.3

1. 12.8 teaspoons $\frac{2 \text{ tsp}}{20 \text{ oz}} = \frac{x \text{ tsp}}{128 \text{ oz (1 gallon)}}$; $(2)(128) = (20)(x); 256 = 20x$; $x = 12.8$

2. 180 eggs $\frac{12 \text{ eggs}}{5 \text{ people}} = \frac{\text{x eggs}}{75 \text{ people}}$; $(12)(75) = (5)(x)$; $900 = 5x; x = 180$

3. 15 quarts $\frac{3 \text{ quarts}}{1 \text{ hour}} = \frac{\text{x quarts}}{5 \text{ hours}}$; $(3)(5) = (1)(x)$; $15 = x$

4. 500 miles $\frac{125 \text{ miles}}{5 \text{ gallons}} = \frac{x \text{ miles}}{20 \text{ gallons}}$; $(125)(20) = (5)(x)$; $2500 = 5x; x = 500$

5. 12 t-shirts, 9 shorts $\frac{4 \text{ shirts}}{4 \text{ days}} = 1$ shirt per day, so 12 shirts for 12 days; $\frac{3 \text{ shorts}}{4 \text{ days}} = \frac{x \text{ shorts}}{12 \text{ days}}$; $(3)(12) = (4)(x); 36 = 4x; x = 9$

6. 130 meals $\frac{60 \text{ veggie}}{90 \text{ customers}} = \frac{x \text{ veggies}}{195 \text{ customers}}$; $(60)(195) = (90)(x); 11700 = 90x$; $x = 130$

7. 330.75 miles $\frac{27 \text{ miles}}{1 \text{ gallon}} = \frac{x \text{ miles}}{12.25 \text{ gallons}}$; $(27)(12.25) = (1)(x)$; $330.75 = x$

8. 4 hours $\frac{90 \text{ boxes}}{1 \text{ hour}} = \frac{360 \text{ boxes}}{\text{x hours}}$; $(90)(x) = (1)(360); 90x = 360$; $x = 4$

9. 36 miles per hour $\frac{20 \text{ minutes}}{12 \text{ miles}} = \frac{60 \text{ minutes (1 hour)}}{\text{x miles}}$; $(20)(x) = (12)(60); 20x = 720; x = 36$

10. 17.37 minutes Find each person's unit rate, then add them. Molly: $\frac{38 \text{ minutes}}{24 \text{ cupcakes}}$; $= \frac{1 \text{ minute}}{\text{x cupcakes}}$; $(38)(x) = (24)(1)$; $38x = 24; x = 0.632$; Jenna: $\frac{32 \text{ minutes}}{24 \text{ cupcakes}}$ $= \frac{1 \text{ minute}}{x \text{ cupcakes}}$; $(32)(x) = (24)(1); 32x = 24$; $x = 0.75$; together: $0.632 + 0.75$ $= 1.382$ cupcakes per minute; $\frac{1.382 \text{ cupcakes}}{1 \text{ minute}} = \frac{24 \text{ cupcakes}}{\text{x minutes}}$; $(1.382)(x) = (1)(24); 1.382x = 24$; $x = 17.37$

11. 4,179,420 hits $\frac{835{,}884 \text{ hits}}{3 \text{ months}} = \frac{x \text{ hits}}{15 \text{ months}}$; $(835{,}884)(15) = (3)(x)$; $12{,}538{,}260 = 3x$; $x = 4{,}179{,}420$

12. 4114 voters $\frac{374 \text{ voters}}{1 \text{ precinct}} = \frac{x \text{ voters}}{11 \text{ precincts}}$; $(374)(11) = (1)(x); 4114 = x$

13. 8.695 miles per hour $\frac{40 \text{ miles}}{2.3 \text{ hours}} = \frac{x \text{ miles}}{1 \text{ hour}}$; $(40)(1) = (2.3)(x); 40 = 2.3x$; $x = 17.39$ miles per hour; $17.39 \div 2 = 8.695$ miles per hour

14. 20.83 minutes $\frac{72 \text{ words}}{1 \text{ minute}} = \frac{1500 \text{ words}}{\text{x minutes}}$; $(72)(x) = (1)(1500); 72x = 1500$; $x = 20.83$

Chapter 10: Percents

Lesson 10.1

1. 20 $\frac{40}{100} = \frac{x}{50}$; $(40)(50) = (100)(x)$; $2000 = 100x; x = 20$

2. 400 $\frac{18}{100} = \frac{72}{x}$; $(18)(x) = (100)(72)$; $18x = 7200; x = 400$

Answers and Explanations

3. 40% $\frac{14}{35} = \frac{x}{100}$; $(14)(100) = (35)(x)$; $1400 = 35x$; $x = 40$

4. 10.2 $\frac{12}{100} = \frac{x}{85}$; $(12)(85) = (100)(x)$; $1020 = 100x$; $x = 10.2$

5. 125 $\frac{40}{100} = \frac{50}{x}$; $40(x) = (100)(50)$; $40x = 5000$; $x = 125$

6. 6.7 $\frac{18}{270} = \frac{x}{100}$; $(18)(100) = (270)(x)$; $1800 = 270x$; $x = 6.7$

7. 21 people $\frac{70}{100} = \frac{x}{70}$; $(70)(70) = (100)(x)$; $4900 = 100x$; $x = 49$; $70 - 49 = 21$

8. 70 cookies $\frac{30}{100} = \frac{21}{x}$; $(30)(x) = (100)(21)$; $30x = 2100$; $x = 70$

9. 2% $\frac{1.5}{75} = \frac{x}{100}$; $(1.5)(100) = (75)(x)$; $150 = 75x$; $x = 2$

Lesson 10.2

1. \$70.00 $\frac{x}{50} = \frac{40}{100}$; $100x = 2000$; $x = 20$; $50 + 20 = 70$

2. \$43.75 $\frac{x}{125} = \frac{35}{100}$; $100x = 4375$; $x = 43.75$

3. \$42.00 $\frac{x}{70} = \frac{40}{100}$; $100x = 2800$; $x = 28$; $70 - 28 = 42$

4. \$72.00 $\frac{x}{160} = \frac{45}{100}$; $100x = 7200$; $x = 72$

Lesson 10.3

1. 30% $\frac{18}{60} = \frac{3}{10} = \frac{x}{100}$; $300 = 10x$; $x = 30$

2. 17 $\frac{20}{100} = \frac{1}{5}$; $\frac{1}{5} \times 85 = 17$

3. 60% $\frac{42}{70} = \frac{3}{5} = \frac{x}{100}$; $300 = 5x$; $x = 60$

4. 27 $\frac{30}{100} = \frac{3}{10}$; $\frac{3}{10} \times 90 = \frac{270}{10} = 27$

5. 12.5% $\frac{16}{128} = \frac{1}{8} = \frac{x}{100}$; $100 = 8x$; $x = 12.5$

6. 25% $\frac{12}{48} = \frac{1}{4} = \frac{x}{100}$; $100 = 4x$; $x = 25$

7. 9 $\frac{15}{100} = \frac{3}{20}$; $\frac{3}{20} \times 60 = \frac{180}{20} = 9$

8. 15% $\frac{24}{160} = \frac{3}{20} = \frac{x}{100}$; $300 = 20x$; $x = 15$

9. 77 $\frac{35}{100} = \frac{7}{20}$; $\frac{7}{20} \times 220 = \frac{7}{1} \times \frac{11}{1} = 77$

10. 20 students $\frac{1}{5} = \frac{x}{100}$; $100 = 5x$; $x = 20$

11. 30% $\frac{75}{250} = \frac{3}{10} = \frac{x}{100}$; $300 = 10x$; $x = 30$

12. 33.3% $\frac{1}{3} = \frac{x}{100}$; $100 = 3x$; $x = 33.3$

Lesson 10.4

1. 25% $\frac{\cancel{5}^{1}}{\cancel{12}_{1}} \times \frac{\cancel{60}^{5}}{\cancel{100}_{20}} = \frac{5}{20} = \frac{1}{4} = 25\%$

2. 49.2% $\frac{3}{5} \times \frac{82}{100} = \frac{246}{500} = \frac{123}{250} = 49.2\%$

3. 66% $\frac{\cancel{6}^{3}}{\cancel{5}_{1}} \times \frac{\cancel{55}^{11}}{\cancel{100}_{50}} = \frac{33}{50} = 66\%$

4. 40% $\frac{\cancel{8}^{2}}{\cancel{25}_{1}} \times \frac{\cancel{125}^{5}}{\cancel{100}_{25}} = \frac{10}{25} = \frac{2}{5} = 40\%$

5. 20% $\frac{\cancel{4}^{1}}{\cancel{15}_{1}} \times \frac{\cancel{75}^{5}}{\cancel{100}_{25}} = \frac{5}{25} = \frac{1}{5} = 20\%$

6. $\frac{1}{5}$ $\frac{\cancel{25}^{5}}{\cancel{100}_{25}} \times \frac{\cancel{4}^{1}}{\cancel{5}_{1}} = \frac{5}{25} = \frac{1}{5}$

7. $\frac{1}{6}$ $\frac{20}{\cancel{100}_{20}} \times \frac{\cancel{5}^{1}}{6} = 1 \times \frac{1}{6} = \frac{1}{6}$

8. $\frac{3}{8}$ $\frac{40}{100} \times \frac{15}{16} = \frac{\cancel{2}^{1}}{\cancel{5}_{1}} \times \frac{\cancel{15}^{3}}{\cancel{16}_{8}} = \frac{3}{8}$

9. $\frac{14}{25}$ $\frac{75}{100} \times \frac{112}{150} = \frac{\cancel{3}^{1}}{\cancel{4}_{1}} \times \frac{\cancel{112}^{28}}{\cancel{150}_{50}} = \frac{28}{50} = \frac{14}{25}$

10. $\frac{8}{25}$ $\frac{60}{100} \times \frac{40}{75} = \frac{\cancel{3}^{1}}{\cancel{5}_{1}} \times \frac{\cancel{40}^{8}}{\cancel{75}_{25}} = \frac{8}{25}$

11. 42% $\frac{7}{\cancel{12}_{1}} \times \frac{\cancel{72}^{6}}{100} = \frac{42}{100} = 42\%$

12. 52.5% $\frac{5}{4} \times \frac{42}{100} = \frac{\cancel{5}^{1}}{4} \times \frac{21}{\cancel{50}_{10}} = \frac{21}{40} = 52.5\%$

Lesson 10.5

1. 76.12%
2. 1.543%
3. 159%
4. 57.21%
5. 0.12%
6. 0.0134%
7. 1045%
8. 189
9. 56.9%
10. 99.99%
11. 0.11%
12. 313.45%
13. 9999%
14. 17.5555578%
15. 18.7%
16. 87%

Lesson 10.6

1. \$600.00 $500 \times 0.08 \times 15 = 600$

2. \$300.00 $500 \times 0.12 \times 5 = 300$

3. \$540.00 $400 \times 0.07 \times 5 = 140; 400 + 140 = 540$

4. \$1,360.00 $1000 \times 0.06 \times 6 = 360; 1000 + 360 = 1360$

5. \$938.66 $2000 \times (1 + 0.08)^5 = 2000 \times (1.08)^5 = 2938.66; 2938.66 - 2000 = 938.66$

6. \$595.56 $500 \times (1 + 0.04)^{20} = 500 \times (1.04)^{20} = 1095.56; 1095.56 - 500 = 595.56$

7. \$6871.95 $2000 \times (1 + 0.28)^5 = 2000 \times (1.28)^5 = 6871.95$

8. 7 years at 12% compound Compound: $500 \times (1 + 0.12)^7 = 500 \times (1.12)^7 = 1105.34$; Simple: $500 \times 0.12 \times 9 = 540; 500 + 540 = 1040$

Chapter 11: Exponents

Lesson 11.1

1. 4^{10} $4^{5+5} = 4^{10}$
2. 7^2 $7^{5-3} = 7^2$
3. 3^{12} $3^{16-4} = 3^{12}$
4. 12^{27} $12^{22+5} = 12^{27}$
5. 11^{12} $11^{7+5} = 11^{12}$
6. 12^{22} $12^{32-10} = 12^{22}$
7. 10^9 $10^{5+4} = 10^9$
8. 23^1 $23^{7-6} = 23^1$
9. 16^{14} $16^{16-2} = 16^{14}$
10. 15^2 $15^{5-3} = 15^2$
11. 11^9 $11^{11-2} = 11^9$
12. 4^{11} $4^{4+7} = 4^{11}$

Lesson 11.2

1. 5^{12} $5^{4\times3} = 5^{12}$
2. 8^{35} $8^{7\times5} = 8^{35}$
3. 14^{70} $14^{10\times7} = 14^{70}$
4. 3^{160} $3^{20\times8} = 3^{160}$
5. 7^{1296} $6^4 = 1296; 7^{1,296}$
6. 8^{16} $2^4 = 16; 8^{16}$
7. 19^{512} $8^3 = 512; 19^{512}$
8. 15^{729} $9^3 = 729; 15^{729}$
9. 8^{24} $8^{3\times8} = 8^{24}$
10. 2^{30} $2^{5\times6} = 2^{30}$
11. 7^{60} $7^{4\times15} = 7^{60}$
12. 13^{15} $13^{5\times3} = 13^{15}$
13. 18^{256} $2^8 = 256; 18^{256}$
14. 277^{1296} $6^4 = 1296; 277^{1,296}$
15. 33^{45} $33^{3\times15} = 33^{45}$
16. 3^{20} $3^{4\times5} = 3^{20}$

Lesson 11.3

1. $\frac{1}{64}$ $4^{-3} = \frac{1}{4^3} = \frac{1}{64}$
2. $\frac{1}{27}$ $3^{-3} = \frac{1}{3^3} = \frac{1}{27}$
3. $\frac{1}{1296}$ $6^{-4} = \frac{1}{6^4} = \frac{1}{1296}$
4. $\frac{1}{3125}$ $5^{-5} = \frac{1}{5^5} = \frac{1}{3125}$
5. $\frac{1}{49}$ $7^{-2} = \frac{1}{7^2} = \frac{1}{49}$
6. $\frac{1}{4}$ $4^{-1} = \frac{1}{4^1} = \frac{1}{4}$
7. $\frac{1}{59049}$ $9^{-5} = \frac{1}{9^5} = \frac{1}{59,049}$
8. $\frac{1}{256}$ $2^{-8} = \frac{1}{2^8} = \frac{1}{256}$
9. 8^{-2} or 2^{-6} or 4^{-3} $64 = 8^2$ or 4^3 or 2^6; $\frac{1}{8^2} = 8^{-2}$; $\frac{1}{4^3} = 4^{-3}$; $\frac{1}{2^6} = 2^{-6}$
10. 9^{-2} or 3^{-4} $81 = 9^2$ or 3^4 $\frac{1}{9^2} = 9^{-2}$; $\frac{1}{3^4} = 3^{-4}$
11. 3^{-2} $9 = 3^2; \frac{1}{3^2} = 3^{-2}$
12. 5^{-2} $25 = 5^2; \frac{1}{5^2} = 5^{-2}$
13. 16 or 4^2 $4^{4+(-2)} = 4^{4-2} = 4^2 = 16$
14. 125 or 5^3 $5^{7+(-4)} = 5^{7-4} = 5^3 = 125$
15. 117,649 or 7^6 $7^{12+(-6)} = 7^{12-6} = 7^6 = 117,649$
16. 38,416 or 14^4 $14^{24+(-20)} = 14^{24-20} = 14^4 = 38,416$

Chapter 12: Roots

Lesson 12.1

1. 7 $\sqrt{49} = \sqrt{7\times7} = 7$
2. 11 $\sqrt{121} = \sqrt{11\times11} = 11$
3. 15 $\sqrt{225} = \sqrt{15\times15} = 15$
4. 9 $\sqrt{81} = \sqrt{9\times9} = 9$
5. 12 $\sqrt{144} = \sqrt{12\times12} = 12$
6. 2 $\sqrt{4} = \sqrt{2\times2} = 2$
7. 1 $\sqrt{1} = \sqrt{1\times1} = 1$
8. 13 $\sqrt{169} = \sqrt{13\times13} = 13$
9. 4 $\sqrt{16} = \sqrt{4\times4} = 4$
10. 6 $\sqrt{36} = \sqrt{6\times6} = 6$
11. 10 $\sqrt{100} = \sqrt{10\times10} = 10$
12. 8 $\sqrt{64} = \sqrt{8\times8} = 8$
13. 1 $1\times1 = 1$
14. 4 $2\times2 = 4$

Answers and Explanations

15. 9 $3 \times 3 = 9$

16. 16 $4 \times 4 = 16$

17. 25 $5 \times 5 = 25$

18. 36 $6 \times 6 = 36$

19. 49 $7 \times 7 = 49$

20. 64 $8 \times 8 = 64$

21. 81 $9 \times 9 = 81$

22. 100 $10 \times 10 = 100$

23. 121 $11 \times 11 = 121$

24. 144 $12 \times 12 = 144$

Lesson 12.2

1. 9 and 10; 9 $\sqrt{81} < \sqrt{89} < \sqrt{100};\ 9 < \sqrt{89} < 10$

2. 6 and 7; 7 $\sqrt{36} < \sqrt{44} < \sqrt{49};\ 6 < \sqrt{44} < 7$

3. 2 and 3; 2 $\sqrt{4} < \sqrt{5} < \sqrt{9};\ 2 < \sqrt{5} < 3$

4. 7 and 8; 7 $\sqrt{49} < \sqrt{50} < \sqrt{64};\ 7 < \sqrt{50} < 8$

5. 9 and 10; 10 $\sqrt{81} < \sqrt{97} < \sqrt{100};\ 9 < \sqrt{97} < 10$

6. 4 and 5; 5 $\sqrt{16} < \sqrt{23} < \sqrt{25};\ 4 < \sqrt{23} < 5$

7. 8 and 9 $\sqrt{64} < \sqrt{73} < \sqrt{81};\ 8 < \sqrt{73} < 9$

8. 13 $\sqrt{144} < \sqrt{154} < \sqrt{169};\ 12 < \sqrt{154} < 13$; she should purchase 13 feet to have enough

Chapter 13: Scientific Notation

Lesson 13.1

1. 1.3×10^{-3} Move the decimal 3 places to the right, so the exponent is negative.

2. 8.10114×10^{2} Move the decimal 2 places to the left, so the exponent is positive.

3. 4.0095×10^{0} The decimal moves 0 places.

4. 5.0×10^{-5} Move the decimal 5 places to the right, so the exponent is negative.

5. 5.851×10^{-1} Move the decimal 1 place to the right, so the exponent is negative.

6. 2.20467×10^{2} Move the decimal 2 places to the left, so the exponent is positive.

7. 4.267×10^{2} Move the decimal 2 places to the left, so the exponent is positive.

8. 1.190155×10^{4} Move the decimal 4 places to the left, so the exponent is positive.

9. 6.06544×10^{-2} Move the decimal 2 places to the right, so the exponent is negative.

10. 8.852×10^{-1} Move the decimal 1 places to the right, so the exponent is negative.

11. 1.488951×10^{3} Move the decimal 3 places to the left, so the exponent is positive.

12. 2.0000199×10^{5} Move the decimal 5 places to the left, so the exponent is positive.

13. 6.66×10^{-4} Move the decimal 4 places to the right, so the exponent is negative.

14. 2.679×10^{-3} Move the decimal 3 places to the right, so the exponent is negative.

15. 1.111×10^{0} The decimal moves 0 places.

16. 3.0075×10^{3} Move the decimal 3 places to the left, so the exponent is positive.

17. 266,990 Move the decimal 5 places to the right.

18. 1,445.5 Move the decimal 3 places to the right.

19. 9,660,317.1 Move the decimal 6 places to the right.

20. 30,302 Move the decimal 4 places to the right.

21. 0.00277 Move the decimal 3 places to the left.

22. 391,918.1 Move the decimal 5 places to the right.

23. 1588 Move the decimal 3 places to the right.

24. 0.010801 Move the decimal 2 places to the left.

Lesson 13.2

1.

Planet	Distance from the Sun (in miles)	Write the distance in scientific notation
Mercury	35,980,000	3.598×10^{7}
Venus	65,240,000	6.524×10^{7}
Earth	92,960,000	9.296×10^{7}
Mars	141,600,000	1.416×10^{8}
Jupiter	483,800,000	4.838×10^{8}
Saturn	888,200,000	8.882×10^{8}
Uranus	1,784,000,000	1.784×10^{9}
Neptune	2,795,000,000	2.795×10^{9}

2. 2 times larger $\frac{1.784 \times 10^9}{8.882 \times 10^8}; \frac{1.784}{8.882} = 0.2;$

$\frac{10^9}{10^8} = 10^1; 0.2 \times 10 = 2$

3. 5 times larger $\frac{4.838 \times 10^8}{9.2960 \times 10^7}; \frac{4.838}{9.2960} = 0.52;$

$\frac{10^8}{10^7} = 10^1; 0.52 \times 10 = 5.2$

4. 9×10^{7}

Answers and Explanations

Chapter 14: Variable Expressions

Lesson 14.1

1. A number divided by two, plus twenty-two
2. A number plus four
3. Four times a number plus three
4. A number times nine-tenths, minus nine
5. A number minus four divided by twenty
6. Three times a number plus seven, minus eight, plus thirty-three
7. Three times a number minus nine
8. Five divided by a number

Lesson 14.2

1. $x = 8$ $x+9-9=17-9;\ x=8$
2. $s = 9$ $17-8=s+8-8;\ 9=s$
3. $z = 35$ $14+z-14=49-14;\ z=35$
4. $f=3$ $17-f+f=14+f;\ 17=14+f;$ $17-14=14+f-14;\ 3=f$
5. $m = 65$ $m-30+30=35+30;\ m=65$
6. $c = 44$ $c-22+22=22+22;\ c=44$
7. $y = 31$ $y+11-11=42-11;\ y=31$
8. $l = 90$ $107-17=17+l-17;\ 90=l$
9. $k = 36$ $k+28-28=64-28;\ k=36$
10. $u = 15$ $28+u-28=43-28;\ u=15$
11. $t = 17$ $59-t+t=42+t;\ 59=42+t;\ 59-42$ $=42+t-42;\ 17=t$
12. $a = 9$ $13-a+a=4+a;\ 13=4+a;$ $13-4=4+a-4;\ 9=a$
13. $b = 30$ $24+b-24=54-24;\ b=30$
14. $e = 32$ $54-e+e=22+e;\ 54=22+e;\ 54-22$ $=22+e-22;\ 32=e$
15. $d = 24$ $15+d-15=39-15;\ d=24$

Lesson 14.3

1. $n=7$ $7n\div 7=49\div 7;\ n=7$
2. $q = 45$ $\frac{q}{5}(5)=9(5);\ q=45$
3. $f=7$ $12f\div 12=84\div 12;\ f=7$
4. $b = 3$ $\frac{42}{b}(b)=14(b);42=14b;42\div 14=14b\div 14;3=b$
5. $k = 13$ $3k\div 3=39\div 3;k=13$
6. $s = 5$ $\frac{55}{s}(s)=11(s);55=11s;\ 55\div 11=11s\div 11;5=s$
7. $m = 120$ $\frac{m}{30}(30)=4(30);m=120$
8. $h = 7$ $16h\div 16=112\div 16;h=7$
9. $x = 90$ $\frac{x}{15}(15)=6(15);x=90$
10. $n = 14$ $4n\div 4=56\div 4;n=14$
11. $m = 4$ $18m\div 18=72\div 18;m=4$
12. $d = 13$ $11d\div 11=143\div 11;d=13$

Lesson 14.4

1. $x = 3$ $10x-7+7=23+7;10x=30;$ $10x\div 10=30\div 10;x=3$
2. $x = 1$ $14-12=12+2x-12;2=2x;$ $2\div 2=2x\div 2;1=x$
3. $x=\frac{7}{4}$ $21+4x-21=28-21;4x=7;$ $4x\div 4=7\div 4;x=\frac{7}{4}$
4. $x = 15$ $200+15x-200=425-200;15x=225;$ $15x\div 15=225\div 15;x=15$
5. $x=\frac{2}{5}$ $5x+39-39=41-39;5x=2;$ $5x\div 5=2\div 5;x=\frac{2}{5}$
6. $z = 6$ $10z+17-17=77-17;10z=60;$ $10z\div 10=60\div 10;z=6$
7. $x = 8$ $65-41=41+3x-41;24=3x;$ $24\div 3=3x\div 3;8=x$
8. $r = 2$ $107-75=75+16r-75;32=16r;$ $32\div 16=16r\div 16;2=r$
9. $d=-\frac{2}{3}$ $49+18d-49=37-49;18d=-12;$ $18d\div 18=-12\div 18;\ d=-\frac{12}{18}=-\frac{2}{3}$
10. $b=\frac{4}{5}$ $15b+18-18=30-18;15b=12;$ $15b\div 15=12\div 15;b=\frac{12}{15}=\frac{4}{5}$
11. $q = -12$ $5q-10q=10q+60-10q;\ -5q=60;$ $-5q\div -5=60\div -5;q=-12$
12. $f=\frac{7}{3}$ $6f+18=32;6f+18-18=32-18;6f=14;$ $6f\div 6=14\div 6;f=\frac{14}{6}=\frac{7}{3}$
13. $j = 7$ $3j-5j=5j-14-5j;\ -2j=-14;$ $-2j\div -2=-14\div -2;j=7$
14. $r = 2$ $23+18r-23=6r+47-23;18r=6r+24;$ $18r-6r=6r+24-=6r;12r=24;$ $12r\div 12=24\div 12;r=2$
15. $k=\frac{1}{9}$ $27k+10=13;27k+10-10=13-10;$ $27k=3;27k\div 27=3\div 27;k=\frac{3}{27}=\frac{1}{9}$
16. $v=-\frac{5}{4}$ $14v-10v=10v-5-10v;4v=-5;$ $4v\div 4=-5\div 4;v=-\frac{5}{4}$

Answers and Explanations

17. 477 — $326\times2.5=815; 326+815+x=1,618;$ $1,141+x=1,618;\ ;x=1,618-1,141=477$

18. 199,111 — $325,000-x=125,889;$ $-x=125,889-325,000;$ $-x=-199,111; x=199,111$

19. 1649 — $1,385+x=3,034; 3,034-1,385=x;$ $x=1,649$

20. 32; 64, 48 — $x+2x+1.5x=144;\ 4.5x=144;$ $x=\frac{144}{4.5}=32;\ 2\times32=64;$ $1.5\times32=48$

21. 3807 — $143+x=3,950; 3,950-143=x; x=3,807$

22. $x=210\div22$

Lesson 14.5

1. Infinite — $0=0$
2. $x=7$ — $4x-7+7=21+7; 4x=28;$ $4x\div4=28\div4; x=7$
3. No solution — $6=2$
4. No solution — $2=7$
5. Infinite — $4=4$
6. $x=3$ — $8x-24+24=0+24; 8x=24;$ $8x\div8=24\div8; x=3$

Chapter 15: Inequalities

Lesson 15.1

1. $x^2\geq25$
2. $x\div5<63$ or $\frac{x}{5}<63$
3. $x+9<12$
4. $643<x+y$
5. $x+2\leq15$
6. $4x>17$
7. $1-x\geq-63$
8. $3x\leq4y$
9. $x\geq2$ — The closed circle shows that the range includes the number 2 on the number line, so any number greater than or equal to 2 is a solution.
10. $x>-2$ — The open circle shows that the range does not include –2, so any number greater than –2 is a solution.

Lesson 15.2

1. $x<11$ — $x+6-6<17-6; x<11$
2. $x<2$ — $25-23>23+x-23; 2>x$
3. $x\leq3.45$ — $7.35+x-7.35\leq10.8-7.35; x\leq3.45$
4. $x\leq0.68$ — $0.9-0.22\geq x+0.22-0.22; 0.68\geq x$
5. $x<31.24$ — $x-4.5+4.5<26.74+4.5; x<31.24$
6. $x>-4,949$ — $5047+x>98-x+x;$ $5047+x>98;$ $5047+x-5047>98-5,047;$ $x>-4,949$
7. $x\geq-42$ — $7-x+x\leq49+x; 7\leq49+x;$ $7-49\leq49+x-49; -42\leq x$
8. $x\leq18.4$ — $1.8+16.63\geq x-16.63+16.63;$ $18.43\geq x$
9. $20\geq14.5+x$; \$5.50 — $20\geq14.5+x; 20-14.5\geq14.5$ $+x-14.5; 5.5\geq x$
10. $x+15\geq23$; 8 pencils — $x+15\geq23; x-15\geq23-15; x\geq8$

Lesson 15.3

1. $x>5$ — $2x+15-15>25-15;$ $2x>10;\ \frac{2x}{2}>\frac{10}{2};\ x>5$
2. $x<13$ — $5+5x<70;\ 5+5x-5<70-5;$ $5x<65;\ \frac{5x}{5}<\frac{65}{5};\ x<13$
3. $x>26.5$ — $8x+8>220;\ 8x+8-8>220-8;$ $8x>212;\ \frac{8x}{8}>\frac{212}{8};\ x>26.5$
4. $x\geq-84$ — $17+\frac{x}{-3}\leq45; 17+\frac{x}{-3}-17\leq45-17;$ $\frac{x}{-3}\leq28;\ \frac{x}{-3}(-3)\geq28(-3);\ x\geq-84$
5. $x\geq-6$ — $34\geq10-4x;\ 34-10\geq10-4x-10;$ $24\geq-4x;\ \frac{24}{-4}\leq\frac{-4x}{-4};\ -6\leq x$
6. $x<175$ — $42>7+\frac{x}{5};\ 42-7>7+\frac{x}{5}-7;$ $35>\frac{x}{5};\ 35(5)>\frac{x}{5}(5);\ 175>x$
7. $x\geq28$ — $232\leq8+8x; 232-8\leq8+8x-8;$ $224\leq8x;\frac{224}{8}\leq\frac{8x}{8}; 28\leq x$
8. $x<-15$ — $63<3-4x; 63-3<3-4x-3;$ $60<-4x;\ \frac{60}{-4}>\frac{-4x}{-4};\ -15>x$
9. $x\geq-108$ — $12\geq-\frac{x}{9};\ 12(-9)\leq-\frac{x}{9}(-9);\ -108\leq x$
10. $x>15.5$ — $3x+5>51.5;\ 3x+5-5>51.5-5;$ $3x>46.5;\frac{3x}{3}>\frac{46.5}{3};\ x>15.5$
11. $x\geq(45)(4);\ x\geq180$
12. $6x\leq100; x\leq16.66$

Answers and Explanations

Chapter 16: Functions

Lesson 16.1

1.

2. A (1, 1); B (4, −4); C (−5, −9); D (9, 5); E (2, 6); F (−1, −2); G (−2, 2); H (−6, 4); I (1, 7); J (−4, 4)

3. A (1, 3); B (2, 5); C (3, 7); D (4, 9); E (3, −6); F (−1, −6); G (−4, 4); H (−6, 5); I (1, 7); J (−3, 3)

Lesson 16.2

1.

x	y
0	1
1	2
2	3
3	4
4	5
5	6

2.

x	y
−2	−2
−1	0
0	2
1	4
2	6
3	8

3.

x	y
0	−4
1	−3
4	0
6	2
8	4
10	6

4.

x	y
−1	−5
0	−3
1	−1
2	1
3	3
5	7

5.

x	y
−2	−3
1	3
0	1
2	5
4	9
6	13

6.

x	y
−4	−1
−2	0
0	1
2	2
4	3
6	4

7. $y = x + 2$

8. $y = 2x + 9$

9. $y = x^2 + 2$

10. $y = x^3$

11.

x	y
−2	−9
−1	−6
0	−3
1	0
2	3
3	6

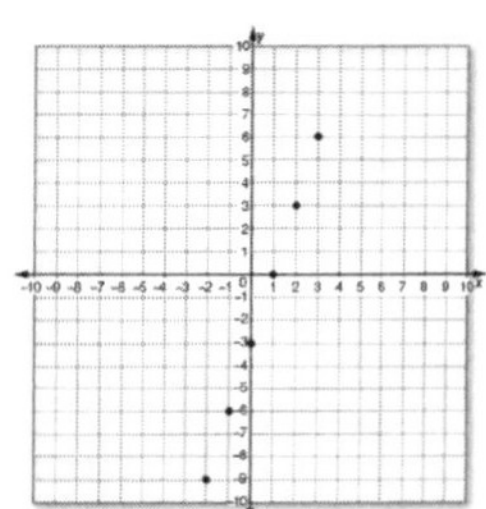

Answers and Explanations

12.

x	y
−3	9
−2	4
−1	1
0	0
1	1
2	4
3	9

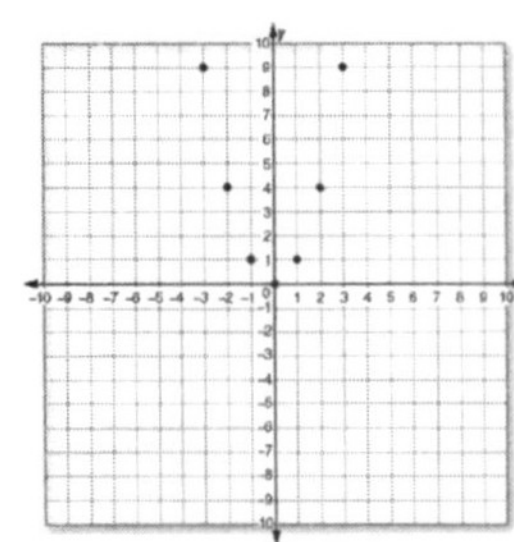

Chapter 17: Graphing Lines and Relationships

Lesson 17.1

1. (2, 5);

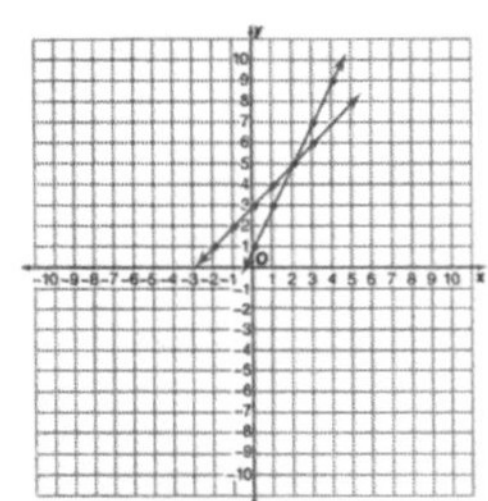

2. (3, −1);

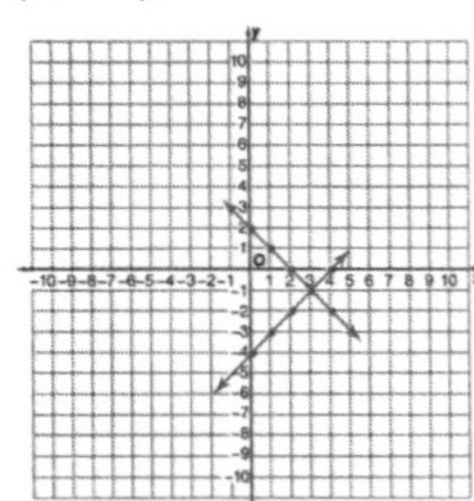

3. (1, 1);

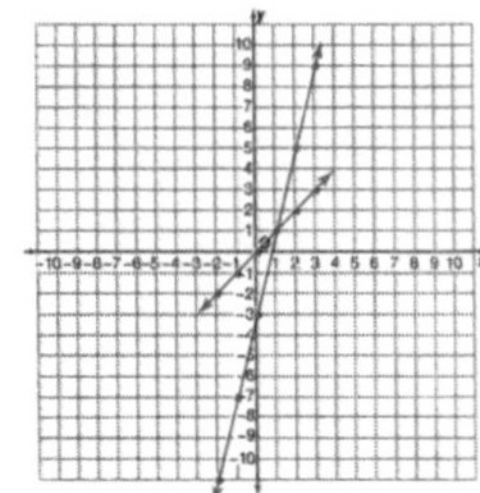

Lesson 17.2

1. $\frac{4}{7}$ Follow the line up from (0,–4) to (0, 0). The rise is 4. Follow the line from (0, 0) out to (7, 0). The run is 7. Slope $= \frac{\text{rise}}{\text{run}} = \frac{4}{7}$.

2. $\frac{-3}{5}$ Follow the line down from (0, 3) to (0, 0). Since the line goes down, the rise is –3. Follow the line from (0, 0) out to (5, 0). The run is 5.
Slope $= \frac{\text{rise}}{\text{run}} = \frac{-3}{5}$.

3. 6 The line is already in $y = mx + b$ form, where m is the slope.

4. 1 Put the line in $y = mx + b$ form by adding x to both sides of the equation: $y = x + 4$.
The slope is 1.

5. $\frac{2}{3}$ Put the line in $y = mx + b$ form.
$-3 = \frac{2}{3}x - y$; $-3 + y = \frac{2}{3}x - y + y$;
$y - 3 = \frac{2}{3}x$; $y - 3 + 3 = \frac{2}{3}x + 3$; $y = \frac{2}{3}x + 3$
The slope is $\frac{2}{3}$.

6. −1 Put the line in $y = mx + b$ form by subtracting x from both sides of the equation: $y = -x - 5$.
The slope is –1.

Lesson 17.3

1. Both frostings are the same shade because the ratio of food coloring to frosting is the same.

2. 6:1; the unit rate is $\frac{6}{1}$

3.

Cups of frosting (y)	Drops of food coloring (x)
$\frac{1}{2}$	3
1	6
$1\frac{1}{2}$	9
2	12

4.

5. The slope is 6.
6. Car A; because the slope of the line is greater
7. 1:30
8. Car A
9. At 1 hour, the car is at 10 miles, so the rate is 10 miles per hour
10. Increasing
11. 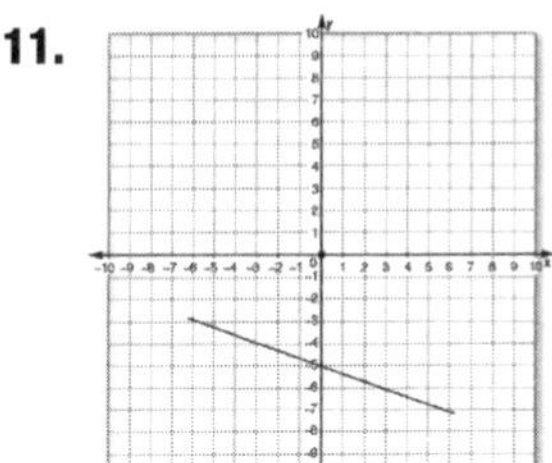
12. Nonlinear

Chapter 18: Customary Units of Measure

Lesson 18.1

1. 6 ft — $72 \div 12 = 6$
2. 144 in. — $12 \times 12 = 144$
3. 44 in. — $3 \text{ ft} \times 12 = 36 \text{ in.}; 36 \text{ in.} + 8 \text{ in.} = 44 \text{ in.}$
4. 16 ft — $192 \div 12 = 16$
5. 1.5 mi — $7920 \div 5280 = 1.5$
6. $5\frac{1}{2}$ yd — $6 \text{ in.} = \frac{1}{2}\text{ft}; 16\frac{1}{2} \div 3 = \frac{33}{2} \times \frac{1}{3} = \frac{33}{6} = 5\frac{1}{2} \text{ yd}$
7. 57 in. — $4 \times 12 = 48 \text{ in.}; 48 + 9 = 57$
8. 0.2 mi — $1{,}056 \div 5280 = 0.2$
9. 50688 in. — $\frac{4}{5} \times 5280 = 4224 \text{ ft};$ $4224 \times 12 = 50{,}688 \text{ in.}$
10. $5\frac{1}{2}$ ft — $66 \div 12 = 5\frac{1}{2}$
11. 18 yd — $648 \div 12 = 54 \text{ ft}; 54 \div 3 = 18 \text{ yd}$
12. $22\frac{1}{2}$ ft = 270 in. — $7.5 \times 3 = 22.5 \text{ ft}; 22.5 \times 12 = 270$
13. $11\frac{2}{3}$ yd — $35 \div 3 = 11\frac{2}{3}$
14. 600 in. — $16 \times 3 = 48 \text{ ft}; 48 + 2 = 50 \text{ ft};$ $50 \times 12 = 600 \text{ in.}$
15. 11469 ft — $2 \times 1760 = 3520 \text{ yd};$ $3520 + 303 = 3823 \text{ yd};$ $3823 \times 3 = 11{,}469 \text{ ft}$
16. 1248 in. — $34 \times 3 = 102 \text{ ft};$ $102 + 2 = 104 \text{ ft};$ $104 \times 12 = 1248 \text{ in.}$
17. 72 sections — $768 \times 3 = 2304 \text{ ft}; 2304 \div 32 = 72$
18. 49 yd; 147 ft — $1764 \div 12 = 147 \text{ ft}; 147 \div 3 = 49 \text{ yd}$

Lesson 18.2

1. 18 qt — $72 \div 2 = 36 \text{ pt}; 36 \div 2 = 18 \text{ qt}$
2. 48 c — $12 \times 2 = 24 \text{ pt}; 24 \times 2 = 48 \text{ c}$
3. 14 c — $3 \times 2 = 6 \text{ pt}; 6 + 1 = 7 \text{ pt}; 7 \times 2 = 14 \text{ c}$
4. 768 qt — $192 \times 4 = 768$
5. 82 gal — $328 \div 4 = 82$
6. 36 c — $2 \times 4 = 8 \text{ qt}; 8 + 1 = 9 \text{ qt};$ $9 \times 2 = 18 \text{ pt}; 18 \times 2 = 36 \text{ c}$
7. 25 c — $6 \times 2 = 12 \text{ pt}; 12 \times 2 = 24 \text{ c}; 24 + 1 = 25 \text{ c}$
8. 13 qt — $52 \div 2 = 26 \text{ pt}; 26 \div 2 = 13 \text{ qt}$
9. 12 c — $\frac{3}{4} \times 4 = 3 \text{ qt}; 3 \times 2 = 6 \text{ pt}; 6 \times 2 = 12 \text{ c}$
10. $8\frac{1}{4}$ gal — $66 \div 2 = 33 \text{ qt}; 33 \div 4 = 8\frac{1}{4} \text{ gal}$
11. 17 c — $4 \times 2 = 8 \text{ pt}; 8 \times 2 = 16 \text{ c}; 16 + 1 = 17 \text{ c}$
12. $1\frac{7}{8}$ gal = 30 c — $7\frac{1}{2} \div 4 = \frac{15}{2} \times \frac{1}{4} = \frac{15}{8} = 1\frac{7}{8} \text{ gal};$ $7\frac{1}{2} \times 2 = 15 \text{ pt}; 15 \times 2 = 30 \text{ c}$
13. 8.9 gal — $35 \times 2 = 70 \text{ pt}; 70 \times 2 = 140 \text{ c};$ $140 + 3 = 143 \text{ c};$ $143 \div 2 = 71.5 \text{ pt};$ $71.5 \div 2 = 35.75 \text{ qt};$ $35.75 \div 4 = 8.94 \text{ gal}$
14. 16 gal — $256 \div 2 = 128 \text{ pt};$ $128 \div 2 = 64 \text{ qt};$ $64 \div 4 = 16 \text{ gal}$
15. 66 pt = 33 qt — $132 \div 2 = 66 \text{ pt}; 66 \div 2 = 33 \text{ qt}$
16. 274 pt — $34 \times 4 = 136 \text{ qt};$ $136 + 1 = 137 \text{ qt};$ $137 \times 2 = 274 \text{ pt}$
17. 24 gal 3 qt — $25 \times 4 = 100 \text{ qt};$ $100 - 1 = 99 \text{ qt};$ $99 \div 4 = 24\frac{3}{4} = 24 \text{ gal } 3 \text{ qt}$
18. 3 qt 3 c — $9 = 3 \times 3, \text{ so } (1 \text{ qt} + 1 \text{ c}) \times 3 = 3 \text{ qt } 3 \text{ c}$

Lesson 18.3

1. $5\frac{3}{8}$ lb — $86 \div 16 = 5\frac{3}{8}$
2. 133 oz — $8 \times 16 = 128 \text{ oz}; 128 + 5 = 133 \text{ oz}$

Answers and Explanations

3. 20,000 lb $10 \times 2000 = 20,000$
4. 1.2 T $2400 \div 2000 = 1.2$
5. $10\frac{3}{8}$ lb $166 \div 16 = 10\frac{3}{8}$
6. 214 oz $13 \times 16 = 208$ oz; $208 + 6 = 214$
7. 500 lb $\frac{1}{4} \times 2000 = 500$
8. 800 lb $\frac{2}{5} \times 2000 = 800$
9. 81 oz $2 \text{ lb} \times 16 = 32$ oz; $32 + 12 = 44$ oz; $2 \text{ lb} \times 16 = 32$ oz; $32 + 5 = 37$ oz; $44 + 37 = 81$ oz
10. 6.5 lb $104 \div 16 = 6.5$
11. $31\frac{1}{8}$ lb $498 \div 16 = 31\frac{1}{8}$
12. 160 lb $167 \times 16 = 2672$ oz; $2672 - 112 = 2560$ oz; $2560 \div 16 = 160$ lbs
13. 19 lb 11 oz First cat: $7 \times 16 = 112$ oz; $112 + 12 = 124$ oz; Second cat: $11 \times 16 = 176$ oz; $176 + 15 = 191$ oz; Together: $124 + 191 = 315$ oz; $315 \div 16 = 19$ lbs 11 oz
14. 65 lb 12 oz $70 + 2.25 - 6.5 = 65.75 = 65$ lbs 12 oz

Lesson 18.4

1. 20 in. $4 + 4 + 6 + 6 = 20$
2. 26 in. $5 + 4 + 7 + 4 + 6 = 26$
3. 108 in. $27 + 36 + 45 = 108$
4. 44 in. $10 + 12 + 10 + 12 = 44$
5. 17 in. $4 + 6 + 4 + 3 = 17$
6. 36 ft $5(4) + 2(8) = 20 + 16 = 36$
7. 81 ft $5 + 4 + 3 + 3 + 3 + 4 + 5 = 27; 3 \times 27 = 81$

Lesson 18.5

1. 30 sq in. $6 \times 5 = 30$
2. 16 sq mi $4 \times 4 = 16$
3. 6 sq in. $\frac{1}{2} \times 3 \times 4 = \frac{1}{2}(12) = 6$
4. 36 sq in. $6 \times 6 = 36$
5. 45 sq ft $9 \times 5 = 45$
6. 62.5 sq in. $\frac{1}{2} \times 25 \times 5 = \frac{1}{2}(125) = 62.5$
7. 9 sq in. $3 \times 3 = 9$
8. 60 sq in. $8 \times 7.5 = 60$

Chapter 19: Metric Units of Measure

Lesson 19.1

1. 0.21 km $210 \div 1000 = 0.21$ km
2. 14.5 cm $145 \div 10 = 14.5$ cm
3. 57300 cm $573 \times 100 = 57,300$ cm
4. 26000 mm $26 \times 100 = 2600$ cm; $2600 \times 10 = 26,000$ mm
5. 0.004 km $400 \div 100 = 4$ m; $4 \div 1,000 = 0.004$ km
6. 40000 cm $400 \times 100 = 40,000$ cm
7. 1600 mm $1.6 \times 100 = 160$ cm; $160 \times 10 = 1600$ mm
8. 2500 m $2.5 \times 1000 = 2500$ m
9. 0.116 m $116 \div 10 = 11.6$ cm; $11.6 \div 100 = 0.116$ m
10. 1,557,000 mm $1.557 \times 1000 = 1557$ m; $1557 \times 100 = 155,700$ cm; $155,700 \times 10 = 1,557,000$ mm
11. 435.5 cm $4355 \div 10 = 435.5$ cm
12. 46670 cm $0.4667 \times 1000 = 466.7$ m; $466.7 \times 100 = 46,670$ cm
13. 3055.6 mm $3.0556 \times 100 = 305.56$ cm; $305.56 \times 10 = 3,055.6$ mm
14. 625 cm $6.25 \times 100 = 625$ cm
15. 775 m $0.775 \times 1000 = 775$ m

Lesson 19.2

1. 0.873 L $873 \div 1000 = 0.873$ L
2. 0.001455 kL $1455 \div 1000 = 1.455$ L; $1.455 \div 1000 = 0.001455$ kL
3. 4750 mL $4.75 \times 1000 = 4750$ mL
4. 7.945 L $7945 \div 1000 = 7.945$ L
5. 0.0001 kL $100 \div 1000 = 0.1$ L; $0.1 \div 1000 = 0.0001$ kL
6. 2.554 L $2554 \div 1000 = 2.554$ L
7. 2.5 mL $0.0025 \times 1000 = 2.5$ mL
8. 7000 mL $0.007 \times 1000 = 7$ L; $7 \times 1000 = 7000$ mL
9. 340 times $3.4 \times 1000 = 3400$ mL; $3400 \div 10 = 340$
10. 4.5 containers $4500 \div 1000 = 4.5$
11. 5.2126 L $5.768 \times 1000 = 5768$ mL; $5768 - 554 - 1.4 = 5212.6$ mL; $5212.6 \div 1000 = 5.2126$ L
12. 1.756 L $256 \div 1000 = 0.256$ L; $0.256 + 1.5 = 1.756$ L

Lesson 19.3

1. 0.4 kg — $400 \div 1000 = 0.4$ kg
2. 225,000,000 mg — $225 \times 1000 = 225,000$ g; $225,000 \times 100 = 22,500,000$ cg; $22,500,000 \times 10 = 225,000,000$ mg
3. 6.6 kg — $6600 \div 1000 = 6.6$ kg
4. 4.505 g — $4505 \div 10 = 450.5$ cg; $450.5 \div 100 = 4.505$ g
5. 21,350,000 mg — $21.35 \times 1000 = 21,350$ g; $21,350 \times 100 = 2,135,000$ cg; $2,315,000 \times 10 = 21,350,000$ mg
6. 0.53 g — $530 \div 10 = 53$ cg; $53 \div 100 = 0.53$ g
7. 0.65 g — $650 \div 10 = 65$ cg; $65 \div 100 = 0.65$ g
8. 7,100,000 cg — $71 \times 1000 = 71,000$ g; $71,000 \times 100 = 7,100,000$ cg
9. 3721 g — $3.721 \times 1000 = 3,721$ g
10. 2.313 kg — $2,313 \div 1000 = 2.313$ kg
11. 0.546 g — $546 \div 10 = 54.6$ cg; $54.6 \div 100 = 0.546$ g
12. 12.305 kg — $12,305 \div 1000 = 12.305$ kg
13. 4.43 g — $4,430 \div 10 = 443$ cg; $443 \div 100 = 4.43$ g
14. 12340 g — $12.34 \times 1000 = 12,340$ g
15. 0.000002 kg — $2 \div 10 = 0.2$ cg; $0.2 \div 100 = 0.002$ g; $0.002 \div 1000 = 0.000002$ kg
16. 300,000,000 mg — $300 \times 1000 = 300,000$ g; $300,000 \times 100 = 30,000,000$ cg; $30,000,000 \times 10 = 300,000,000$ mg
17. 25.8 cg — $258 \div 10 = 25.8$ cg
18. 0.065 kg — $65 \div 1000 = 0.065$
19. 1.1394 g — $5,599.4 \div 10 = 559.94$ cg; $559.94 \div 100 = 5.5994$ g; $0.0034 \times 1000 = 3.4$ g; $5.5994 - 1.06 - 3.4 = 1.1394$ g
20. The first hive; 18.315 grams — Hive 1: 1,678.616 g; Hive 2: $1.6 \times 1000 = 1,600$ g; Hive 3: $1,660,301 \div 10 = 166,030.1$ cg; $166,030.1 \div 100 = 1,660.301$ g; $1,678.616 - 1,660.301 = 18.315$ g

Lesson 19.4

1. 40 cm; 100 sq cm — $10(4) = 40; 10 \times 10 = 100$
2. 38 cm — $9 + 2 + 3 + 4 + 6 + 14 = 38$
3. 20.8 cm; 26.4 sq cm — $4.4(2) + 6(2) = 8.8 + 12 = 20.8$; $4.4 \times 6 = 26.4$
4. 36 meters; 72 sq meters — $12(2) + 6(2) = 24 + 12 = 36; 12 \times 6 = 72$
5. 90 sq m — $\frac{1}{2}(12)(15) = (6)(15) = 90$
6. 24 sq m — $\frac{1}{2}(12)(4) = (6)(4) = 24$
7. \$226.80; 14.4 m — $4.2 \times 3 = 12.6; 12.6 \times 18 = \$226.80$; $4.2(2) + 3(2) = 8.4 + 6 = 14.4$

Chapter 20: Equivalent Measures

Lesson 20.1

1. 35.56 cm — $14 \times 2.54 = 35.56$
2. 4.575 m — $15 \times 0.305 = 4.575$
3. 10.968 m — $12 \times 0.914 = 10.968$
4. 3.656 m — $4 \times 0.914 = 3.656$
5. 4.827 km — $3 \times 1.609 = 4.827$
6. 0.948 L — $4 \times 0.237 = 0.948$
7. 1.419 L — $3 \times 0.473 = 1.419$
8. 8.514 L — $9 \times 0.946 = 8.514$
9. 13.2475 L — $3.5 \times 3.785 = 13.2475$
10. 325.314 mL — $11 \times 29.574 = 325.314$
11. 396.9 g — $14 \times 28.35 = 396.9$
12. 1.362 kg — $3 \times 0.454 = 1.362$
13. 170.1 g — $6 \times 28.35 = 170.1$
14. 3218 m — $2 \times 1.609 = 3.218$ km; $3.218 \times 1000 = 3,218$ m
15. 2.607 L — $11 \times 0.237 = 2.607$
16. 4.8 lbs of silver — $4.8 \times 0.454 = 2.1792$ kg; $2.1792 \times 1000 = 2179.2$ g
17. 36.6 meters — $120 \times 0.305 = 36.6$
18. 7568 mL — $8 \times 0.946 = 7.568$ L; $7.568 \times 1000 = 7568$ mL

Lesson 20.2

1. 0.936 in. — $24 \times 0.039 = 0.936$
2. 56.342 in. — $143 \times 0.394 = 56.342$
3. 118.11 in. — $3 \times 39.37 = 118.11$
4. 2.484 mi — $4 \times 0.621 = 2.484$
5. 0.7 oz — $20 \times 0.035 = 0.7$
6. 6.342 qt — $6 \times 1.057 = 6.342$
7. 792.6 gal — $3 \times 264.2 = 792.6$

Answers and Explanations

8. 9.9225 lb — $4.5 \times 2.205 = 9.9225$
9. 9.44 in. — $242 \times 0.039 = 9.438$
10. 458.64 oz — $13 \times 2.205 = 28.665$ lbs; $28.665 \times 16 = 458.64$ oz
11. 42.9 in. — $1100 \times 0.039 = 42.9$
12. 71.68 oz — $2 \times 2.205 = 4.41$ lbs; $4.41 \times 16 = 70.56$ oz; $32 \times 0.035 = 1.12$ oz; $1.12 + 70.56 = 71.68$
13. The 6 ft 4 in. volleyball players are taller on average — $6 \times 12 = 72; 72 + 4 = 76$ in.; $76 \div 0.394 = 192.89$ cm
14. 6.21 miles — $10 \times 0.621 = 6.21$

Lesson 20.3

1. 302°F — $150°C \times \frac{9}{5} + 32 = 270 + 32 = 302°F$
2. 65.6°C — $(150°F - 32) \times \frac{5}{9} = 118 \times \frac{5}{9} = 65.6°C$
3. 32°F — $0°C \times \frac{9}{5} + 32 = 0 + 32 = 32°F$
4. −17.8°C — $(0°F - 32) \times \frac{5}{9} = -32 \times \frac{5}{9} = -17.8°C$
5. 102.2°C — $(216°F - 32) \times \frac{5}{9} = 184 \times \frac{5}{9} = 102.2°C$
6. 221°F — $105°C \times \frac{9}{5} + 32 = 189 + 32 = 221°F$
7. 22.2°C — $(72°F - 32) \times \frac{5}{9} = 40 \times \frac{5}{9} = 22.2°C$
8. 86°F — $30°C \times \frac{9}{5} + 32 = 54 + 32 = 86°F$
9. −31.7°C — $(-25°F - 32) \times \frac{5}{9} = -57 \times \frac{5}{9} = -31.7°C$
10. 1.7°C — $(35°F - 32) \times \frac{5}{9} = 3 \times \frac{5}{9} = 1.7°C$
11. 98.6°F — $37°C \times \frac{9}{5} + 32 = 66.6 + 32 = 98.6°F$
12. 1742°F — $950°C \times \frac{9}{5} + 32 = 1710 + 32 = 1742°F$
13. 792.8°C — $(1219°F - 32) \times \frac{5}{9} = 1.187 \times \frac{5}{9} = 659.4°C$; $(2646°F - 32) \times \frac{5}{9} = 2,614 \times \frac{5}{9} = 1,452.2°C$; $1452.2 - 659.4 = 792.8°C$
14. 100.4°F — $38°C \times \frac{9}{5} + 32 = 68.4 + 32 = 100.4°F$

Chapter 21: Basic Concepts of Geometry

Lesson 21.1

1. C D
2. Q R
3. Point D
4. $\overleftrightarrow{AB}, \overleftrightarrow{GH}, \overleftrightarrow{HG}, \overleftrightarrow{BA}$
5. A line drawn through point J and point K
6. C

Lesson 21.2

1. Y X
2. $\overline{XZ}, \overline{ZX}, \overline{XY}, \overline{YX}, \overline{ZY}, \overline{YZ}, \overline{YM}, \overline{MY}, \overline{LY}, \overline{YL}, \overline{XL}, \overline{LX}, \overline{ZL}, \overline{LZ}$;
   Ray $\overrightarrow{XL}, \overrightarrow{ZL}, \overrightarrow{YL}, \overrightarrow{ML}, \overrightarrow{LM}, \overrightarrow{LX}, \overrightarrow{LZ}, \overrightarrow{LY}, \overrightarrow{XM}, \overrightarrow{XY}, \overrightarrow{XZ}, \overrightarrow{ZY}, \overrightarrow{ZM}, \overrightarrow{YM}$
3. $\overline{ED}, \overline{DE}, \overline{EA}, \overline{AE}, \overline{DC}, \overline{CD}, \overline{AB}, \overline{BA}, \overline{BC}, \overline{CB}$
4. A B

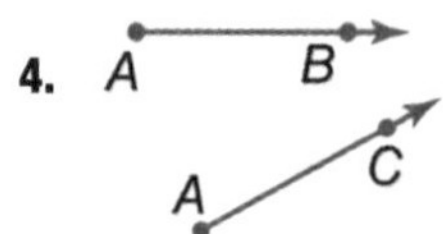

5. $\overline{CD}, \overline{NP}, \overline{PN}, \overline{DC}$

Lesson 21.3

1. Acute
2. Right
3. Acute
4. Obtuse
5. Acute
6. Obtuse
7. Right
8. Obtuse

Lesson 21.4

1. Complementary:
   ∠AGB; ∠BGC and ∠DGE; ∠EGF;
   Supplementary:
   ∠BGC and ∠BGF; ∠BGA and ∠AGE;
   ∠CGA and ∠FGA; ∠AGF and ∠FGD
   Vertical:
   ∠AGB and ∠DGE; ∠DGF and ∠AGC;
   ∠CGD and ∠AGF; ∠BGC and ∠FGE;
2. Complementary:
   ∠DFE and ∠DFC; ∠CFB and ∠BFA;
   Supplementary:
   ∠AFC and ∠CFE; ∠AFB and ∠BFE; ∠AFD and ∠DFE

3. Yes; sum of the angles = 90°
4. $\angle a = \angle c = \angle g = \angle e$
5. $\angle a = 125°$; $\angle b = 55°$;
$\angle c = 125°$; $\angle e = 125°$;
$\angle f = 55°$; $\angle h = 55°$

Lesson 21.5

1. $\angle a = 108°$, $\angle b = 72°$, $\angle c = 108°$, $\angle d = 72°$, $\angle e = 108°$, $\angle f = 72°$, $\angle g = 108°$ — All of the small angles are equal, so they are all 72°. $\angle e$ and 72° are supplementary, so $\angle e = 180° - 72° = 108°$. All the large angles are equal, so they are all 108°.
2. $\angle 1 = 48°$; $\angle 2 = 132°$; $\angle 3 = 48°$; $\angle 4 = 132°$; $\angle 5 = 48°$; $\angle 6 = 132°$; $\angle 7 = 48°$; $\angle 8 = 132°$ — All of the small angles are equal, so they are all 48°. $\angle 4$ and 48° are supplementary, so $\angle 4 = 180° - 48° = 132°$. All the large angles are equal, so they are all 132°.
3. $\angle a = 125°$; $\angle b = 55°$; $\angle c = 125°$; $\angle d = 55°$; $\angle e = 125°$; $\angle g = 125°$; $\angle h = 55°$ — All of the small angles are equal, so they are all 55°. $\angle g$ and 55° are supplementary, so $\angle g = 180° - 55° = 125°$. All the large angles are equal, so they are all 125°.
4. $\angle FOE = 46°$, — $\angle FOE + \angle GOF = 90°$; $90° - 44° = 46°$

$\angle EOC = 90°$, — $\angle EOC$ and $\angle EOG$ are supplementary, and $\angle EOG = 90°$; $180° - 90° = 90°$

$\angle BOC = 44°$ — $\angle BOC = \angle FOG = 44°$

Chapter 22: Triangles

Lesson 22.1

1. Acute
2. Obtuse
3. Right
4. Obtuse
5. Right
6. Acute
7. Equilateral
8. Isosceles
9. Scalene

Lesson 22.2

1. Congruent: equal angles and sides
2. Neither: sides and angles are not equal
3. Similar: Equal angles but not sides
4. Similar: Proportionate sides
5. Similar: equal angles not sides
6. Congruent: equal angles and sides

Lesson 22.3

1. 10 — $6^2 + 8^2 = c^2$; $36 + 64 = c^2$; $c^2 = 100$; $c = \sqrt{100} = 10$
2. $9\sqrt{2}$ — $9^2 + 9^2 = c^2$; $81 + 81 = c^2$; $c^2 = 162$; $c = \sqrt{162} = \sqrt{81 \times 2} = 9\sqrt{2}$
3. 26 — $10^2 + 24^2 = c^2$; $100 + 576 = c^2$; $c^2 = 676$; $c = \sqrt{676} = 26$
4. 12 — $9^2 + b^2 = 15^2$; $81 + b^2 = 225$; $b^2 = 225 - 81$; $b^2 = 144$; $b = \sqrt{144} = 12$
5. 8 — $a^2 + 6^2 = 10^2$; $a^2 + 36 = 100$; $a^2 = 100 - 36$; $a^2 = 64$; $a = \sqrt{64} = 8$
6. 13 — $12^2 + 5^2 = c^2$; $144 + 25 = c^2$; $c^2 = 169$; $c = \sqrt{169} = 13$
7. HI = 50 ft; KL = 30 ft; JL = 78 ft — $120^2 + HI^2 = 130^2$; $14{,}400 + HI^2 = 16{,}900$; $HI^2 = 16{,}900 - 14{,}400$; $HI^2 = 2{,}500$; $HI = \sqrt{2500} = 50$

$\frac{KL}{HI} = \frac{72}{120}$; $\frac{KL}{50} = \frac{72}{120}$; $KL(120) = (50)(72)$;

$KL(120) = 3600$; $KL = 3600 \div 120 = 30$

$\frac{JL}{GI} = \frac{72}{120}$; $\frac{JL}{130} = \frac{72}{120}$; $JL(120) = (130)(72)$;

$JL(120) = 9360$; $KL = 9360 \div 120 = 78$

8. LN = 25m; PQ = 21 m; OQ = 35 m — $20^2 + 15^2 = LN^2$; $400 + 225 = LN^2$; $625 = LN^2$; $LN = \sqrt{625} = 25$

$\frac{PQ}{MN} = \frac{28}{20}$; $\frac{PQ}{15} = \frac{28}{20}$; $PQ(20) = (15)(28)$;

$PQ(20) = 420$; $PQ = 420 \div 20 = 21$

$\frac{OQ}{LN} = \frac{28}{20}$; $\frac{OQ}{25} = \frac{28}{20}$; $OQ(20) = (25)(28)$;

$OQ(20) = 700$; $OQ = 700 \div 20 = 35$

Answers and Explanations

9. RT = $5\sqrt{2}$ in.; VW = 20 in.; UW = $20\sqrt{2}$ in.

$5^2+5^2=RT^2;$
$25+25=RT^2;$
$50=RT^2;$
$RT=\sqrt{50}=$
$\sqrt{25\times2}=5\sqrt{2}$

$\frac{VW}{ST}=\frac{20}{5};\ \frac{VW}{5}=\frac{20}{5};VW(5)=(5)(20);$

$VW(5)=100;VW=100\div5=20$

$\frac{UW}{RT}=\frac{20}{5};\ \frac{UW}{5\sqrt{2}}=\frac{20}{5};UW(5)=(5\sqrt{2})(20);$
$UW(5)=100\sqrt{2};UW=100\sqrt{2}\div5=20\sqrt{2}$

10. 16 ft $\frac{x}{12}=\frac{20}{15};x(15)=(12)(20);$
$15x=240;x=240\div15=16$

Chapter 23: Geometric Figures

Lesson 23.1

1. Square
2. Trapezoid
3. Rectangle
4. Rectangle
5. Trapezoid
6. Square
7. Rhombus
8. Kite
9. Rectangle

Lesson 23.2

1. Polygon
2. Not a polygon
3. Polygon
4. Polygon
5. Polygon
6. Polygon
7. Polygon
8. Polygon
9. Polygon

Lesson 23.3

1. 2 cm $d=2r;d=2(1)=2$
2. 14 in. $d=2r;d=2(7)=14$
3. 4 ft $d=2r;8=2r;r=4$
4. d
5. 3 in. $d=2r;6=2r;r=3$
6. $\overline{AO}$, $\overline{OB}$
7. Area 100π, Circumference 20π $A=\pi r^2;$ $A=\pi(10^2)=100\pi;$ $C=\pi d=20\pi$
8. Circumference 14π, Radius 7 $A=\pi r^2;\ 49\pi=\pi r^2;$ $49=r^2;r=\sqrt{49}=7;$ $C=\pi d=14\pi$
9. Diameter 10 cm; Area 25π sq cm; Circumference 10π cm $d=2r=10;\ A=\pi r^2;$ $A=\pi(5^2)=25\pi;$ $C=\pi d=10\pi$
10. Circumference 12π cm; Area 36π sq cm $C=\pi d=12\pi;\ A=\pi r^2;$ $A=\pi(6^2)=36\pi$
11. 100π inches or 314 in. $C=\pi d=25\pi;$ $4\times25\pi=100\pi$ $=100(3.14)=314$
12. 10π km Route A: $C=\pi d=10\pi;$ Route B: $C=\pi d=30\pi;$ $30\pi-20\pi=10\pi$

Lesson 23.4

1. Translation
2. Rotation
3. Reflection
4. Projection
5. Dilation
6. Rotation
7. Reflection
8. Translation
9. 4
10. 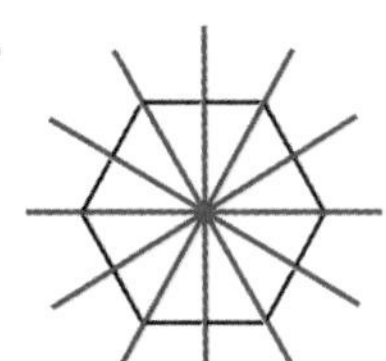

Chapter 24: Solid Figures

Lesson 24.1

1. 96 sq cm $SA=2(4\times4)+2(4\times4)+2(4\times4)$ $=2(16)+2(16)+2(16)$ $=32+32+32=96$
2. 160 sq in $SA=2(10\times2)+2(2\times5)+2(10\times5)$ $=2(20)+2(10)+2(50)$ $=40+20+100=160$

3. 72 sq m $SA = 2(6\times2)+2(2\times3)+2(6\times3) = 2(12)+2(6)+2(18) = 24+12+36 = 72$

4. 56π sq in. $SA = 2\pi r^2 + 2\pi rh$; $SA = 2\pi(2^2)+2\pi(2)(12) = 8\pi + 48\pi = 56\pi$

5. 440 sq cm $SA = 2(10\times6)+2(10\times6)+2(10\times10) = 2(60)+2(60)+2(100) = 120+120+200 = 440$

6. 114π sq in. $SA = 2\pi r^2 + 2\pi rh$; $SA = 2\pi(3^2)+2\pi(3)(16) = 18\pi + 96\pi = 114\pi$

Lesson 24.2

1. 90π cu ft $V = \pi r^2 h = \pi(3^2)(10) = \pi(9)(10) = 90\pi$
2. 36 cu ft $V = lwh = (2)(3)(6) = 36$
3. 64 cu m $V = lwh = (4)(4)(4) = 64$
4. 432π cu in. $V = \pi r^2 h = \pi(6^2)(12) = \pi(36)(12) = 432\pi$
5. 140 cu cm $V = lwh = (4)(7)(5) = 140$
6. 16π cu ft $V = \pi r^2 h = \pi(2^2)(4) = \pi(4)(4) = 16\pi$
7. 480 cu ft $V = \frac{1}{3}lwh = \frac{1}{3}(12)(12)(10) = \frac{1}{3}(1440) = 480$
8. 32π cu ft $V = \frac{1}{3}\pi r^2 h = \frac{1}{3}\pi(4^2)(6) = \frac{1}{3}\pi(16)(6) = \frac{1}{3}(96)\pi = 32\pi$
9. 32 cu yd $V = \frac{1}{3}lwh = \frac{1}{3}(4)(4)(6) = \frac{1}{3}(96) = 32$
10. 120π cu ft $V = \frac{1}{3}\pi r^2 h = \frac{1}{3}\pi(6^2)(10) = \frac{1}{3}\pi(36)(10) = \frac{1}{3}(360)\pi = 120\pi$
11. 140 cu ft $V = \frac{1}{3}lwh = \frac{1}{3}(5)(7)(12) = \frac{1}{3}(420) = 140$
12. 33π cu ft $V = \frac{1}{3}\pi r^2 h = \frac{1}{3}\pi(3^2)(11) = \frac{1}{3}\pi(9)(11) = \frac{1}{3}(99)\pi = 33\pi$

Chapter 25: Data Presentation

Lesson 25.1

1. Red
2. April, May
3. Most: December; Least: July
4. Carl, Elaine
5. Drama
6. Most: Rapid Rail; Least: Motor Bus
7. The number of visitors grew from 1995–1997 then fell off 1998 and 1999

Lesson 25.2

1. June is the rainiest month
2. Wednesday, Saturday, Sunday
3. Friday, Saturday, Wednesday
4. David gets worse the later he plays in the day
5. The value of the car falls rapidly until 60,000 miles and then declines more moderately
6. Thursday

Lesson 25.3

1. Car A; the longer it goes the closer it gets to Taree
2. Town A
3. Internet use surpassed television use
4. People continue to move from the country to the cities.

Lesson 25.4

1. Housing, Transportation, and Other
2. Region 1 and Region 2, or Region 2 and Region 3

Chapter 26: Visualizing Statistics and Probabilities

Lesson 26.1

1. Put the data in order: 1, 2, 3, 4, 5, 6, 7, 8, 9.

   Mean: $\frac{1+2+3+4+5+6+7+8+9}{9} = \frac{45}{9} = 5$; Median: 5;

   Range: $9-1=8$; Mode: n/a

2. Put the data in order: 10, 10, 10, 15, 20, 45, 60, 110

   Mean: $\frac{10+10+10+15+20+45+60+110}{8} = \frac{280}{8} = 35$;

   Median: $\frac{15+20}{2} = \frac{35}{2} = 17.5$; Range: $110-10=100$;

   Mode: 10

3. Put the data in order: 1, 2, 23, 23, 24, 25, 32, 48, 56

   Mean: $\frac{1+2+23+23+24+25+32+48+56}{9} = \frac{234}{9} = 26$;

   Median: 24; Range: $56-1=55$; Mode: 23

4. Put the data in order: –20, –20, –10, 0, 10, 20, 20

   Mean: $\frac{-20+-20+-10+0+10+20+20}{7} = \frac{0}{7} = 0$;

   Median: 0; Range: $20-(-20)=40$; Mode: -20 and 20

5. 117,850 $114{,}564 + 113{,}098 + 125{,}888 = 353{,}550$; $353{,}550 \div 3 = 117{,}850$

6. 114 bags $1710 \div 15 = 114$

Answers and Explanations

7. 21 tomatoes $252 \div 12 = 21$

8. 4 days $324 \div 81 = 4$

Lesson 26.2

1. 39, 40, 41, 45, 47, 47, 47, 49, 52, 56, 56, 56

2. 120, 125, 128, 128, 130, 131, 132, 134, 136, 137, 139, 141, 142, 143, 145, 145, 149, 161, 165

3. Median: 35.5; Range: 80; Mode n/a.
There are 10 values, so the median is the average of values 5 and 6: $\frac{34+37}{2} = \frac{71}{2} = 35.5$; the range is $81 - 1 = 80$; each value appears only once, so there is no mode

4.

Shrubs Collected by Students	
Stem	Leaf
0	4 8
1	2 6
2	1 1 3

Lesson 26.3

1. 70

2. 38, 60–22 = 38

3.

5 6 7 8 9 10 11 12 13 14 15 16 17 18 19 20

4. Range: 90–50 = 40; Median 76–77

Lesson 26.4

1. 12; 3

1 — H — 1H
1 — T — 1T
2 — H — 2H
2 — T — 2T
3 — H — 3H
3 — T — 3T
4 — H — 4H
4 — T — 4T
5 — H — 5H
5 — T — 5T
6 — H — 6H
6 — T — 6T

2. 36; 12

Shirts Pants Shoes Outcome

blue — black — black — blue, black, black
brown — blue, black, brown
red — blue, black, red
blue — tan — black — blue, tan, black
brown — blue, tan, brown
red — blue, tan, red
blue — white — black — blue, white, black
brown — blue, white, brown
red — blue, white, red
black — black — black — black, black, black
brown — black, black, brown
red — black, black, red
black — tan — black — black, tan, black
brown — black, tan, brown
red — black, tan, red
black — white — black — black, white, black
brown — black, white, brown
red — black, white, red
red — black — black — red, black, black
brown — red, black, brown
red — red, black, red
red — tan — black — red, tan, black
brown — red, tan, brown
red — red, tan, red
red — white — black — red, white, black
brown — red, white, brown
red — red, white, red
yellow — black — black — yellow, black, black
brown — yellow, black, brown
red — yellow, black, red
yellow — tan — black — yellow, tan, black
brown — yellow, tan, brown
red — yellow, tan, red
yellow — white — black — yellow, white, black
brown — yellow, white, brown
red — yellow, white, red

Lesson 26.5

1.

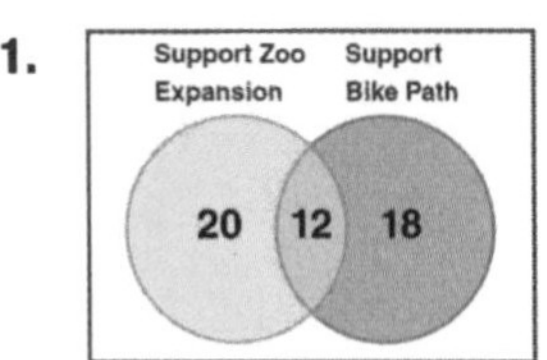

20 zoo only;
18 bike path only

2.

Stone Washed
Boot Cut
40
20
60

20 jeans both;
40 stone washed not boot cut;
60 boot cut not stone washed

Lesson 26.6

1. $\frac{7}{14}$ or $\frac{1}{2}$ 7 red out of 14 total $= \frac{7}{14} = \frac{1}{2}$

2. $\frac{15}{35}$ or $\frac{3}{7}$ 15 females out of 35 total $= \frac{15}{35} = \frac{3}{7}$

3. $\frac{212}{525}$ 212 club members out of 525 total $= \frac{212}{525}$

4. $\frac{3}{156}$ or $\frac{1}{52}$ 3 boxes of hard-boiled eggs out of 156 total $= \frac{3}{156} = \frac{1}{52}$

Notes

Notes